MARKET-SHARE ANALYSIS

International Series in Quantitative Marketing

Editor:

Jehoshua Eliashberg
The Wharton School
University of Pennsylvania
Philadelphia, Pennsylvania, U.S.A.

Market-Share Analysis
EVALUATING COMPETITIVE MARKETING EFFECTIVENESS

Lee G. Cooper
ANDERSON GRADUATE SCHOOL OF MANAGEMENT
UNIVERSITY OF CALIFORNIA, LOS ANGELES

Masao Nakanishi
SCHOOL OF BUSINESS ADMINISTRATION
KWANSEI GAKUIN UNIVERSITY
NISHINOMIYA-SHI, JAPAN

Kluwer Academic Publishers
BOSTON DORDRECHT LONDON

Distributors for North America:
Kluwer Academic Publishers
101 Philip Drive, Assinippi Park
Norwell, Massachusetts 02061 USA

Distributors for the UK and Ireland:
Kluwer Academic Publishers
Falcon House, Queen Square
Lancaster LA1 1RN, UNITED KINGDOM

Distributors for all other countries:
Kluwer Academic Publishers Group
Distribution Centre
Post Office Box 322
3300 AH Dordrecht, THE NETHERLANDS

Library of Congress Cataloging-in-Publication Data

Cooper, Lee G., 1944–
    Market-share analysis: evaluating competitive marketing effective-
ness / Lee G. Cooper, Masao Nakanishi.
        p.   cm. – – (International series in quantitative marketing)
    Bibliography: p.
    Includes index.
    ISBN 0–89838–278–5
    1. Marketing — Decision making — Mathematical models.
I. Nakanishi, Masao, 1936–   . II. Title. III. Series.
HF5415.135.C66 1988
658.8'02—dc 19   88–12092
                                                                      CIP

Contents

List of Tables

ix

List of Figures

Foreword

In April 1971, Los Angeles and its satellite cities were treated
to one of its least interesting and least publicized elections in
years. Nothing seemed to be hotly contested. A few Los
Angeles city councilmen were up for reelection as were some
members of the Board of Education and the Board of Trustees
of the Community Colleges.

– Nakanishi, Cooper and Kassarjian [1974]

Our colleague, Professor Harold H. Kassarjian, ran for one of the
seats on the Board of Trustees and received 17,286 votes. While he
lost the election, he had collected the data which he felt characterized
voting in such *low-involvement* cases. He asked us to join him in writing
a follow-up to a study of a similar election which had been published
the previous fall in *Public Opinion Quarterly*. Neither of us was content
with the methods and models used in the prior study. Shares are different
than other criteria, be they vote shares, market shares or retail stores'
shares of customers. Different methods are needed to reflect their special
nature. And thus began a research collaboration, running 17 years, so
far.

Though our combined research efforts have covered diverse areas of
consumer choice behavior, in recent years we came to the realization that
our models and analytical methods might be very profitably employed
in the analysis of market-share figures for consumer products. So we
decided to write a book on market-share analysis which was intended
to give not only graduate students in marketing an introduction to the
topic but also front-line managers a practical guide to the various stages
of analysis.

The latter objective was a bit of a problem. Neither of us had extensive business experience, but once our focus was set we learned rather
quickly. We found that so-called optical scanner data (or POS data, as
it is called in Japan) were becoming the major data source for market-
share figures for many packaged consumer goods. We also found that to
be of practical use to front-line managers the data base, the analytical
and interpretive models, and the planning process must all be integrated
into a comprehensive system of data management and computation.

In the course of writing this book one of the authors undertook
a rather ambitious project to develop computer software which is essentially a miniature market information system designed to facilitate

market-share analysis, with a special emphasis on the utilization of optical scanner data. We are happy to note that the end product of this project, CASPER, was the Grand Prize Winner of the Ashton-Tate Framework Applications Contest, co-sponsored (and judged) by PC Magazine. The development of CASPER led us to contact many practitioners, and brought us a deeper understanding of what is involved in market-share analysis in business contexts.

We now feel that this book offers front-line managers a combination of good theory and implementable models, as well as a prototype market information system from which real-world systems may be developed. To graduate students this book should be a good reference source for consumer choice models, market-share models, and new techniques in competitive mapping. In addition, CASPER may be used as a brand-planning game, through which the students may experience the complexities of market response under highly competitive conditions. We tried to give the reader a balanced treatment of the theoretical and the practical. We put much of the mathematical and theoretical material into appendices, so as not to interrupt the flow of ideas. An (*) at the beginning of a section heading signals advanced statistical or theoretical content which may be skipped by those readers who are bent on practical applications.

We thank the many colleagues who have assisted the development of this book. In particular we acknowledge the contributions of Penny Baron, J. Dennis Bender, Gregory S. Carpenter, Carl T. Finkbeiner, Sunil Gupta, Dominique M. Hanssens, Charles F. Hofacker, Barbara E. Kahn, Harold H. Kassarjian, Hotaka Katahira, Robert J. Meyer, David F. Midgley, Yutaka Osawa, Jagmohan S. Raju, Burton E. Swanson and John C. Totten. We appreciate the efforts of the Series Editor, Jehoshua Eliashberg, who along with the reviewers he recruited made valuable suggestions on the first draft of the book. We thank Zachary Rolnik, Editor, for his encouragement and support through the administrative part of creating a book, Marjorie Payne, Production Manager, for her assistance in producing a better manuscript, and Leah Jackson for copy editing. We are also grateful to Information Resources, Inc. which provided the scanner data used in the coffee-market example in the latter half of this book, to Quaker Oats for a grant which helped get us started with scanner data in 1983, to the Marketing Science Institute which, in 1987, aided in the development of brand-planning software used in Chapter 7, to Beatrice Foods and an anonymous consumer-products firm which provided exposure to and experience with large-scale commercial data, and to an anonymous retailer which aided our understanding of how scanner-based operations affect the organization of retail activities. We acknowledge the financial assistance of Cooper Research Inc. for support in producing the camera-ready version of this manuscript.

Dedication

We dedicate this book to Ann, Joseph and Daniel Cooper, and to Hiroko and Tauto Nakanishi. The support, love and indulgence of our families has made the crucial difference in our efforts. We will always remember and be thankful.

August 1988

Lee G. Cooper
Santa Monica, California, USA

Masao Nakanishi
Nishinomiya-shi, JAPAN

MARKET-SHARE ANALYSIS

Chapter 1

Scope and Objectives

1.1 Interest in Market-Share Analysis

In this era of intense competition, both world-wide and domestic, business firms of all sizes and varieties have become more and more concerned with the market-share figures they achieve in the marketplace. From our personal experience, some managers appear interested as much, if not more, in market shares as profits or returns on investment. For product and brand managers in particular, the sense of urgency associated with the gains and losses of market shares for the product/brand in their charge may be likened to what winning or losing of a war front means to generals or the general staff. Though such military analogies are not to be taken literally, one fact seems obvious: Market shares command the attention of business managers as key indices for measuring the performance of a product or brand in the marketplace. Many individuals in business indeed keep a close watch over day-by-day changes in market shares, so much so that market-share movement to them is almost synonymous to market information.

To the extent that market shares are used as market performance indices, it is clearly desirable for the individuals concerned to have thorough knowledge of the processes which generate market-share figures and to be able to analyze the impact of their own actions on market shares, as well as their profit implications. Lacking such knowledge, one might be tempted to oversimplify the cause-and-effect relationships between market shares and marketing variables, or to equate market shares to profitability (a not unusual tendency even among seasoned businessmen) and fall into deadly traps of blindly competing for market shares

1

for their own sake. Despite the obvious importance associated with it in many firms, the approach of many managers to market-share analysis may be described as casual.

The interest in market-share analysis has received new impetus in recent years, especially since the advent of optical-scanning systems — *POS* (point of sale) systems — at the retail level. A *POS* system collects sales records (essentially in the form of customer-by-customer receipts) at check-out counters of retail establishments with optical scanners which read *bar codes* of merchandise labels. It then puts the sales records in a computer (i.e., *store controller*) where sales records are tabulated into item-by-item sales summaries. *POS* systems were originally introduced in retail stores to improve the efficiency and accuracy of store personnel at the check-out counters and in the backroom and have achieved a considerable degree of success in speeding up check-out operations and in improving inventory control. *POS*-generated sales data also have an obvious potential as the database for merchandising and store management. Some authors even suggest that, by linking *POS* systems with electronic ordering systems (*EOS*) which handle order processing as well as inventory control, *store automation* will soon become a reality.

POS systems also open up a new source of market-share data at the retail level for manufacturers of consumer products. *POS* data have many advantages over traditional sources of market-share information such as retail audit, warehouse withdrawal, and consumer panel data, in that they are fast, accurate, low cost, and detailed. Already various marketing-research agencies are in the business of gathering *POS* data from a sample of stores and supplying manufacturers with summaries of them. In addition, several research agencies operate *optical-scanner panels* (or *scanner panels*) of consumers in a number of communities which generate purchase histories per household. It is often pointed out that scanner panels are superior to the traditional diary panels in their accuracy and speed. (We will give a more detailed description of those and other data collection techniques in Chapter 4.)

Though much has been said of the wonderful powers of *POS* systems, we believe that so far *POS* data have been underutilized for marketing-planning purposes. Considering the apparent advantages of *POS* data, this statement may seem improbable to the reader. Yet the current usage of *POS* data, whether it be in inventory control or in merchandising planning, is mainly on an item-by-item basis, and little attention has been paid to the interrelationships between items. Single-item summaries and analyses of *POS* data are no doubt useful for many purposes, but they ignore the complex pattern of interactions which exist among product classes, brands within a product class, and items within a brand. Market-share analysis focuses on the competitive interrelations among brands, and is one area in which *POS* data are not fully utilized. In our opinion, the chief reason why the application of *POS* data is so lagging in the analysis of competitive interactions, including market-share analysis, is that the analyst's understanding of the nature of *POS* data is lacking. How does one describe the competitive structure among products, brands, and items within a store? Unless we understand clearly the process that generates *POS* or scanner-panel data, we will not be able to analyze them correctly. Here is a case for having a clear conception before we can embark on market-share analysis.

Consider the following conversation between the marketing V.P. (or division manager) and a brand manager.

- Marketing V.P.: What happened to Serve-Right last month?

- Brand Manager: It's OK, though our share went down by two percentage points.

- Marketing V.P.: You mean we now have only a 13% share of the market? We've been losing our share three months in a row!

- Brand Manager: Yes, but our volume is up by 2% over the same month last year.

- Marketing V.P.: Yeah, but that may be because we are just coming out of a recession. How are Dominant and Superior?

- Brand Manager: Superior gained three percentage points last month. They started a heavy trade promotion two months ago. Dominant is in the same boat as we are. They've been losing their share, but their volume is up.

- Marketing V.P.: Haven't we been giving the trade a 15% rebate for three months?

- Brand Manager: Right, but the stores aren't cutting their prices as much as we thought they would. Superior gives them rebates and allowances for cooperative advertising, and that may be what we need to do to get the stores to pass the rebates through to the consumers.

- Marketing V.P.: Our retail prices are already lower than either Dominant or Superior. Maybe we are not getting enough shelf space.

- Brand Manger: Well, I've thought of that too. Perhaps we can do more TV spots in major markets to let the stores know that we are serious about pushing Serve-Right.

- Marketing V.P.: Look, I can't give Serve-Right any more media budget. I have other brands to think about! Get your act together by Friday, and tell me how you propose to improve our market position.

This conversation is, of course, hypothetical (we hope that no real-world brand manager would be this naive!), but points to the complexities and difficulties associated with market-share analysis. Much confusion seems to arise from the fact that the market share for a firm's brand/product is affected not only by the firm's own actions but also by the actions of competitors. Moreover, there are influences of such factors as seasonal variations in sales and general economic conditions which affect the performance of all brands in the industry. The plight of the brand manager in the above example may be attributable to his inability to isolate the effects of his firm's own actions from the effects of all other variables including competitors' actions. What is lacking here is a systematic approach to market-share analysis.

In part, the preoccupation of many managers with market shares may be the making of the *strategic market-planning* school of marketing thought, which has been promulgated by such authors as Abell and Hammond[1] and Buzzell,[2] since the 1970s. They emphasize the importance of market shares so much that, if one accepts their tenets naively, securing market shares will be the primary objective in any firm's marketing strategies. This stance may be justifiable in a new, growing industry, since, according to *experience analysis* which forms the core of their theory, maintaining the market-share leadership in a new, growing industry will automatically assure a firm the largest *experience* (i.e., cumulative sales volume) and therefore the lowest production and marketing costs. However, the determination to pursue the largest share in an industry

---

[1] Abell, D. F. and J. S. Hammond [1979], *Strategic Market Planning: Problems & Analytical Approaches*, Englewood Cliffs, New Jersey: Prentice-Hall.

[2] Robert D. Buzzell, Bradley T. Gale & Ralph G. M. Sultan [1975], "Market-Share — A Key to Profitability," *Harvard Business Review*, January-February, 97-106.

may not be optimal in those situations where the market for a product is already at a saturation level, for the share expansion for one brand may be achieved only at excessive costs in such a situation. Market-share leadership is clearly not a universal objective in every situation.

Though this is an admittedly simplistic description of the strategic market-planning concept, we need to examine more carefully whether such importance attached to market-share expansions is justified, as this school of marketing thought suggests. Again, we will need a conceptual framework in order to perform such an examination.

1.2 Need for a Analytical Framework

Market-share analysis is inherently more complex than the sales analysis for a single product/brand simply because one is required to take the competitive factors into account. To a mind which is used to analyzing the performance of one product/brand at a time, the complexity involved in market-share analysis, as described in the preceding paragraphs, might look formidable indeed. However, it is the authors' view that the difficulties lie in the analyst's state of mind rather than in the lack of analytical methodology. We posit that the analyst's task will be greatly facilitated, if he/she has a reasonably accurate view of the market and competition. In a sense, taking a product/brand at a time for analysis represents an extremely distorted view of the market, in which the analyst implicitly assumes that the product/brand (either word would mean the same in this case) partially monopolizes the market. Any strategy or plan based on this implicit assumption is bound for failure sooner or later, if the structure of actual markets tend toward what economists call *oligopoly* and *monopolistic competition*. Many have learned this fact, in some cases painfully, by watching their best-laid plans crumble in front of their eyes because of competitors' unexpected responses. It is like taking a picture of competition through a telephoto lens. While one brand may be in excellent focus, the foreground or background are either excluded or out of focus. As pretty as the picture may seem, too much is ignored by this view.

In this book we shall attempt to provide those individuals who are interested in analyzing market shares for some products or brands with a framework for analysis, which in our opinion promises a most meaningful view of the market and competitive structure. The reader will find various models of the market and competition, the most prominent of which is called a "Multiplicative Competitive Interaction (MCI) Model" or an "Attraction Model" and has the following general structure.

$$s_i = \frac{\mathcal{A}_i}{\sum_{j=1}^{m} \mathcal{A}_j} \tag{1.1}$$

$$\mathcal{A}_i = \prod_{k=1}^{K} f_k(X_{ki})^{\beta_k} \tag{1.2}$$

where:

s_i = the market share of brand i

$\mathcal{A}_i$ = the attraction of brand i

m = the number of brands

X_{ki} = the value of the kth explanatory variable X_k for brand i (e.g., prices, product attributes, expenditures for advertising, distribution, sales force)

K = the number of explanatory variables

f_k = a monotone transformation on X_k, $(f_k(\cdot) > 0)$

β_k = a parameter to be estimated.

A detailed discussion of the above model will be given in Chapter 2, and therefore we will only note here that the model is based on a simple idea that market shares are equal to the shares of attractions of respective brands, and that marketing instruments interact to determine, at least partially, the attraction of each brand. We will illustrate throughout this book how using appropriate market-share models such as the MCI model not only increases the analyst's understanding of the market and helps the planning process but also facilitates the analyst's tasks considerably in doing so. Furthermore, we will show that the communication of the results of market-share analysis within a firm will be greatly facilitated by the adoption of a meaningful model. As an illustration consider the following conversation between Marketing V.P. and Brand Manager in another firm.

- Marketing V.P.: What happened to Superior last month?

- Brand Manager: It is doing all right. Our share is three percentage points up. Would you like to see the trend? (Hit a key to select from a graph menu on a workstation on the desk.)

- Marketing V.P.: (Looking at the display) I see Dominant and Serve-Right are down. Is it because we've done the trade promotion?

- Brand Manger: Yes, that and our quality. We can price Superior 5% higher than our competition and still increase our share. The rest of the market is very price-competitive, but we are relatively well protected.

- Marketing V.P.: Show me the (competitive) map for price. (Brand Manager hits several keys, and a diagram emerges on the screen.)

- Marketing V.P.: The quality improvement sure has changed the picture. At shelf price, we are no longer directly competing against Dominant. We have a lot of clout on Serve-Right pricewise, but we don't want to start a price war. When they promote heavily, it hurts our share.

- Brand Manager: As I said, we needn't worry about retail prices. We can show the stores that pricing Superior 3% higher than Dominant will improve their profits. By the way, we can stop the rebates now. The trade promotion has given us a pretty good store penetration, and we will keep it even if we stop rebates.

- Marketing V.P.: How do you know?

- Brand Manager: With our share going up to 30% in many stores, they don't want to drop us, and, by pricing Superior 3% higher, they can get more margin from us than from Dominant. We will keep the promotional allowance, though. It doesn't cost us much because the stores and we split the costs. It is good to have some exposure in newspapers.

- Marketing V.P.: You mean it is better to put money in newspapers than in TV spots? Show me the elasticities for promotion. (Brand Manager selects several tables and flicks them on the display.)

- Brand Manager: You see that the elasticities for (newspaper) features are higher than those for TV spots or magazine ads. We may

want a big splash in December when the promotional elasticities
are higher, but until then cooperative ads will do fine.

- Marketing V.P.: Let's see the provisional Income Statement for the
  next month. (Brand Manager shows another table on the display.)
  OK, we seem to be doing just as well as we can do. Keep up the
  good work and I'll see you next month.

The above conversation is, of course, hypothetical, and may sound
suspiciously like science fiction. The authors have no intention of creating
an illusion that marketing decision making can be mechanized or even
automated by using computers. However, note that in this case both the
product manager and brand manager are looking at the situation from
the same analytical framework. In fact, a computer is not an essential
element in this conversation. Although the *marketing workbench* as a set
of powerful computer-based tools and models is a growing reality,[3] no
workstation or personal computer will help if the individuals involved do
not share a common understanding of the market and competition.

The persons in the above conversation are primarily thinking in terms
of *elasticities* (an economic concept which many readers no doubt consider as abstract as demand curves). They are communicating well
enough because both of them have the same understanding of this term.
We may add that nothing is said about *models* in this conversation. The
concept of elasticities is *generic* in the sense that it does not depend on
a specific model of the market or competition. A model comes into the
picture when one tries to estimate actual elasticities or predict future
ones. The MCI (attraction) model mentioned above will give one set of
estimates; other models will give other estimates. To the extent that
one model is accepted by the managers in a firm as a meaningful view
of the market and competition, elasticity estimates based on the model
will be also acceptable as the basis for marketing decisions. This is why
we believe that decision processes, as well as communication processes,
in a firm will be greatly facilitated by the organizational acceptance of
a model of the market and competitive structure.

Formally adopting an analytical framework has another advantage:
it will help the firm to build an effective *market information system*.
The emphasis in this marriage between information-systems concepts
and market-response modeling is simply that structuring data so that

---

[3]See McCann, John M. [1986], *The Marketing Workbench: Using Computers for
Better Performance*, Homewood, IL: Dow Jones–Irwin.

they are relatable to consumer demand provides a powerful organizing principle for the information system and provides the potential for addressing issues such as the effectiveness of marketing efforts. As will be discussed in more detail later, what data should be collected and how they are analyzed are largely dependent on the firm's view of the market and competition. If, for example, the market is seen as virtually consisting of a single segment, the analyst's task will be greatly simplified. Or if the firm sees competition as having negligible effects on the performance of its product/brand, there will be no sense in collecting competitive data. But such simplistic views are often inadequate. If the firm accepts that there are distinct and heterogeneous consumer segments and that the marketing instruments of the firm and its competitors all interact to create the attractiveness of the products/brands to these segments, the analyst will have to collect the types of data which will allow him/her to perform more comprehensive analyses of the effectiveness of the firm's marketing activities in a competitive environment. Thus an analytical framework, i.e., a view of the market and competition, determines essentially the requirements for a firm's information and analysis system.

The reader should be reminded that there is no single correct analytical framework for market-share analysis. The preponderance of the MCI model (or any other model for that matter) in this book should not suggest the authors' insistence that this model is *the* correct view of the market. A model is merely one approximation to the reality of the market and competition, and it would be unwarranted to insist one model represents the *truth*. Even though we believe that the MCI model allows us rich interpretation of market-share data without imposing heavy demand on our analytical capacity, the analyst will have to choose consciously among several alternative representations (i.e., models) of the structure of market and competition which fits best the specific conditions he/she faces. This requires a thorough understanding of the characteristics and implications of each model. In the next two chapters of this book, basic concepts necessary to analyze market-share data and several alternative models will be explained as comprehensively as possible. The deeper the reader's understanding of necessary concepts and models, the easier it will be for him/her to follow the subsequent discussions of data requirements and collection techniques (Chapter 4) and parameter-estimation techniques (Chapter 5).

1.3   The Process of Market-Share Analysis

Before we begin to describe the methodology of market-share analysis, it is perhaps beneficial to define its basic characteristics so that the reader will not be misled as to its relevance and eventual applicability to his or her own problems. The three key characteristics are that market-share analysis is *competitive*, *descriptive* as well as predictive, and *profit-oriented*.

First, market-share analysis is *competitive*. This implies that the effects of one's actions must be analyzed in conjunction with the market positions and actions of competitors. (In economic jargon, the marginal effect of a marketing variable is a function of competitors' actions and their market shares.) This also means that one will have to distinguish those factors which affect one's product/brand from more general factors which affect the entire industry (e.g., seasonality in product usage, and business and economic conditions). Finally, this means that, given competitors who are free to adopt any marketing strategies, market-share prediction also involves the prediction of competitors' future actions, which is a difficult undertaking in itself. Many experienced managers know that their best-laid plans mean little if they fail to predict correctly the courses of action the competitors are going take.

At this juncture we emphasize that the market-share analysis we explore in this book is basically for products in either the growth or maturity (i.e., saturation) stages of their product life cycle. In this context, it is important for one to distinguish between a *new brand* for a firm in an established industry and an entirely *new product* which is creating a new industry. We do not belittle the importance of being able to predict the future shares for a new product, but we envision that the analytical approach for predicting the performance of a new product is substantially different from that for an established product. When a radically new product is introduced by a firm in the market, it usually holds a temporarily monopolistic position due to technological advantages or legal protection (i.e., patents). Because the structure of the market and competition in the introductory stage of the product life cycle is so different from that in either the growth or maturity stages, the approaches to market-share analysis in this book may not be directly applicable to new products.

Second, market-share analysis must be *descriptive* as well as predictive. A common tendency among business managers is that if they can make good forecasts of market shares, they expect nothing more. The ability to make accurate predictions of future shares is indeed a major contribution of market-share analysis, but we do not believe that it is enough. Market-share analysis should provide the managers with much-needed information on the structure of the market and competition and the influence of marketing actions on brand performance — all of which are indispensable for them to be able to establish viable marketing strategies. An example is given by the competitive-map analysis of Chapter 6. Knowing that competitor A is vulnerable to our actions, but competitor B is not, or knowing one's share is much affected by the actions of competitor C, clearly gives a manager a better sense of competitive moves he/she can make in order to deal successfully with competitors.

Third, market-share analysis is *profit-oriented* in the sense that any firm is interested in not only market-share movement, but also its profit consequences. One might talk about a plan to expand the market share for a firm's product/brand, by improving quality, reducing price, advertising more, employing more sales persons, etc. But the key question obviously is, "Is it worth our effort to increase the market share?" *Experience analysis*, for example, tells us to try to expand one's market share if the increase in share allows the firm to have the leading position on the *experience curve*, that is, if the resultant share is the largest among the competitors. This in turn suggests that for firms with currently small shares the mad rush to become the industry leader may have dire consequences. The ability to predict the cost of achieving a certain market-share level should be as valuable for a firm as the ability to estimate the likelihood of achieving that share. We will return to this theme in the brand-planning exercises in Chapter 7 of this book.

Based on the above characterization, we assert that the basic goal of market-share analysis is to evaluate the effectiveness of marketing actions in a competitive environment. We propose the following scenario for the process of market-share analysis. (See also Figure 1.1.)

1.3.1 Stage 1: Specification of Models

This stage is for the selection of appropriate models for describing market-share movement and changes in overall (industry) sales volume. (In a simplest specification, a firm's sales volume is equal to the product of industry sales volume and its market share.) At the time when a firm is developing a system for market-share analysis, this stage is indispensable since the models determine data requirements in the data-collection stage. If the firm already has an ongoing data stream, the specification

Figure 1.1: The Process of Market-Share Analysis

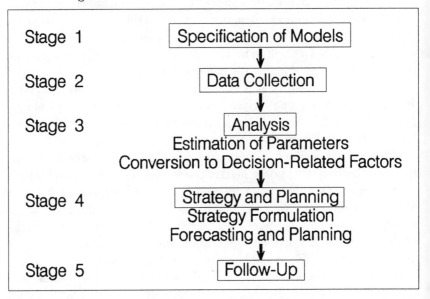

task becomes one of choosing a model which will allow the analyst to assess the impact of the variables in the data stream on demand. After the initial specification, this stage is only repeated when the analyst feels that the underlying structure of the market and competition is changing or has changed, and that it is necessary to modify or recalibrate the model. Modification may also be motivated by new data becoming available or by the desire for a more comprehensive explanation or assessment. Techniques for this specification step, such as time-series and experimental analyses, can help address issues concerning the duration of marketing effects and whether marketing instruments interact.

1.3.2   Stage 2: Data Collection and Review

Market-share data may be obtained from many sources. A traditional source was the so-called retail store-audit data, but since the adoption of optical scanners (i.e., POS systems) more data at the retail level are being generated by scanners. Wholesale warehouse withdrawals are also used as a source of market-share data for many consumer products. Consumer surveys and diary panels are sometimes used for market-share estimation. For many firms the only way to get own market-share figures is to divide the firm's own sales volume by what it can estimate of the industry sales volume for the same period and area.

One critical problem with the data collection stage for market-share analysis is the need for information on marketing activities of competitors as well as the firm's own activities. Any reasonably designed market information system should be able to meet adequately the information requirement on the firm's own activities, but the information on competitors' activities is a different matter. This requires careful monitoring of competitors' activities in the market and compiling a comprehensive file for each competitor.

Optical scanner data at the retail level, if they are available, are capable of supplying competitive information for a limited set of marketing variables such as shelf price and store displays. These data may be combined with available information on newspaper features, and manufacturers' and stores' coupons. Advertising expenditures or benchmarks such as target-audience rating points (TARPs) or gross rating points (GRPs) can be used to assess how these efforts relate to demand. Scanner panels can be tapped for measures such as brand inventories in panel households, indices of brand loyalty or time-since-last-purchase. These panels are also rich sources for potential segmentation by usage frequency or style, or demographic characteristics.

Simple, graphical summary relating market shares to other collected data can reveal a great deal about the nature of market response and competition.

1.3.3   Stage 3: Analysis

Once necessary data are collected for an adequate number of periods and/or areas (to give sufficient *degrees of freedom*), the analyst can proceed to:

1. **Estimation of Model Parameters**: Once the appropriate models are chosen, the next step is to estimate the parameters of the models. Statistical techniques such as log-linear regression analysis and maximum-likelihood estimation will be used in this step. Even though the model specification is not changed, it may be necessary to re-estimate parameters periodically. This is desirable not only for the purpose of adapting parameter values to changing conditions but also for the purpose of improving the accuracy of estimates.

2. **Conversion to Decision-Related Factors**: Model parameters themselves provide the analyst or manager with little information as to

the structure and occurrences in the market and competition. From a decision maker's viewpoint, more immediately useful information may be the responsiveness of market shares toward marketing activities of the own firm and competitors as summarized by market simulators. Or it may be the visual presentation (*map*) of the relative market positions of competing products/brands. It takes some ingenuity to produce a representation that is easily understood by managers who are not quantitatively oriented.

1.3.4   Stage 4: Strategy and Planning

The planning stage may be divided into two steps.

1. **Strategy Formulation**: In this step the information obtained in the analysis stage is used for the formulation of marketing strategies.[4] It is hoped that descriptive, rather than predictive, types of analysis will give the analyst and manager(s) concrete suggestions for formulating marketing strategies. The graphic summaries, for example, may suggest more effective marketing strategies.

2. **Forecasting and Planning**: Future market shares and sales volumes will be forecasted on the basis of a marketing plan. It will be nonsensical to speak of forecasts without an explicitly stated plan. Market simulators require, for example, explicit assumptions about competitive activities. Consequently, they produce *conditional forecasts* (i.e., *conditional* on these assumptions). A plan can be evaluated against various competitive scenarios. Also, it is theoretically possible, but not always practical, to search for an optimal (i.e., *profit-maximizing*) plan.

1.3.5   Stage 5: Follow-Up

It is critically important that the analyst reviews the performance of the firm's product/brand after marketing plans are put into effect. A careful review of one's plans and actual performance will improve not only future planning but also the techniques for market-share analysis. In doing a follow-up, it is not enough just to look at whether market shares were accurately forecasted. Market shares and consequently actual sales volume differ from the forecasted values for three basic reasons.

---

[4]In this book the term *strategy* is used in a rather loose sense, and *strategy* and *tactics* will be used interchangeably. Since an understanding of tactical response is fundamental to strategy formulation, and given the short-term nature of market-share analysis, maintaining the distinction would be too tedious.

1. Forecasts of industry sales volume were off.

2. Forecasts of market shares were off.

3. Marketing activities were not carried out as planned.

If the actual performance is at variance with the planned, It is essential for the analyst to pin-point the cause of variance by careful analysis. The so-called *variance analysis*[5] may be a useful technique for this purpose.

We have summarized here the process of market-share analysis as we view it. The reader will find that the organization of Chapters 2 through 7 of this book follows closely the stages of this process. Chapters 2 and 3 describe issues related to modeling (Stage 1: Specification of Models). Chapter 4 deals with the issues related with data collection and aggregation (Stage 2: Data Collection). Chapter 5 describes various techniques of parameter estimation (Stage 3: Analysis. Parameter Estimation). Chapter 6 (Competitive Maps) is related to reduction of data to decision-related factors (Stage 3: Analysis. Conversion to Decision-Related Factors). Chapter 7 is devoted to decision-support systems for planning (Stage 4: Strategy and Planning). Stage 5: Follow-Up is also dealt with in Chapter 7. Chapter 8 will discuss various remaining problems associated with market-share analysis and the potential avenues for future research in this area.

---

[5]Hulbert, James & Norman Toy [1977], "A Strategic Framework for Marketing Control," *Journal of Marketing*, 41 (April), 12–20.

Chapter 2

Understanding Market Shares

2.1 Market Shares: Definitions

What do we mean by *market share*? An obvious definition of a firm's market share might be "that share of the market commanded by a firm's product (or brand)." But this is merely a tautology and not a definition, and therefore does not help us understand market shares. Its basic difficulty lies in the ambiguity of the term *market*. One normally thinks of a market being a collection of persons (or institutions) who are likely to purchase a certain class of product. For consumer products and services, the market is a group of consumers who are potential buyers of a product or service, such as detergent, air travel, or coffee. (For simplicity, the term *product* is to be understood to encompass services hereafter, unless otherwise specified.) Those consumers who never buy a product are *out of the market*. If we define *market* in this manner, market shares should mean *shares of potential consumers*.

However, clearly this is not the common usage of the term. In most cases, market shares mean shares of the actual sales (either in quantity sold or dollar volume) for a product in a given period and in a given geographical area. *Market* in those situations should be taken as the sales performance of a product class in the market, rather than a collection of buyers for the product. In this book the term *market shares* will be used mostly in this latter sense. This concept of market shares may be

17

more explicitly stated in the following manner.

$$s_i = \frac{Q_i}{Q} \qquad (2.1)$$

where:

s_i = the market share of firm i

Q_i = the sales (quantity sold or dollar volume) of firm i's product

Q = the total sales (quantity sold or dollar volume) for the market

$Q = \sum_{j=1}^{m} Q_j$

m = the number of competing firms.

The quantity Q in the above equation is commonly called the *industry sales*, and we will follow this convention. Note that in this formulation market shares are a temporally and spatially specific concept, that is, defined and measured only for a specific period and a specific geographical area. It does not make much sense for one to talk about a firm's share in general; one must say instead a firm's share of the U. S. market in 1986, that of the European market in 1987, etc. This is because both the numerator and denominator of equation (2.1) are time- and area-specific, and will have to be matched for the same period and geographical area.

We shall have occasion also to refer to shares of potential buyers, but they will be denoted as *consumer shares* or *buyer shares*, so that there will be no confusion. Note that television audience *ratings* are consumer shares in this sense. In addition, a retail store's share of consumers who come to the shopping district in which it is located will be called a *shopper share* to distinguish it from its share of consumers from a certain geographical area or segment (e.g., *consumer share*). Most analytical techniques for market-share analysis will be directly applicable to the analysis of consumer shares with slight changes in the interpretation of equation (2.1), where Q_i and Q are replaced by the number of consumers, N_i and N, respectively. These points will be further clarified in a later section.

A further issue which should be addressed at this point is concerned with the choice of the *level* of distribution channel from which sales figures are obtained for computing market shares. When a manufacturer uses both wholesalers and retailers in its channel of distribution, it may possible to obtain three sets of sales figures, one each at the factory, wholesale, and retail levels. Complications arise since the sales figures at those three levels do not generally coincide. It is, of course, easy for the manufacturer to get sales (or *shipment*) data at the factory level, but are they meaningful for the purpose of market-share analysis? Some channels of distribution are notorious for their insensitivity to the changes in consumer demand. After all, aren't retail-sales figures more directly indicative of the firm's performance in the market? Isn't one of the most basic questions in market-share analysis how consumers are influenced by prices and promotions at the retail level? Or lacking retail-sales figures (which is not an uncommon condition for many firms), are wholesale (withdrawal) figures more appropriate than factory-shipment figures? Those are the questions which must be answered by the analyst before market shares may be computed. Much is dependent on the nature of products and services and the firm's ability to collect appropriate data. But, since assessing the effectiveness of marketing instruments in influencing consumer demand is one of the most importance uses of market-share analysis, the general principle should be to measure market shares as close as possible to the consumer-demand level.

2.2 Defining *Industry* Sales

We have defined market shares on the basis of sales performance of products and services, but this definition is not concrete enough. In order for one to be able actually to compute market shares for one's firm or brand, it is necessary to measure the denominator of equation (2.1), which is commonly called the *industry* sales. There are several problems associated with this measurement. First and foremost, what is a relevant *industry*? As the first approximation, let's say that an industry is composed of a set of firms which are competing for the same group of (potential) buyers.[1] But how does one know which firms are competing for the same group of buyers? Here we will have to leave the matter pretty much to the experience and judgment of the analyst.

In many business contexts the market boundaries are known quite well. But even in the absence of such knowledge, or in times when it is proper to question prior assumptions, there is a principle to guide the analyst in *delineating* the boundaries for an industry, that is, choosing a set of firms which compete against each other. We know that the indus-

---

[1]Note that the number of competitors in an industry is given by m in equation (2.1).

try boundaries change, depending on what level(s) of buyer needs and wants for which firms compete. The more basic the needs for which firms compete, the greater will be the number of firms in an industry. Conversely, the more specific the attributes (of products and services) with which firms choose to compete, the smaller will be the number of firms in an industry. To illustrate, if we assume that firms compete for the basic human need of personal transportation, all firms which produce automobiles, motorcycles, and bicycles (even skateboards!) compete against each other and therefore form an industry. On the other hand, if we narrowly select those firms which choose to compete solely on the basis of the luxury of interior fixture of a vehicle, only a small number of firms will be in an industry.

But the principle is not easily translated into practice. There are techniques (such as multidimensional scaling) which may be used for delineating industry boundaries, but in the authors' opinion they are more exploratory than definitive. Instead, we will propose in this book a more developmental approach. Since the models in this book are able to give the analyst a basis for evaluating industry boundaries, why not use them empirically to form the relevant boundaries for an industry? In this approach, the analyst will first proceed with tentative boundaries for an industry, and, with the increase in experience and additional data, keep modifying the boundaries to converge eventually on a workable definition of an industry. If the focus is on understanding the effectiveness of one's marketing efforts, one wants an industry definition broad enough to include all threats to one's marketing program, but narrow enough that the same set of measures of marketing effort and performance can be applied to all competitors. We will illustrate this with the Coffee-Market Example presented in Chapters 5 – 7.

Second, even if one is successful in defining an industry, it may not be possible to know the sales (quantity sold or dollar volume) of firms other than one's own. Fortunate are those few industries for which trade associations or governmental agencies regularly gather data on industry sales. (The automobile industry is a prime example.) There are also those consumer products for which some agencies maintain continuous measurement of sales at the retail level for nearly all competing firms in the market (see Chapter 4). Lacking such associations/agencies, the estimation of industry sales may pose to the analyst a difficult research problem. One may survey buyers for their purchases (in a period) and estimate industry sales by multiplying average purchase size by the number of potential buyers. Or one may deduce industry sales from an indicator which is known to have a high correlation with them. With whatever technique one chooses, it may be only possible to estimate one's own share, but impossible to estimate the shares of competitors. As is shown in later chapters, this inability to estimate competitors' shares seriously compromises the efficacy of market-share analysis.

To summarize, the definition of relevant industry boundaries is not always a simple and precise operation. It requires subjective judgment of the analyst based on his or her experience and thorough knowledge of product, market, and competitors. But if industry definition is not a straightforward operation, one might be better off to select models which do not heavily depend on the correct definition of a relevant industry. As will be shown later, the MCI model and its relatives are less sensitive to how an industry is defined than the linear or multiplicative models are, since the former is adaptable to the so-called *hierarchical market segments* (see Chapter 3).

2.3   Kotler's *Fundamental Theorem*

With the preliminaries in the last two sections, we are now in a position to explore further the relationship of a firm's market shares with its marketing activities. For the time being we shall assume that a relevant industry is defined and industry sales are measured. Kotler[2] posits that a firm's market share is proportional to the *marketing effort* of its product. In mathematical notation, this supposition may be written as:

$$s_i = k \cdot M_i \tag{2.2}$$

where:

M_i = the marketing effort of the product of firm i

k = a constant of proportionality.

This is not a bad assumption. If a firm's marketing effort were measurable, one would think (hope?) that the greater the marketing effort of one's firm the greater should be its market share.

For equation (2.2) to be useful, setting aside for the time being the question of how one might measure marketing effort, one must know the

---

[2]Kotler, Philip [1984], *Marketing Management: Analysis, Planning, and Control,* Fifth Edition, Englewood Cliffs, NJ: Prentice-Hall, Inc.

value of proportionality constant, k. But market shares for an industry must sum to one, i.e.,

$$\sum_{i=1}^{m} s_i = 1 \ .$$

This implies that

$$\sum_{i=1}^{m} k \cdot M_i = 1$$

or

$$\sum_{i=1}^{m} M_i = \frac{1}{k} \ .$$

Hence

$$k = \frac{1}{\sum_{i=1}^{m} M_i} \ .$$

By substituting this value of k in equation (2.2), we have

$$s_i = \frac{M_i}{\sum_{j=1}^{m} M_j} \ . \tag{2.3}$$

This last equation says that the market share of firm i is equal to the firm's marketing effort divided by the sum of marketing effort for all competitors in the industry. In other words, it says that a firm's market share is equal to its share of marketing effort, a statement which certainly seems plausible. Equation (2.3) is what Kotler calls the *fundamental theorem* of market share (Kotler [1984], p. 231).

It is interesting to note that this formulation is so basic that a whole series of variations may be devised from it. For example, if firms tended to differ in terms of the effectiveness of their marketing effort, one may write

$$s_i = \frac{\alpha_i \cdot M_i}{\sum_{j=1}^{m} \alpha_j \cdot M_j} \tag{2.4}$$

where α_i is the effectiveness coefficient for firm i's marketing effort. This implies that, even if two firms expend the same amount of marketing effort, they may not have the same market share. If one firm's marketing effort is twice as effective as that of the other, the former will achieve a market share twice as large as the other's share.[3]

So far we stepped aside the question of how one goes about measuring the marketing effort for a firm's product. Here Kotler additionally

---

[3]For other variations, see Kotler [1984], pp. 224-237.

assumes that a firm's marketing effort is a function of its marketing mix, both past and current. Mathematically, we may write,

$$M_i = f(P_i, A_i, D_i, \ldots) \qquad (2.5)$$

where:

P_i = the price of firm i's product

A_i = the advertising expenditures of firm i

D_i = the distribution efforts (e.g., trade allowances given by firm i).

There are wide choices in the specification of the functional form for equation (2.5). For example, if we choose it to be a multiplicative function

$$M_i = P_i^{p_i} \cdot A_i^{a_i} \cdot D_i^{d_i}$$

where p_i, a_i, d_i are parameters to be estimated, and substitute this expression in (2.3) or (2.4), the resultant market-share model will be an MCI model (see Chapter 1). Or if we choose an exponential function

$$M_i = \exp(p_i \cdot P_i + a_i \cdot A_i + d_i \cdot D_i)$$

the market-share model is called the multinomial logit (MNL for short) model. We will have more to say on the choice of functional forms.

2.3.1 A Numerical Example

At this point a numerical example may help the reader understand the nature of the models proposed by Kotler. Table 2.1 gives a hypothetical industry with three firms, with the values of the marketing mix for each and computed market shares.

The model used here is a basic MCI model (equation (2.4) and the multiplicative function for M_i). The share of firm 1 is computed in the following manner.

$$
\begin{aligned}
M_1 &= 0.9 \times 10.50^{-1.8} \times 80,000^{0.6} \times 54,000^{0.8} &&= 69802.47 \\
M_2 &= 1.2 \times 11.30^{-1.8} \times 90,000^{0.6} \times 48,000^{0.8} &&= 79648.67 \\
M_3 &= 1.0 \times 9.80^{-1.8} \times 70,000^{0.6} \times 65,000^{0.8} &&= 94011.84 \\
s_1 &= 69802.47/(69802.47 + 79648.67 + 94011.84) &&= 0.2867 \; .
\end{aligned}
$$

In this example price is the most dominant factor. Firm 2 has a higher marketing-effort effectiveness, but its share is less than firm 3 because of a higher price. Compare Table 2.1 with Table 2.2 in which firm 2 reduced its price to $10.00. Now its share is the largest.

Table 2.1: Numerical Example of Kotler's Fundamental Theorem

Firm	Marketing Effectiveness Coefficient	Price ($)	Advertising Expenditure ($)	Trade Allowances ($)	Market Shares (%)
1	0.9	10.50	80,000	54,000	28.67
2	1.2	11.30	90,000	48,000	32.72
3	1.0	9.80	70,000	65,000	38.61
Parameters		−1.8	0.6	0.8	

Table 2.2: Numerical Example — The Effect of Reducing Price

Firm	Marketing Effectiveness Coefficient	Price ($)	Advertising Expenditure ($)	Trade Allowances ($)	Market Shares (%)
1	0.9	10.50	80,000	54,000	26.54
2	1.2	10.00	90,000	48,000	37.73
3	1.0	9.80	70,000	65,000	35.74
Parameters		−1.8	0.6	0.8	

2.4   *Market-Share Theorem

Kotler's *fundamental theorem* gives us one justification for accepting equation (2.3) as a valid representation of the relationship between a firm's marketing mix and its market share. This *market-share-as-share-of-marketing-effort* representation makes a lot of intuitive sense, but there are other ways than Kotler's to derive such a representation. We will review some of them in a later section, and only look at one important theorem derived by Bell, Keeney and Little[4] here.

Bell, Keeney, and Little (BKL hereafter) consider a situation where, in making a purchase of a product, consumers must choose one brand from a set of alternative brands available in the market. They posit that the only determinant of market shares is the *attraction* which consumers feel toward each alternative brand, and make the following assumptions about attractions. Letting $\mathcal{A}_i$ be the attraction of brand i

---

[4]Bell, David E., Ralph L. Keeney & John D. C. Little [1975], "A Market Share Theorem," *Journal of Marketing Research*, XII (May), 136–41.

$(i = 1, 2, \ldots, m)$ and s_i be its market share,

Axiom A 2.1 $\mathcal{A}_i \geq 0$ *for all i and $\sum_{i=1}^{m} \mathcal{A}_i > 0$ (i.e., attractions are nonnegative and their sum is positive).*

Axiom A 2.2 $\mathcal{A}_i = 0 \Longrightarrow s_i = 0$. *(The symbol $\Longrightarrow$ should read "implies," i.e., zero attraction implies zero market share.)*

Axiom A 2.3 $\mathcal{A}_i = \mathcal{A}_j \Longrightarrow s_i = s_j$ *($i \neq j$) (i.e., equal attraction implies equal market share).*

Axiom A 2.4 *When $\mathcal{A}_j$ changes by Δ, the corresponding change in s_i ($i \neq j$) is independent of j (e.g., a change in attraction has a symmetrically distributed effect on competitive market share).*

From those four *axioms* they show that the following relationship between attractions and market shares may be derived.

$$s_i = \frac{\mathcal{A}_i}{\sum_{j=1}^{m} \mathcal{A}_j} \qquad (2.6)$$

Perhaps no one would argue the fact that equation (2.6) and equation (2.3) are extremely similar. True, equation (2.3) and (2.6) represent two rather distinct schools of thought regarding the determinants of market shares (a firm's marketing effort for the former and consumer attraction for the latter). But an additional assumption that the attraction of a brand is proportional to its marketing effort (which is not unreasonable) is all that is required to reconcile two equations. It is rather comforting when the same expression is derivable from different logical bases.[5]

BKL also show that a slightly different set of assumptions also yield equation (2.6). Let C be the set of all alternative brands from which consumers make their choice.

Axiom B 2.1 $\mathcal{A}_i \geq 0$

Axiom B 2.2 *The attraction of a subset $S(\subseteq C)$ is equal to the sum of the attractions of elements in S.*

Axiom B 2.3 *$\mathcal{A}_i$ is finite for all i and non-zero for at least one element in C.*

---

[5] Axiom A 2.4 is has been the subject of critical discussion, as will be developed later.

Axiom B 2.4 *If the attractions of subsets $S^{(1)}$ and $S^{(2)}$ are equal, their market shares are equal.*

The last axiom establishes the relationship between attractions and market shares. BKL observe that, if we add an assumption that

$$\sum_{i=1}^{m} \mathcal{A}_i = 1$$

in lieu of B 2.4, $\mathcal{A}_i$ in this set of axioms satisfies the assumptions for probabilities in a finite (discrete) sample space. Because of this BKL suggest that attractions may be interpreted as *unnormalized probabilities*. However, this in turn suggests that if attractions were to follow axioms B 2.1 through B 2.4, by normalizing the $\mathcal{A}_i$'s through (2.6), market shares (s_i) may be interpreted as probabilities. This latter interpretation seems to confuse an *aggregate* concept (that is, market shares) with an *individual* (or *disaggregated*) concept (that is, probabilities). Only when the market is homogeneous (i.e., not composed of systematically different consumer segments), can market shares and choice probabilities be used interchangeably. We will return to this point in section 2.8.

2.5 Alternative Models of Market Share

The previous two sections gave the rationales behind the MCI model and its close cousin, the MNL model. We now give explicit specifications to those models.

MCI Model:

$$\mathcal{A}_i = \exp(\alpha_i) \cdot \prod_{k=1}^{K} X_{ki}^{\beta_k} \cdot \epsilon_i \qquad (2.7)$$

$$s_i = \frac{\mathcal{A}_i}{\sum_{j=1}^{m} \mathcal{A}_j}$$

MNL Model:

$$\mathcal{A}_i = \exp(\alpha_i + \sum_{k=1}^{K} \beta_k \cdot X_{ki} + \epsilon_i) \qquad (2.8)$$

$$s_i = \frac{\mathcal{A}_i}{\sum_{j=1}^{m} \mathcal{A}_j}$$

where:

α_i = a parameter for the constant influence of brand i

ϵ_i = an error term

and the other terms are as previously defined in Chapter 1. In the following parts of this book, we will use *attraction*, rather than *marketing effort*, to describe $\mathcal{A}_i$, because it is a more accepted terminology, keeping in mind that this implies the assumption that attraction is proportional to marketing effort. Note that the MCI model above is a version of the general MCI (attraction) model in Chapter 1 in that the monotone transformation, f_k, is an identity transformation. The MNL model is another version of the general model where f_k is an exponential transformation.[6]

But the MCI and MNL models are not the only models of market shares. A common formulation is that of the *linear model* which assumes simply that a brand's market share is a linear function in marketing-mix variables and other relevant variables. Another common form is the *multiplicative model*, where market shares are given as a product of a number of variables (raised to a suitable power). Although there are other more complicated market-share models, for our purposes at present it is sufficient to define explicitly the following three alternative models.

Linear Model:

$$s_i = \alpha_i + \sum_{k=1}^{K} \beta_k \cdot X_{ki} + \epsilon_i \tag{2.9}$$

Multiplicative Model:

$$s_i = \exp(\alpha_i) \cdot \prod_{k=1}^{K} X_{ki}^{\beta_k} \cdot \epsilon_i \tag{2.10}$$

Exponential Model:

$$s_i = \exp(\alpha_i + \sum_{k=1}^{K} \beta_k \cdot X_{ki} + \epsilon_i) \tag{2.11}$$

The reader should note that the five models — MCI, MNL, linear, multiplicative, and exponential — are closely related to each other. For example, if we take the logarithm of both sides of either the multiplicative or exponential model, we will have a linear model (linear in the

---

[6]Those models will be referred to *raw-score* MCI or MNL models in later chapters of this book.

parameters of the respective models, and not in variables). In other words, the difference between the linear model and the multiplicative and exponential models is merely one of the choice of transformations for variables, that is, whether or not the logarithmic transformation is applied to variables. (The specification for the error term may be different in those three models, but this is a rather fine technical point which will be addressed in Chapter 5.)

The most interesting relationship is, however, the one between the MCI and multiplicative models, which is also duplicated between the MNL and exponential models. The multiplicative model, of course, assumes that market shares are a multiplicative function in explanatory variables, while in the MCI model attractions are multiplicative in variables and market shares are computed by normalizing attractions (i.e., by making the sum of market shares to be equal to one). Obviously, the key difference between the two is normalization. In this connection, Naert and Bultez [1973] proposed the following important condition for a market-share model.

1. Estimated market shares from the model are nonnegative.

2. The sum of estimated market shares is greater than zero and less than or equal to one.

These conditions, commonly known as the *logical-consistency requirements*, are clearly not met by either the multiplicative or exponential model, but are met by their respective normalized forms (i.e., MCI and MNL), which must be a clear advantage for MCI and MNL models. Note that the linear model does not satisfy the logical-consistency requirements.

Why, then, are the MCI and MNL models not used more extensively? The answer is that for a time both of those models were considered to be intrinsically nonlinear models, requiring estimation schemes which were expensive in analysts' time and computer resources. This, however, turned out to be a hasty judgment because those models may be changed into a linear model (in the model parameters) by a simple transformation. Take the MCI model, for example. First, take the logarithm of both sides.

$$\log s_i = \alpha_i + \sum_{k=1}^{K} \beta_k \log X_{ki} + \log \epsilon_i$$

$$-\log\{\sum_{j=1}^{m}(\alpha_j \prod_{k=1}^{K} X_{kj}^{\beta_k}\epsilon_j)\}$$

If we sum the above equation over i ($i = 1, 2, \ldots, m$) and divide by m, we have

$$\log \tilde{s} = \bar{\alpha} + \sum_{k=1}^{K} \beta_k \log \tilde{X}_k + \log \tilde{\epsilon}$$

$$-\log\{\sum_{j=1}^{m}(\alpha_j \prod_{k=1}^{K} X_{kj}^{\beta_k}\epsilon_j)\}$$

where $\tilde{s}$, $\tilde{X}_k$ and $\tilde{\epsilon}$ are the geometric means of s_i, X_{ki} and ϵ_i, respectively. Subtracting the above from the previous equation, we obtain

$$\log\left(\frac{s_i}{\tilde{s}}\right) = \alpha_i^* + \sum_{k=1}^{K} \beta_k \log\left(\frac{X_{ki}}{\tilde{X}_k}\right) + \epsilon_i^* \qquad (2.12)$$

where:

$$\alpha_i^* = (\alpha_i - \bar{\alpha})$$

$$\epsilon_i^* = \log(\epsilon_i/\tilde{\epsilon}).$$

The last equation is linear in model parameters α_i^* ($i = 1, 2, \ldots, m$) and β_k ($k = 1, 2, \ldots, K$). (In addition, there is another parameter σ_ϵ^2, the variance of ϵ_i, to be estimated, but this parameter does not concern us until Chapter 5.) This transformation will be called the *log-centering transformation* hereafter.[7] Note that, if we apply the log-centering transformation to the MNL model, we obtain the following linear form.

$$\log\left(\frac{s_i}{\tilde{s}}\right) = (\alpha_i - \bar{\alpha}) + \sum_{k=1}^{K} \beta_k(X_{ki} - \bar{X}_k) + (\epsilon_i - \bar{\epsilon})$$

where $\bar{\alpha}$, $\bar{X}_k$ and $\bar{\epsilon}$ are the arithmetic means of α_i, X_{ki} and ϵ_i, respectively. If we let $\alpha_i^* = (\alpha_i - \bar{\alpha})$ and $\epsilon_i^* = (\epsilon_i - \bar{\epsilon})$,

$$\log\left(\frac{s_i}{\tilde{s}}\right) = \alpha_i^* + \sum_{k=1}^{K} \beta_k(X_{ki} - \bar{X}_k) + \epsilon_i^* \qquad (2.13)$$

---

[7]The importance of this transformation is that we can estimate the parameters of the original nonlinear model using linear-regression techniques.

Both equations (2.12) and (2.13) are linear functions in model parameters, and hence called *log-linear* models. Recall that the multiplicative and exponential models are also log-linear models. In other words, both the MCI and MNL models are really special cases of log-linear models. This point may be dramatically illustrated by the following comparisons among the *reduced forms* of these models.[8]

Linear Model:

$$s_i = \alpha_i + \sum_{k=1}^{K} \beta_k X_{ki} + \epsilon_i$$

Multiplicative Model:

$$\log s_i = \alpha_i + \sum_{k=1}^{K} \beta_k \log X_{ki} + \log \epsilon_i$$

Exponential Model:

$$\log s_i = \alpha_i + \sum_{k=1}^{K} \beta_k X_{ki} + \epsilon_i$$

MCI Model:

$$\log \left(\frac{s_i}{\tilde{s}} \right) = \alpha_i^* + \sum_{k=1}^{K} \beta_k \log \left(\frac{X_{ki}}{\tilde{X}_k} \right) + \epsilon_i^*$$

MNL Model:

$$\log \left(\frac{s_i}{\tilde{s}} \right) = \alpha_i^* + \sum_{k=1}^{K} \beta_k (X_{ki} - \bar{X}_k) + \epsilon_i^*$$

In the above, the multiplicative and exponential models are shown in the log-linear form. In all five equations the right-hand side is linear in both α_i $(i = 1, 2, \ldots, m)$ and β_k $(k = 1, 2, \ldots, K)$. The left-hand side is either a market share, the logarithm of a market share, or a log-centered form of a market share. We will defer the discussion on the specification of the error term (ϵ_i, $\log \epsilon_i$ and ϵ_i^*) till Chapter 5, but, since the number of parameters in the five formulations are the same, one would expect that those models would be just as accurate in predicting the

---

[8] The *reduced forms* of these models contain variables transformed so that they made be directly submitted to a multiple-regression routine.

dependent variable, namely, the left-hand side of each equation. Many readers would then ask, "Which one makes the most accurate prediction of market shares?" We report that many studies on predictive accuracy of market-share models[9] found the logical-consistency property of the MCI and MNL models to produce only marginally better predictions than the linear and multiplicative models. Why then all this fuss about the MCI and MNL models? First, these test did not include the more sophisticated versions of the models (see Chapter 3). And second, as was stated in Chapter 1, we do not believe that predictive accuracy is the only important criterion for judging the value of a model. We would rather find the answer in the *construct validity* (i.e., intrinsic meaningfulness) of those models, which is discussed in the next section.

2.6   Market-Share Elasticities

There is a common yet perplexing question which often arises on the part of a product/brand manager, that is, "How much will our brand share change if we change a marketing-mix variable by a certain amount?" The answer to this question is obviously vital to those who develop short-term marketing plans. After all, a brand manager must decide what price to charge and how much the firm should spend in advertising, sales promotion, trade allowances, etc. If the market responses to the changes in marketing-mix variables were known, his/her job would become in many ways immensely simpler.[10] But this is one of the most difficult pieces of information to obtain. It might be said that in a sense this entire book is devoted to answering this difficult question.

Before we begin the discussion of how one predicts actual changes in market shares, let us first look into a theoretical concept, *market-share elasticity*, which will help us in measuring responses toward marketing-mix variables. Simply stated, *market-share elasticity is the ratio of the relative change in a market share corresponding to a relative change in*

---

[9]See Brodie, Roderick & Cornelius A. de Kluyver [1984], "Attraction Versus Linear and Multiplicative Market Share Models: An Empirical Evaluation," *Journal of Marketing Research*, 21 (May), 194–201. Ghosh, Avijit, Scott Neslin & Robert Shoemaker [1984], "A Comparison of Market Share Models and Estimation Procedures," *Journal of Marketing Research*, 21 (May), 202–10. Leeflang, Peter S. H. & Jan C. Reuyl [1984], "On the Predictive Power of Market Share Attraction Models," *Journal of Marketing Research*, 21 (May) 211–15.

[10]The planning process would still require a substantial effort as is discussed in Chapter 7.

a *marketing-mix variable.* Expressed mathematically,

$$e_{s_i} = \frac{\Delta s_i / s_i}{\Delta X_{ki} / X_{ki}} = \frac{\Delta s_i}{\Delta X_{ki}} \cdot \frac{X_{ki}}{s_i} \qquad (2.14)$$

where s_i is the market share, and X_{ki} is the value of the kth marketing-mix variable, for brand i. The symbol Δ indicates a change in respective variables. There is nothing conceptually difficult in market-share elasticity. For example, if a brand's share increased 10% corresponding to a price reduction of 5%, the above equation would give a (price) elasticity of -2; or if advertising expenditures were increased by 3% and as a result the share increased by 1%, the (advertising) elasticity would be 0.33; and so forth. We say that a brand's market share is *elastic* with respect to X_{ki} if the (absolute) value of e_{s_i} is greater than one; *inelastic* if it is less than one. It is also obvious that one may predict the changes in market share from the knowledge of market-share elasticity. If e_{s_i} is 0.5, then we know that a 10% increase in X_{ki} will produce a 5% increase in market share. In absolute terms, if the current share is 30% and the current advertising expenditure (per period) is $1 million, a $100,000 increase in advertising expenditure will result in a 1.5% increase in market share.

No one would deny that share elasticities would give one a clear perspective on the effect of marketing-mix variables on market shares. And this is not just a theoretical concept, either. It is not far-fetched if we said that, even if product/brand managers might not know the exact magnitude of market response to the change in a marketing-mix variable, they might have a reasonably good idea of market-share elasticities for their product/brand, at least to the extent that market shares are either elastic or inelastic to changes in marketing-mix variables. As will be shown later, it is sometimes difficult for one to separate market-share elasticities from the elasticities regarding the *industry* sales, but, even so, experienced managers should have a fair grasp of market-share elasticities. If a manager had no idea of whether a 5% change in price or advertising expenditures would bring about a less than, equal to, or more than 5% change in the market share, how could he/she even approach to making short-term marketing plans?

No matter how experienced a manager is, however, he/she seldom knows the exact magnitude of elasticities. One of the reasons for such general states of uncertainty is that share elasticities change over time depending on the share levels and the intensity of competitive activities at that time. A manager might be able to get a reasonable idea of share elasticities for his/her brand through experience if they were relatively stable over time, but the fact is that elasticities are not constant over time. In general, the greater the share of a brand, the smaller one expects the elasticities for its share to be. (The reader will find that this is the basic reason for rejecting the Multiplicative model because it implies constant elasticities.) It is obvious that, if a brand has a 95% share of market, say, it cannot gain more than 5 percentage points even if the magnitude of X_{ki} is increased by more than 5%. Also one would generally expect that a brand's share changes will be affected by what other brands do. If the competitors are relatively inactive, a brand may gain a large share by lowering its price. But, if competitors retaliate quickly, a brand may not gain any share at all for the same amount of price reduction. To summarize, the necessity to take share levels and competitive reactions into account puts the manager at a severe disadvantage in knowing market-share elasticities accurately.

Market-share models discussed in the preceding section will help managers by providing them with the estimates of elasticities. This, we believe, is one of the most important contributions of those models. Stated differently, there is no way to estimate elasticities directly from empirical data without adopting a model. This may not be intuitively clear because the formula for computing elasticities (2.14) appears to contain only those terms which may be empirically measurable. But note that the Δs_i term in equation (2.14) must correspond to the change in a specific marketing-mix variable, ΔX_{ki}. Suppose that one observed that a brand's share increased 3% in a period. How does one know how much of that increased share is due to price reduction? Or due to increased advertising? To assess those so-called *partial effects* one needs a market-share model.

The reader may be cautioned at this point that the estimated values of elasticities vary from one model to the other, and hence one must choose that model which fits the situation best. To illustrate, we will derive the share elasticity with respect to X_{ki} for the simplest version of each model. For that purpose, however, one needs another concept of share elasticity which is slightly different from the one defined by (2.14). Technically, (2.14) is called the *arc elasticity*. This is because both Δs_i and ΔX_{ki} span a range over the market-response curve which gives the relationship between market shares and marketing-mix variables. The other elasticity formula is called the *point elasticity* and takes the following form.

$$e_{s_i} = \frac{\partial s_i}{\partial X_{ki}} \cdot \frac{X_{ki}}{s_i} \ . \tag{2.15}$$

Note that the only difference between the two formulas is that $(\Delta s_i/\Delta X_{ki})$ in equation (2.14) is replaced by $(\partial s_i/\partial X_{ki})$ in (2.15). Formula (2.15) utilizes the slope of the market-response curve at a specific value of X_{ki}. The reason for using the point-elasticity formula than the arc formula is that the former gives much simpler expressions of share elasticity. We may add that (2.15) is a close approximation of (2.14) for a small value of ΔX_{ki}, that is, when the change in X_{ki} is very small. The point elasticity for each model is given below. For convenient formulas for computing point elasticities see Appendix 2.9.1.

Linear Model:

$$e_{s_i} = \beta_k X_{ki}/s_i$$

Multiplicative Model:

$$e_{s_i} = \beta_k$$

Exponential Model:

$$e_{s_i} = \beta_k X_{ki}$$

MCI Model:

$$e_{s_i} = \beta_k(1 - s_i)$$

MNL Model:

$$e_{s_i} = \beta_k(1 - s_i)X_{ki}$$

Though the five market-share models are similar in the sense that they are either linear or log-linear models, the share elasticities implied from the models are quite different. One may wish to disqualify some models on the basis of those expressions on some a priori grounds. In the following we will only present verbal discussions, but the interested reader is referred to a more mathematical treatment of the properties of market-share elasticities given in Appendix 2.9.2.

First, one would expect that a brand's share elasticity approaches zero as the share for that brand approaches one. The Multiplicative model implies that share elasticity is constant regardless of the share level, and therefore seems rather inappropriate as a market-share model.

Second, it is generally accepted that it becomes harder to gain market shares as a firm increases its marketing effort. In other words, one would expect market-share elasticity to approach zero as X_{ki} goes to infinity (or minus infinity depending on the variable in question). But the Exponential model implies an opposite: share elasticity may be increased indefinitely as the value of X_{ki} increases. This is an uncomfortable situation, especially if variable X_{ki} is a promotional variable (such as advertising expenditures, number of salesmen, etc.). In addition, the Exponential model has the same problem as the Multiplicative model: for a fixed value of X_{ki}, e_{s_i} is constant for all levels of s_i.

Note that the elasticity expression for the Linear model reflects that share elasticity declines as the share increases, but, when the share approaches one, the elasticity does not approach zero. In fact, share elasticity approaches 1 as X_{ki} increases to infinity (or minus infinity, as the case may be). Thus the Linear model produces a highly unreasonable share-elasticity expression.

Considering what we expect from share elasticities, one may conclude that the Linear, Multiplicative, and Exponential models are not proper market-share models for use in marketing decision making. This leaves us the MCI and MNL models as feasible alternatives. Figure 2.1 shows the change in share elasticity over the positive range of X_{ki} values.

Figure 2.1: Share Elasticities for MCI and MNL Models

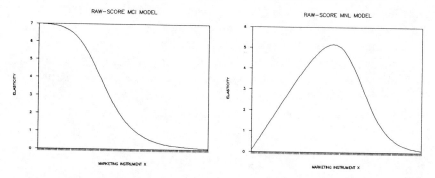

The share is assumed to increase as X_{ki} increases over the range. Accounting for this share increase, the share elasticity for the MCI model monotonically declines as X_{ki} increases (Figure 2.1 (a)), while that for the MNL model increases to a point and then declines.

The reader will ask which expression is a better one for share elasticity. The answer is, "It depends on variable X_{ki}." The relevant issue here is how share elasticity should behave for low values of the variable. If X_{ki} is product price, for example, it is more likely that share elasticity is fairly large even when price is near zero. Hence, one would be inclined to use the MCI model for price. On the other hand, if the variable is advertising expenditure, it is not unreasonable to assume that, at an extremely low level of expenditure, advertising is not very effective. (This is to say that there is a threshold effect for advertising.) This assumption, of course, leads to the adoption of the MNL model for advertising expenditure. Indeed, it is the authors' position that the choice between the MCI and MNL models is not one or the other; both models may be mixed in a single formulation for market shares. The reader may recall that a general MCI (attraction) model of the following type was presented in Chapter 1.

General MCI (Attraction) Model:

$$\mathcal{A}_i = \prod_{k=1}^{K} f_k(X_{ki})^{\beta_k} \tag{2.16}$$

$$s_i = \frac{\mathcal{A}_i}{\sum_{j=1}^{m} \mathcal{A}_j}$$

where f_k is a monotone transformation of X_{ki}. It is obvious that, if one chooses an identity transformation for k (that is, $f_k(X_{ki}) = X_{ki}$), (2.16) becomes the MCI model; if f_k is an exponential function (that is, $f_k(X_{ki}) = \exp(X_{ki})$), then (2.16) becomes the MNL model. But there is no reason for one to have to choose either the identity or exponential transformation for all the f_k's in (2.16). Depending on the nature of variable X_k, one should be free to choose either the identity or exponential transformation (or any other appropriate monotone transformation, for that matter). This is why in (2.16) f_k has subscript k. For the remainder of this book, we will use a mixture of MCI and MNL models.

2.7   Sales-Volume Elasticities

The reader is perhaps convinced by now that market-share elasticities play a significant role in market-share analysis, but we must add that they are not the only important concept in marketing planning. It may be superfluous to say that the product/brand manager is interested not in forecasting market-share changes themselves, but in forecasting the changes in sales volume of the firm's product corresponding to the changes in marketing-mix variables. For this latter purpose, knowing share elasticities is not enough. Since a brand's sales volume is a product of its market share and the relevant industry sales, one would also need information on how much industry sales change due to the firm's marketing activities.

There is a rather interesting relationship between the share, industry-sales, and sales-volume elasticities for a firm. One may define *point sales elasticity* in the manner analogous to (2.15).

$$e_{Q_i} = \frac{\partial Q_i}{\partial X_{ki}} \cdot \frac{X_{ki}}{Q_i} \tag{2.17}$$

where Q_i is the sales volume (in units sold) for firm i. Similarly, *point industry-sales elasticity* may be defined as follows.

$$e_Q = \frac{\partial Q}{\partial X_{ki}} \cdot \frac{X_{ki}}{Q} \tag{2.18}$$

where Q is the sales volume for the entire industry. It is well known that the following simple relationship exists among e_{s_i}, e_{Q_i}, and e_Q.[11]

$$e_{Q_i} = e_{s_i} + e_Q \ . \tag{2.19}$$

This equation shows that sales elasticity for firm i is merely the sum of the firm's share elasticity and industry-sales elasticity.[12] For example, if share elasticity is 0.6 and industry-sales elasticity is 0.1, the sales elasticity is 0.7. In other words, if a firm increased a marketing-mix variable by 10%, say, and as a result increased its share by 6% and at the same time succeeded in expanding the industry sales by 1%, then its sales volume should increase by approximately 7%.[13] Equation (2.19) combines the essential elements of interbrand competition. In order to expand a firm's brand sales, one will have to increase either industry sales or the market share for the brand, or both. But one would expect that in many cases the industry sales will be rather inelastic to a single firm's marketing activities. If this were indeed the case, brand sales could

---

[11]Lambin, Naert & Bultez [1975], "Optimal Marketing Behavior in Oligopoly," *European Economic Review*, 6, 105-28.

[12]This assumes no systematic competitive reactions. This assumption is relaxed in section 6.3.

[13]The numerical result is approximate because equation (2.19) holds for *point* elasticities only. If the change in X_{ki} is relatively large as in this example, the relationship should be expressed by *arc* elasticities as follows:

$$e_{Q_i} = \frac{\Delta Q_i}{\Delta X_{ki}} \cdot \frac{X_{ki}}{Q_i} = e_{s_i}(1 + \frac{\Delta Q}{Q}) + e_Q \ .$$

When $\frac{\Delta Q}{Q}$ is relatively small, $e_{Q_i} \approx e_{s_i} + e_Q$ as in the case of point elasticities.

be expanded only if the firm's share could be increased. Suppose that $e_{s_i} = 0.6$ and $e_Q = 0.1$. In order to increase the brand sales by 10%, the market share will have to be increased by more than 8.5% ($10 \times 0.6/0.7$). On the other hand, if industry sales were reasonably responsive to a firm's marketing mix, the increase in brand sales could be achieved with relatively small increase in market share. If $e_{s_i} = 0.6$ and $e_Q = 0.3$, say, a 6.7% ($10 \times 0.6/0.9$) share increase results in a 10% increase in brand sales.

To summarize, when industry-sales elasticities are near zero, it is clear that firms in an industry will be fighting for a share of a *fixed pie*. The reliance on market-share increases in improving a firm's sales will undoubtedly leads to a more intense competition. If industry-sales elasticities are reasonably large, firms will not have to be too sensitive about taking shares from others (or others taking one's share), resulting in more complacent competitive relationships among firms. Thus the knowledge of industry-sales elasticities is helpful to marketing managers in assessing competitive pressures existing in an industry. We will turn to the estimation of industry-sales elasticities in Chapter 5 and the effects on brand planning are discussed in Chapter 7.

2.8   *Market Shares and Choice Probabilities

So far we have chosen to treat market shares as an aggregate quantity, namely, the ratio of a firm's (brand) sales to the relevant industry sales. But, since aggregate sales are composites of many purchases made by individual buyers (consumers and industrial buyers), market-share figures must be related to individual buyers' choices of various brands. In fact, one frequently encounters measures of market shares which are based on data obtained from individual buyers. The market-share figures computed from the so-called *consumer-diary panels* or *optical-scanner panels*[14] are prime examples of such individual-based market-share measures. But such individual-based market-share measures are estimates of actual market shares, and, if one had actual share figures, why should one bother with those measures? In this section we will look at the relationships between market shares and choices made by individual buyers and examine the importance of individual-based market-share data.

In analyzing the relationships between market shares and individual

---

[14]These are consumer panels whose purchase records are maintained by utilizing optical scanners located at selected retail stores.

choice probabilities, we will have to consider the variability of two factors — *choice probabilities* and *purchase frequency* for individual buyers — over the population of buyers in the market. Let us first define those two concepts.

Suppose that each buyer purchases a number of units of the product per period. We will assume that the *purchase frequency* (i.e., the number of purchases per period) by an individual buyer is a random variable which has a statistical distribution. We shall call this distribution an individual *purchase-frequency* distribution, since it is defined for each buyer in the market. The specific form of this distribution does not concern us here except that it has its mean (*mean purchase frequency*).

Let's assume, not unreasonably, that a buyer does not always purchase the same brand from a set of alternative brands (this is the relevant *industry* in our previous definition). In addition, it is assumed that a buyer's choice of a brand at one *purchase occasion* is made independently from his/her previous purchase and the buyer's selection is governed by probabilities specific to each brand.[15] The set of probabilities for alternative brands in the industry is called *individual choice probabilities*.

In our view, whether or not the buyer's behavior is truly probabilistic or deterministic is not an issue here. A buyer's choice behavior may be totally deterministic, but the environmental conditions surrounding purchase occasions may be such that they involve probabilistic elements which, from the viewpoint of an outside observer, make the buyers' choices appear probabilistic. We also posit that the attractions of alternative brands affect choice probabilities. This is to be consistent with our position that brand attractions are the determinants of market shares. We refer the reader to Appendix 2.9.3 for how individual choice probabilities are determined from attractions of alternative brands.

We distinguish four cases regarding the homogeneity (or heterogeneity) of the buyer population with respect to *individual choice probabilities* and *purchase frequencies*.

Case 1: Homogeneous Purchase Frequencies and Choice Probabilities

If mean individual purchase frequencies are equal for all buyers and the brand selection of every buyer in the market is governed by the same set of choice probabilities, it is rather obvious that the market share of a brand will be approximately equal to the choice probability for the

---

[15]This is to say, each buyer's brand selection in a period follows a Bernoulli process.

brand. (Actually, it is the expected value of the market share of a brand which will be equal to the choice probability for the brand.) In this case market shares may be interpreted as individual choice probabilities without much difficulty. For example, if the market share for a brand is 0.3, one may say that each buyer chooses this brand with a 0.3 probability.

Case 2: Homogeneous Purchase Frequencies and Heterogeneous Choice Probabilities

The interpretation of market shares will have to be changed a little if each buyer has a different set of choice probability values for alternative brands. We still assume that mean purchase frequencies are equal for all buyers in the market. Under those assumptions it is easy to show that the expected value of a brand's market share is equal to the (population) average of choice probabilities for that brand. In other words, a market share of 0.3 may be interpreted that the average of choice probabilities across the buyer population is 0.3.

Case 3: Heterogeneous Purchase Frequencies and Homogeneous Choice Probabilities

This is the case where, while a common set of choice probabilities is shared by all buyers, mean purchase frequencies vary over buyers and have a statistical distribution over the buyer population. In this case the expected value of a brand's market share is still equal to its choice probability.

Case 4: Heterogeneous Purchase Frequencies and Choice Probabilities

In this case both choice probabilities and purchase frequencies are assumed to be variable over the buyer population. We need to distinguish further two cases within this.

(a) Uncorrelated Case: choice probabilities and purchase frequencies are uncorrelated (i.e., independently distributed) over the buyer population.

(b) Correlated Case: choice probabilities and purchase frequencies are correlated over the buyer population.

Let's first look at the uncorrelated case. If purchase frequencies and choice probabilities are uncorrelated, the expected value of market shares are, as is shown later, still equal to population averages of choice probabilities (as in the case of homogeneous purchase frequencies). Turning to the correlated case, one finds that market shares are no longer directly related to choice probabilities. This is perhaps more realistic for most products, since one often hears that so-called *heavy users* and *light users* exhibit remarkably different purchase behavior. Heavy users are said to be more discriminating in taste, more price conscious, and tend to purchase *family-size* or economy packages, etc. It is not surprising, then, to find heavy users preferring some brands or brand/size combinations to those preferred by light users. If there were differences in the value of choice probability for a brand between heavy and light users, individual purchase frequencies and choice probabilities would be correlated and the market share for the brand will be biased toward the choice probability values for heavy users simply because they purchase more units of the brand. Thus market shares and choice probabilities generally do not coincide in this case. Table 2.3 illustrates those points.

Table 2.3: Effect of Correlation Between Purchase Frequencies and Choice Probabilities

(a) Uncorrelated Case

Buyer	Purchase Frequency	Choice Probabilities		Expected Number of Purchases	
		Brand 1	Brand 2	Brand 1	Brand 2
1	1	0.2	0.8	0.2	0.8
2	3	0.2	0.8	0.6	2.4
3	2	0.8	0.2	1.6	0.4
Average	2	0.4	0.6	0.8	1.2
Market Share				0.4	0.6

(b) Correlated Case

Buyer	Purchase Frequency	Choice Probabilities		Expected Number of Purchases	
		Brand 1	Brand 2	Brand 1	Brand 2
1	1	0.2	0.8	0.2	0.8
2	2	0.2	0.8	0.4	1.6
3	3	0.8	0.2	2.4	0.6
Average	2	0.4	0.6	1.0	1.0
Market Share				0.5	0.5

Table 2.3 (a) shows the case where purchase frequencies and choice probabilities are uncorrelated. In this case the expected market shares are equal to the averages of choice probabilities. In Table 2.3 (b) there

is a moderate degree of correlation between purchase frequencies and choice probabilities, as heavy buyer 3 prefers brand 1 while light buyers 1 and 2 prefer brand 2. In this case market share for brand 1 is greater than the average of choice probability for the brand. The results above may be stated more formally as follows.

The expected value of unit sales for brand i is obtained by averaging (over the buyer population) individual purchase frequencies multiplied by the individual's choice probability for the brand. Hence the expected value of market share for brand i is given by:

$$\text{Market Share }_i = \frac{\text{Average Number of Units Purchased for Brand } i}{\text{Average Purchase Frequency (for All Brands)}}$$

or

$$E(s_i) = \frac{1}{\bar{\mu}} \int_0^\infty \int_0^1 \mu \pi_i g(\mu, \pi_i) d\pi_i d\mu \tag{2.20}$$

where:

$E(s_i) =$ the expected value of market share for brand i

$\mu =$ the mean purchase frequency per period (per individual)

$\bar{\mu} =$ the population mean of μ

$\pi_i =$ the individual choice probability for brand i

$g(\mu, \pi_i) =$ the joint density function for μ and π_i.

Equation (2.20) shows that the expected value of market share for brand i is a weighted average of choice probabilities (weights are individual mean purchase frequencies) divided by average mean purchase frequency $\bar{\mu}$. From (2.20) we directly obtain the following result.

$$E(s_i) = \bar{\pi}_i + cov(\mu, \pi_i)/\bar{\mu}$$

where:

$\bar{\pi}_i =$ the population mean of π_i

$cov(\mu, \pi_i) =$ the covariance of μ and π_i.

This is because, by definition, $cov(\mu, \pi_i) = \bar{\mu} E(s_i) - \bar{\mu} \bar{\pi}_i$. This equation shows that in general $E(s_i)$ is not equal to $\bar{\pi}_i$. Since $cov(\mu, \pi_i)$ may be positive or negative, one cannot say if market shares are greater or smaller than population mean of choice probabilities. But if μ and π_i

are positively correlated, $E(s_i)$ is greater than $\bar{\pi}_i$. If the correlation is negative, $E(s_i)$ is less than $\bar{\pi}_i$. Note also that, if $cov(\mu, \pi_i) = 0$ (that is, if there is no correlation between the market share and choice probability), then the expected market share and the average choice probability are equal. In other words, in the uncorrelated case the expected value of a brand's market share is equal to its average choice probability ($\bar{\pi}_i$). The foregoing results are summarized in Table 2.4.

Table 2.4: Relations Between Market Shares and Choice Probabilities

	Purchase Frequencies	
Choice Probabilities	Homogeneous	Heterogeneous
Homogeneous	Case 1: $E(s_i) = \pi_i$	Case 3: $E(s_i) = \pi_i$
Heterogeneous	Case 2: $E(s_i) = \bar{\pi}_i$	Case 4 (a) Uncorrelated: $E(s_i) = \bar{\pi}_i$ Case 4 (b) Correlated: $E(s_i) = \bar{\pi}_i + cov(\mu, \pi_i)/\bar{\mu}$

It is apparent from the table that the only case where there is no correspondence between market shares and choice probabilities is Case 4 (b). This fact might tempt one to look at this case as an exception or anomaly, but this is probably the most prevalent condition in the market. A practical implication of the preponderance of Case 4 (b) is that, for the purpose of market-share forecasts, it is not sufficient for one to be able to predict the choice behavior of individuals accurately; rather it becomes necessary for one to be able to predict choice probabilities for each different level of purchase frequencies.

Of course, the situation cannot be changed by merely assuming that μ and π_i are uncorrelated over the buyer population (Case 4 (a)). Since μ and π_i are arithmetically related, that is, $\pi_i = \mu_i/\mu$ where μ_i is the expected number of units of brand i purchased by an individual, and $\sum_{i=1}^{m} \mu_i = \mu$ where m is the number of alternative brands in the industry, the assumption that $cov(\mu, \pi_i) = 0$ (for all i) implies a very restrictive form of joint distribution for μ and π_i. Indeed, it may be shown that μ is distributed as a Gamma function and the π_i's are jointly distributed as a Dirichlet distribution. No other distributional assumption will give $cov(\mu, \pi_i) = 0$. See Appendix 2.9.4 for the proof of this result. The reader will find that the assumption that the processes which generate individual purchase frequencies are independent of the processes which determine individual choice probabilities is very common in modeling consumer choice behavior. But note that this practice is equivalent to assuming no correlation between μ and π_i and hence should be made only in limited circumstances where those restrictive distributional assumptions are justified.

What does all this argument about the relationship between purchase frequencies and choice probabilities suggest to analysts and marketing managers? If the correlation between purchase frequencies and choice probabilities are suspect, it is clearly advisable to segment the market in terms of purchase frequencies and analyze each segment separately. One may discover that marketing instruments have different effects on different segments and may be able to allocate marketing resources more efficiently. Also forecasting of brand sales and market shares will become more accurate if market shares are forecast for each segment and weighted by the mean purchase frequencies for the segments to obtain the estimate of overall market shares. Segmentation analysis of this type, however, requires more refined data than usual aggregate market share data, such as consumer-diary or scanner-panel data. Individual-based market-share estimates obtained from such data sets may become increasingly important if the data are accompanied by measures of the individual buyers' characteristics and allow the analyst to look into how buyer profiles are related to purchase frequencies. We will deal with the issues related to market-share data more extensively in Chapter 4.

2.9   Appendices for Chapter 2

2.9.1   *Calculus of Market-Share Elasticities

The point elasticities of market share s_i with respect to a marketing variable X_{kj} are given by

$$e_{s_i \cdot j} = \frac{\partial s_i / s_i}{\partial X_{kj} / X_{kj}} = \frac{\partial s_i}{\partial X_{kj}} \cdot \frac{X_{kj}}{s_i} \qquad (2.21)$$

The calculation of elasticities may be rather cumbersome for specific market-share models. In this appendix several formulas which are useful in calculating market-share elasticities are derived. In the following $e_{y \cdot x}$ indicates the elasticity of variable y with respect to variable x.

Chain Rule for a Compound Function:

If $Y = f(X)$ and $Z = g(Y)$, then

$$e_{z.x} = \frac{dZ}{Z} \cdot \frac{X}{dX} = \frac{dZ}{Z} \cdot \frac{Y}{dY} \cdot \frac{dY}{Y} \cdot \frac{X}{dX} = e_{z.y} e_{y.x}$$

Elasticity for a Sum of Variables:
If $W = Y + Z$, then

$$
\begin{aligned}
e_{w.x} &= \frac{dW}{dX} \cdot \frac{X}{W} = \left(\frac{dY}{dX} + \frac{dZ}{dX}\right) \cdot \frac{X}{W} \\
&= \frac{dY}{dX} \cdot \frac{X}{Y} \cdot \frac{Y}{W} + \frac{dZ}{dX} \cdot \frac{X}{Z} \cdot \frac{Z}{W} \\
&= e_{y.x} \frac{Y}{W} + e_{z.x} \frac{Z}{W}
\end{aligned}
$$

Elasticity for a Product of Variables:
If $W = Y \cdot Z$, then

$$
\begin{aligned}
e_{w.x} &= \frac{dW}{dX} \cdot \frac{X}{W} = \left(\frac{dY}{dX} Z + \frac{dZ}{dX} Y\right) \cdot \frac{X}{W} \\
&= \frac{dY}{dX} \cdot \frac{X}{Y} + \frac{dZ}{dX} \cdot \frac{X}{Z} \\
&= e_{y.x} + e_{z.x}
\end{aligned}
$$

Elasticity for an Inverse of a Variable:
If $Y = 1/Z$, then

$$
\begin{aligned}
e_{y.x} &= \frac{dY}{dX} \cdot \frac{X}{Y} = \frac{d}{dX} Z^{-1} \cdot \frac{X}{Z^{-1}} \\
&= -Z^{-2} \frac{dZ}{dX} X Z = -\frac{dZ}{dX} \cdot \frac{X}{Z} = -e_{z.x}
\end{aligned}
$$

2.9.2 *Properties of Market-Share Elasticities

Market-share elasticities have the following properties.

1. Since $Q_i = Q \cdot s_i$, we readily see that $e_{Q_i.x} = e_{Q.x} + e_{s_i.x}$, from the elasticity formula for a product of variables in Appendix 2.9.1.

2. If s_i is an increasing function in X, $e_{s_i.x} \to 0$ as $s_i \to 1$. This is because, as $s_i \to 1$, $Q_i \to Q$ and therefore $e_{Q_i.x} \to e_{Q.x}$ in (1).

3. If s_i is a strictly increasing function in X, $e_{s_i.x} \to 0$ as $X \to \infty$. This is derived from (2), since as $X \to \infty$, $s_i \to 1$. If s_i is an increasing function in X but approaches a constant (< 1) as $X \to \infty$, then $e_{s_i.x} \to 0$ (since $ds_i/dX \to 0$).

Not all market-share models satisfy the above three properties of market-share elasticities. Compare the following five models and the corresponding elasticities with respect to variable X.

Linear Model:

$$e_{s_i} = \beta X / s_i$$

Multiplicative Model:

$$e_{s_i} = \beta$$

Exponential Model:

$$e_{s_i} = \beta X$$

MCI Model:

$$e_{s_i} = \beta(1 - s_i)$$

MNL Model:

$$e_{s_i} = \beta(1 - s_i)X$$

If β is positive, it is clear that neither the linear, the multiplicative, nor the exponential model satisfies property (2) and (3). Only the MCI and MNL models satisfy all properties. This is one of the basic justifications for our choice of the latter models for market-share analysis.

2.9.3   *Individual Choice Probabilities

We have not discussed how individual choice probabilities are determined. The focus of this appendix is to relate individual choice probabilities to attractions of alternative brands. We can of course assume that the choice probability for a brand is proportional to its attraction, and obtain a result similar to Kotler's *fundamental theorem* discussed in section 2.3. But there are other more axiomatic approaches to deriving choice probabilities, and here we will be dealing with two basic models which are closely related to each other. It may be added that the terms *attraction* and *utility* will be used interchangeably in this appendix.

*Constant-Utility Models

The simplest model for choice probabilities is the constant-utility model which is also called the Luce model or Bradley-Terry-Luce model. Its basic assumption (or *axiom*) may be stated as follows.

Axiom 1 *Let an object, x, be an element of the* choice set *(i.e., set of choice alternatives), C, and also of a subset of C, S (i.e., $S \subseteq C$). The probability that x is chosen from C is equal to the product of the probability that x is chosen from S and the probability that (an element of) S is chosen from C.*

Luce calls this assumption the *individual choice axiom*, which may be expressed mathematically as:

$$Prob(x \mid C) = Prob(x \mid S)Prob(S \mid C)$$

where $Prob(x \mid C)$ is read "the probability that x is chosen from C."

This *axiom* for choice probabilities leads to results similar to that of the Market-Share Theorem for market shares. If we let

$$u_x = \frac{Prob(x \mid C)}{Prob(z \mid C)}$$

for an arbitrary object in C, then for two objects x and y in C

$$\frac{u_x}{u_y} = \frac{Prob(x \mid C)}{Prob(y \mid C)}$$

and this ratio does not change with the choice of z. Also, since

$$\sum_{y \in C} Prob(y \mid C) = Prob(x \mid C) \sum_{y \in C} \frac{u_y}{u_x} = 1$$

we have

$$Prob(x \mid C) = u_x / \sum_{y \in C} u_y \ .$$

The quantity u_x is called the *constant utility* of object x, and presumably determined for each individual as a function of marketing activities for x.

This model formed a basis of various models of individual choice behavior,[16] and was also implicitly adopted for many market-share models. But the model exhibits the so-called *Independence from Irrelevant*

---

[16] Huff, David L. [1962], *Determination of Intraurban Retail Trade Areas*, Los Angeles: Real Estate Research Program, University of California, Los Angeles. Haines, George H., Jr. Leonard S. Simon & Marcus Alexis [1972], "Maximum Likelihood Estimation of Central-City Food Trading Areas," *Journal of Marketing Research*, 9 (May), 154–59. Nakanishi, Masao & Lee G. Cooper [1974], "Parameter Estimation for a Multiplicative Competitive Interaction Model — Least Squares Approach," *Journal of Marketing Research*, 11 (August), 303–11.

Alternatives (IIA) property which produces some quite counterintuitive results. From the axiom we have

$$\frac{Prob(x \mid C)}{Prob(y \mid C)} = \frac{Prob(x \mid S)}{Prob(y \mid S)}$$

for any subset of $S \subseteq C$ which contain both x and y. Since this relationship must hold for set $\{x, y\}$,

$$\frac{u_x}{u_y} = \frac{Prob(x \mid \{x, y\})}{Prob(y \mid \{x, y\})} \, .$$

This ratio is independent of the choice of z. Since z is supposedly irrelevant to the odds of choosing x over y, this has been called the *Independence of Irrelevant Alternatives* (IIA) property. The classic counter examples are from Debreu.[17] Although Debreu proposed a record-buying situation, the issues are more clearly illustrated using a transportation-choice example. Suppose a person is indifferent between riding on a *red bus* (RB) versus a *blue bus* (BB) if offered just these two alternatives, but prefers riding a *taxi* (T) four-to-one over a *red bus*, if offered this pair or four-to-one over a *blue bus*, if offered that pair of alternatives. The choice axiom would summarize this case by noting that $Prob(RB \mid \{RB, BB\}) = .5$, $Prob(T \mid \{T, RB\}) = .8$, and $Prob(T \mid \{T, BB\}) = .8$. While it seems clear that the probability of choosing a taxi shouldn't decrease if it is offered in a choice set along with both a red bus and a blue bus (i.e., $Prob(T \mid \{RB, BB, T\})$ should still be .8), the choice axiom insists that $Prob(T \mid \{RB, BB, T\}) = .67$ and $Prob(RB \mid \{RB, BB, T\}) = .16$. The choice axiom forces this so that the *ratio* of the utility of RB to T is *constant* regardless of the choice set in which they are offered.

The concept of *constant utility* and the IIA property are really two sides of the same coin. If we think of *utility* is a inherent property of an object which doesn't change regardless of the context in which a choice is made, we will be trapped by the IIA property into counterintuitive positions.

There are two ways out of this problem. First, we can explicitly consider how the context in which choices are made affect the attraction of the alternatives. This is the path we follow in Chapter 3 when discussing the distinctiveness of marketing efforts (see section 3.8). Second, we can

---

[17]Debreu, Gerard [1960], "Review of R. D. Luce's *Individual Choice Behavior: A Theoretical Analysis, American Economic Review*, 50 (1), 186–8.

consider *utility* to be a random variable, rather than a constant. This is the topic of the next section.

*Random-Utility Models

A broad group of choice models is based on the assumption that utilities which an individual feels toward various objects (in our application, brands in an industry) at each purchase occasion are random variables, and the individual selects that brand which happens to have the largest utility value among the alternatives at that occasion. This model, known as a *random-utility model*, is defined as follows. Let $U_1, U_2, \ldots, U_m$ be the utilities for alternative brands where m is the number of brands in the choice set, C,[18] and $g(U_1, U_2, \ldots, U_m)$ be the joint density function for them. The probability that brand i is chosen at a purchase occasion is given by

$$Prob(i \mid C) = Prob(U_i \geq U_j \text{ for all } j \in C) \ .$$

In order to evaluate this probability, however, one must evaluate an integral function. For three brands, the probability that brand 1 is chosen is given by the following integral.

$$Prob(1 \mid C) = \int_{-\infty}^{\infty} \int_{-\infty}^{u_1} \int_{-\infty}^{u_1} g(u_1, u_2, u_3) du_3 du_2 du_1 \qquad (2.22)$$

Similarly, $Prob(2 \mid C)$ and $Prob(3 \mid C)$ are given by suitably changing the upper limits of integration. Integral (2.22) may be defined for any number of choice objects (e.g., brands).

A large number of variants of random utility models may be created from this definition by selecting different specifications for g. However, the usefulness of random utility models is limited because, unless the density function g is so very special as to give an analytical solution, the evaluation of this integral will in general require numerical integration. For example, if g is a joint normal density (known as a *probit* or *multivariate-probit* model), there is no analytical (or closed-form) solution to this integral. The probit model is a reasonable model for many applications, but its use has been hampered by the fact that the evaluation of (2.22) for a large number of objects involves tedious numerical integration.

---

[18]C is the set of all competing brands in the industry.

There is one exception, however, to the need for cumbersome numerical integration of (2.22). McFadden[19] showed that, if the joint distribution for random utilities $\{U_1, U_2, \ldots, U_m\}$ is a so-called multivariate *extreme-value distribution* of type I, then integral (2.22) has a closed-form solution. A multivariate extreme-value distribution takes the following form.

$$G(u_1, u_2, \ldots, u_m) = \prod_{i=1}^{m} \exp[-\exp(\alpha_i - u_i)]$$

where α_i $(i = 1, 2, \ldots, m)$ are parameters. This distribution is convenient because the maximum value among a sample of random utilities $\{u_1, u_2, \ldots, u_m\}$ from this distribution is also distributed as an extreme-value distribution of the following form.

$$F(u_{\max}) = \exp[-\exp(-u_{\max}) \sum_{i=1}^{m} \exp(\alpha_i)]$$

where $u_{\max}$ is a realization of a new random variable,

$$U_{\max} = \max(U_1, U_2, \ldots, U_m) \ .$$

Using this property, the distribution function for random variable

$$U_{\max^* i} = \max\{U_j : \text{for all } j \neq i\}$$

is given by

$$F(u_{\max^* i}) = \exp[-\exp(-u_{max^* i}) \sum_{j \neq i}^{m} \exp(\alpha_j)] \ .$$

Then the probability that brand i is chosen at a purchase occasion is given by

$$
\begin{aligned}
Prob(i \mid C) &= Prob(U_i > U_{max^* i}) &\qquad (2.23)\\
&= \int_{-\infty}^{\infty} \int_{-\infty}^{u_i} dG(u_i) dF(u_{\max^* i})\\
&= \int_{-\infty}^{\infty} \exp[-\exp(\alpha_i - u_i)] \cdot
\end{aligned}
$$

[19]McFadden, Daniel [1974], "Conditional Logit Analysis of Qualitative Choice Behavior." In Paul Zarembka (editor), *Frontiers in Econometrics*, New York: Academic Press, 105–42.

$$\exp(\alpha_i - u_i)\exp[-\exp(u_i)\sum_{j\neq i}^{m}\exp(\alpha_j)]du_i$$

$$= \exp(\alpha_i)/\sum_{j=1}^{m}\exp(\alpha_j) \ .$$

The reader will recall that, if we let the attraction of brand i, $\mathcal{A}_i$, be equal to $\exp(\alpha_i)$, this expression is similar to an MNL model. Indeed the foregoing argument has been used to derive MNL models for individual choice behavior. However, one may derive an expression similar to more straightforward attraction models (2.6), if, instead of an extreme-value distribution of type I, one chooses an extreme-value distribution of type II, namely,

$$G(u_1, u_2, \ldots, u_m) = \prod_{i=1}^{m}\exp[-\mathcal{A}_i u_i^{-b}]$$

where $\mathcal{A}_i$ $(i = 1, 2, \ldots, m)$ are parameters. To show this, first note that the distribution function for random variable

$$U_{\text{max}^* i} = \max\{U_j : \text{ for all } j \neq i\}$$

is given by

$$F(u_{\text{max}^* i}) = \exp[-u_{max^* i}^{-b}\sum_{j\neq i}^{m}\mathcal{A}_j] \ .$$

Using this,

$$
\begin{aligned}
Prob(i \mid C) &= Prob(U_i > U_{\text{max}^* i}) && (2.24)\\
&= \int_{-\infty}^{\infty}\int_{-\infty}^{u_i} dG(u_i)dF(u_{\text{max}^* i})\\
&= \int_{-\infty}^{\infty}\exp[-\mathcal{A}_i u_i^{-b}](\mathcal{A}_i b u_i^{-b-1})\exp[-u_i^{-b}\sum_{j\neq i}^{m}\mathcal{A}_j]du_i\\
&= \mathcal{A}_i/\sum_{j=1}^{m}\mathcal{A}_j \ .
\end{aligned}
$$

This demonstrates the fact that MCI models as well as MNL models are derivable if extreme-value distributions are assumed for the joint distribution of random utilities.

Although both equations (2.24) and (2.25) are derived for individual choice probabilities, one may derive an attraction model for aggregate market shares, if the definition of distribution functions is slightly changed. Suppose that random utilities for alternative brands, U_1, U_2, $\ldots$, U_m, are jointly distributed over the population of individual buyers, rather than within an individual. Each individual has a set of realized values for utilities, $u_1, u_2, \ldots, u_m$, and will select that brand which has the maximum utility value among m brands. Cast in this manner, the problem is to find the proportion of buyers who will purchase brand i, but equations (2.24) and (2.25) give precisely this proportion (that is, market share) for two extreme-value functions. Thus McFadden's argument may be used to give another justification for using an attraction model.

Although random utility models in general do not have the IIA property, it should be noted that some random utility do have it. Yellott[20] proved that a random utility model is equivalent to a constant utility model (and hence possesses the IIA property) if and only if the joint distribution of random utilities follows a multivariate extreme-value distribution. The basic forms of MNL and MCI models happen to belong to this special case. But we wish to emphasize that it is possible to construct attraction-type models of probabilistic choice which do not have the IIA property. We will discuss two such models — the *fully extended* and *distinctiveness* models — in Chapter 3.

2.9.4   *Multivariate Independent Gamma Function

It was stated in section 2.8 that the condition that $cov(\mu, \pi_i) = 0$ occurs for a very restricted case where μ is distributed as a Gamma function and the π_i's are jointly distributed as a Dirichlet function. In this appendix we will give a proof for this statement. Let μ_i be the expected number of purchases of brand i by an individual. By definition $\mu_i = \mu \pi_i$ (or $\pi_i = \mu_i / \mu$). We seek a joint distribution of μ_i ($i = 1, 2, \ldots, m$), where m is the number of alternative brands, for which μ and each $\mu_i / \mu (= \pi_i)$ are mutually independent. But, since μ and its inverse are usually negatively correlated, one would expects that μ and μ_i / μ will be correlated for most random variables. This suggests that we are indeed looking for a rather special distribution for the μ_i's.

Lukacs[21] showed that, for mutually independent nonnegative random

---

[20]Yellott, John I. [1977], "The Relationship between Luce's Choice Axiom, Thurstone's Theory of Comparative Judgment, and the Double Exponential Distribution," *Journal of Mathematical Psychology*, 15, 109–44.

[21]Lukacs, E. [1965], "A Characterization of the Gamma Distribution," *Annals of Mathematical Statistics*, Vol. 26, 319-24.

variables X_1 and X_2, if $(X_1 + X_2)$ and $X_1/(X_1 + X_2)$ are mutually independent, both X_1 and X_2 must be Gamma variates with a common shape parameter (but not necessarily a common location parameter). We will use this result to show the following propositions.

Proposition 1 *If the μ_i's $(i = 1, 2, \ldots, m)$ are mutually independent Gamma variates with density function*

$$g(\mu_i) = \exp(-\mu_i/\beta)\mu_i^{\alpha_i-1}/\beta^{\alpha_i}\Gamma(\alpha_i)$$

then μ and the π_i's are independently distributed.

Proposition 2 *If the μ_i's are mutually independent nonnegative random variables and μ and $\mu_i/\mu(= \pi_i)$ are independent, then the μ_i's are jointly distributed as multivariate (independent) Gamma function.*

Proof 1 By the change-of-variable formula, the joint density of μ and $\pi_1, \pi_2, \ldots, \pi_{m-1}$ is given by

$$\begin{aligned}
g(\mu, \pi_1, \pi_2, \ldots, \pi_{m-1}) &= g(\mu_1, \mu_2, \ldots, \mu_m)J \\
&= g(\mu_1, \mu_2, \ldots, \mu_m)\mu^{m-1}
\end{aligned}$$

where J is the Jacobian determinant associated with the transformation of the μ_i's to μ and the π_i's. Hence

$$\begin{aligned}
g(\mu, \pi_1, \pi_2, \ldots, \pi_{m-1}) &= \prod_{i=1}^{m} g(\mu_i)\mu^{m-1} \\
&= \prod_{i=1}^{m} \exp(-\mu_i/\beta)\mu_i^{\alpha_i-1}/\beta^{\alpha_i}\Gamma(\alpha_i)\mu^{m-1} \\
&= [\exp(-\mu/\beta)\mu^{\alpha_.-1}/\beta^{\alpha_.}\Gamma(\alpha_.)] \cdot \\
&\quad [\Gamma(\alpha_.)\prod_{i=1}^{m} \pi_i^{\alpha_i-1}/\Gamma(\alpha_i)]
\end{aligned}$$

where

$$\alpha_. = \sum_{i=1}^{m} \alpha_i .$$

Thus $g(\mu, \pi_1, \pi_2, \ldots, \pi_{m-1})$ can be factored into two parts: the first is a Gamma density function for μ with parameters $\alpha_.$ and β, and the second is a Dirichlet density function for $\pi_1, \pi_2, \ldots, \pi_{m-1}$ (and $\pi_m = 1 - \pi_1 - \pi_2 - \ldots - \pi_{m-1}$) with parameters α_i $(i = 1, 2, \ldots, m)$. Therefore μ and $\pi_1, \pi_2, \ldots, \pi_m$ are independent.

Proof 2 Let, for an arbitrary index j^* ($j^* \in C$), M_{j^*} be the sum of the μ_i's except μ_j, i.e.,

$$M_{j^*} = \sum_{j^* \neq j}^{m} \mu_{j^*} = \mu - \mu_j \ .$$

By the assumption, μ_j and M_{j^*} are independently distributed nonnegative random variables and also μ_j and $\mu_j/\mu = \mu_j/(\mu_j + M_{j^*})$ are independent. By Lukacs' result μ_j and M_{j^*} are both Gamma variates with a common shape parameter. Since index j was chosen arbitrary, this result applies for all j, that is, all μ_j's are Gamma variates sharing a common shape parameter. Q.E.D.

Chapter 3

Describing Markets and Competition

3.1 Market and Competitive Structure

In the preceding chapter we viewed competition among brands in an industry in the simplest possible way, that is, with the assumption that every brand is directly competing against all other brands in the industry. But competition in the actual market place may take more complex patterns. It is not unusual to find some grouping of brands such that within a group competition among its members are intense, but competition is not intense or even nonexistent between the groups.

Consider the toothpaste industry. Brands belonging to it may be subdivided into at least three groups: family use, breath care, and tar removers (for smokers). Each group emphasizes a different product attribute: the first group emphasizing decay-preventive ingredients, the second, breath fresheners, and the third, tar control, etc. The three groups serve different *segments* of buyers, and therefore do not directly compete with each other, although brands in a group tend to be highly competitive in the sense that the action of one brand affects the market shares of others.

Then why can't we treat the three brand groups of the toothpaste industry as three separate industries? It is because, at the retail level at least, the shares of three groups are often observed to be interdependent. A price deal for a brand in the family-use group, say, may affect the demand of brands in other brand groups. The reason is not difficult to find. Though three groups of toothpaste are used by different user groups, they are often bought by the same person in a family. A mild degree of interdependencies among three groups makes it necessary to treat them as a single industry.

Our purpose in this chapter is to create a framework that may be used to describe the market and competitive structures existing in an industry. By a *market and competitive structure* we mean the structure of interdependencies among competitors in an industry, as expressed by grouping patterns of brands. We could simply call such a pattern a *competitive* structure, but a competitive structure may be a reflection of the underlying pattern of buyer demand in the market. If it were found that brand A directly competed with brand B but not with brand C, it might be because the buyers perceive brand A and B as alternatives, but not brand A and C. Since we mostly utilize aggregate market-share data in determining grouping patterns of brands, we will not know if such a conjecture is true or false. The choice of the cumbersome expression *market and competitive structures* reflects our lack of information about the underlying perception of buyers.

In this chapter we will examine various approaches for looking at and modeling market and competitive structures among brands. Of particular interest are the phenomena: differential effectiveness of marketing actions, asymmetry of competitive interactions, and variations between market segments. We will also deal with two topics of considerable importance — the distinctiveness of brands and time-series issues — related to the description of market and competitive structures.

3.2   Asymmetries in Market and Competition

An even cursory observation of competitive interactions in the market place reveals that some firms (brands) are capable of exerting inordinately strong influence over the shaping of demand and competition, while other firms (brands) are not. One often sees some *price leaders* who can reduce their prices and obtain a large gain in market share, seemingly oblivious to their competitors' reactions. Other firms can create strong buyer loyalties, albeit for only a short term, with splashy promotional campaigns. It appears that such notable marketing *clout* is not possessed by all firms in an industry and, interestingly, are not the sole property of larger firms. There are fairly large firms in many industries which have difficulties in increasing their shares, even if they reduce prices below those of their price-aggressive competitors. Furthermore, the impact of one competitor's action may affect one rival or one group of rivals more than another. For example, a price cut by Hewlett-Packard in the personal computer market may disproportionately draw more market share from Apple than from another major brand, say, IBM.

The imparity in competitive interdependencies are perhaps more pronounced in the retail trade. Retailers with experience know that which brands they should use for *loss-leaders* (i.e., brands whose price is cut to increase store traffic) and which brands to feature in newspapers for the maximum effect. And they do not cut prices or feature arbitrarily, either. Retailers seem to share pretty much the same opinion as to which brands are candidates for loss-leaders or newspaper features.

Those observations illustrate both differential effectiveness of brands and asymmetries in market and competitive structures. Differential effectiveness among brands reflects that firms (brands) have different degrees of effectiveness in carrying out their marketing activities. That such differences exist in real markets is obvious, but differential effectiveness alone does not create or reflect asymmetries. Asymmetries are reflected in differential crosseffects among brands. Firms are, it appears, differentially effective not only with respect to their own shares and sales, but also with respect to their ability (that is, *clout*) to influence the shares and sales of other brands. Furthermore, firms seem to differ in the degree to which they are influenced by other brands' actions (that is, *vulnerability*). We will deal with those two aspects of competition in the following sections.

3.3 Differential Effectiveness

We have already discussed this issue of differential effectiveness in Chapter 2, and a solution at that time was to include some parameters in market-share models to take account of the overall *marketing effectiveness* of each brand. The reader will recall, in the now-familiar specification of attraction models,

$$
\mathcal{A}_i = \exp(\alpha_i + \epsilon_i) \prod_{k=1}^{K} f_k(X_{ki})^{\beta_k}
$$

$$
s_i = \mathcal{A}_i / \sum_{j=1}^{m} \mathcal{A}_j
$$

where parameters α_i $(i = 1, 2, \ldots, m)$ represent the marketing effectiveness of respective brands.

The inclusion of the α's in attraction models, however, does not fully account for differential effectiveness among brands. The differential effectiveness may be specific to each marketing instrument, such as a brand which has a particularly effective pricing policy or an effective advertising campaign. The α_i's do not appear in the elasticity formulas for a particular marketing instrument, X_k (namely, $e_{s_i} = \beta_k(1 - s_i)$ for MCI models and $e_{s_i} = \beta_k X_{ki}(1 - s_i)$ for MNL models). The *marketing-effectiveness* parameters may reflect differences in the *brand franchise* or *brand loyalty*. Literally, they are the constant component of each brand's attraction, but they have nothing to do with elasticities. As a result, elasticity formulas for simple attraction models do not reflect differential effectiveness. If we are to insist that share elasticities must also reflect differential effectiveness, those elasticity formulas will have to be modified.

If it is decided to modify market-share elasticities to account for differential effectiveness, the reader will find that this may be achieved in only one way, that is, by specifying parameters β_k's in such a manner that each brand has a special parameter, β_{ki}, for variable X_k. The attraction models will have to be respecified as follows.

$$\mathcal{A}_i = \exp(\alpha_i + \epsilon_i) \prod_{k=1}^{K} f_k(X_{ki})^{\beta_{ki}} \tag{3.1}$$

$$s_i = \mathcal{A}_i / \sum_{j=1}^{m} \mathcal{A}_j$$

This is the differential-effects version of attraction models. This modification does not change the basic structure of direct and cross elasticities for attraction models. For example,

MCI Model:

$$e_{s_i} = \beta_{ki}(1 - s_i)$$

MNL Model:

$$e_{s_i} = \beta_{ki} X_{ki}(1 - s_i) \ .$$

As variable X_{ki} increases, the elasticity decreases for MCI models, but it increases and then decreases for MNL models. By expanding the parameterization of the model we are now able to capture brand-by-brand differences in market responsiveness to each element of the marketing mix. If all brands are equally effective then $\beta_{ki} = \beta_{kj} = \beta_k$ $\forall$ i, j, and the elasticity expressions reduce to those for simple attraction models.

3.4 Differential Cross Elasticities

In the preceding chapters we presented elasticities as a key concept in market-share analysis, but what do they tell us of the effects that a firm may exert with its actions on the sales and shares of other firms in the same industry? The share, sales, and industry-volume elasticities described in Chapter 2 — known as *direct elasticities* — are not sufficient, if the analyst is interested in knowing what effects other brands' actions will have on his/her brand's share, or what effects his/her actions will have on other brands' shares. For the purpose of analyzing differential crosseffects among brands we will need a new concept — *cross elasticities*. Let us give a more precise definition to this new concept.

Suppose that brand j changed variable X_{kj} by a small amount ΔX_{kj}. The cross elasticity of brand i's ($i \neq j$) share with respect to variable X_{kj} may be verbally expressed as "the ratio of the proportion of change in market share for brand i corresponding to the proportion of change in variable X_k for brand j," and is defined as follows.

$$e_{s_i \cdot j} = \frac{\Delta s_i / s_i}{\Delta X_{kj} / X_{kj}} = \frac{\Delta s_i}{\Delta X_{kj}} \frac{X_{kj}}{s_i} \qquad (3.2)$$

Note that $e_{s_i \cdot j}$ has two subscripts: the first indicates the brand which is influenced and the second, the brand which influences. This is an *arc* cross-elasticity formula and the *point* cross elasticity is defined as:[1]

$$e_{s_i \cdot j} = \frac{\partial s_i / s_i}{\partial X_{kj} / X_{kj}} = \frac{\partial s_i}{\partial X_{kj}} \frac{X_{kj}}{s_i} \ . \qquad (3.3)$$

We now turn to the forms of point elasticities for specific market-share models. Point cross elasticities for differential-effects attraction models take the following forms.

MCI Model:

$$e_{s_i \cdot j} = -\beta_{kj} s_j$$

---

[1] As in the case of direct elasticities, the above formula is for variable X_{kj}, but for the sake of simplicity no superscript or subscript k will be attached to $e_{s_i \cdot j}$. It will be clear from the context which variable is being referenced.

MNL Model:

$$e_{s_i.j} = -\beta_{kj}X_{kj}s_j$$

It may be added that, for simple-effects attraction models, β_{kj} in the above formulas are replaced by a common parameter β_k.

Let us consider what the above formulas imply. For the raw-score versions of both MCI and MNL models cross elasticities with respect to variable X_{kj} are constant for any brand i ($i \neq j$). This means that the relative changes of other brands' shares (i.e.,$\partial s_i/s_i$) caused by brand j's actions are the same for any brand, though actual changes in shares (i.e., ∂s_i) are different from one brand to another, depending on the current share level for each brand (i.e., s_i). A numerical example may help to illustrate this point. Suppose that there are four brands and their respective shares are 0.3, 0.1, 0.2 and 0.4. Assuming that an MCI model is applicable and β_{k1} is 0.5, the value of cross elasticity for brand i ($i \neq 1$) with respect to the change in X_{k1} is given by

$$e_{s_i.1} = -0.5 \times 0.3 = -0.15 \ .$$

If no other variables have been changed, a 10% increase in variable X_{k1} will bring about a 1.5% reduction in any other brand's share, i.e.,

$$\Delta s_i/s_i = e_{s_i.1} \times (\Delta X_{k1}/X_{k1}) = -0.15 \times 0.1 = -0.015 \ .$$

If brand 2 has a 20% share of market, the actual loss of its share will be by 0.3 percentage points, i.e.,

$$s_2 = -0.015 \times 20\% = -0.3\% \ .$$

These calculations are summarized in Table 3.1.

Though share cross elasticities are equal for brands 2, 3, and 4, the actual change in a brand's share varies, reflecting its current level. (The sum of actual changes in shares is zero for all brands in the industry, as it should be.) Note that the competitive positions of brands 2, 3, and 4 relative to each other have not changed by the reduction in their shares. In fact, the new share of any brand other than 1 may be simply calculated by

New Share of Brand i = (1 − New Share of Brand 1) × Old Share of Brand i.

We may add that, for an MNL model, relative and actual changes in s_i are a function of the current value of X_{kj}, but the value of $e_{s_i.j}$ for this model is identical for any other brand i.

Table 3.1: Numerical Example of Cross Elasticities for MCI Model

Brand	Current Share	Share Elasticity	Relative Change in Share	Actual Change in Share	New Share
1	.3	0.35^a	0.035	0.0105	.3105
2	.2	−0.15	−0.015	−0.0030	.1970
3	.1	−0.15	−0.015	−0.0015	.0985
4	.4	−0.15	−0.015	−0.0060	.3940

a. Direct elasticity is $e_{s_1.1} = \beta_{k1}(1 - s_1)$.

From those calculations one can see that simple attraction models specify a rather peculiar pattern of competition in that the relative effects of a brand's actions on another brand's share are identical for any brand in the industry. This equality of cross elasticities implied by such simple attraction models does not fit what we observe in the marketplace. There are brands which seem to be nearly immune from other brands' price changes; some firms seem to be able to ignore promotional activities of other brands with little loss of their shares, while others seem to be greatly affected by such activities, and so forth. Examples of this kind may be found in many industries. It is therefore desirable to introduce in market-share models the inequality of cross elasticities, if we are to analyze differential cross effects among brands. There are two ways to attack this problem. On one hand, we could reflect the asymmetries which might arise from the *temporal distinctiveness* of marketing efforts. This is pursued in section 3.8. On the other hand, we could extend the parameters of the attraction model to reflect asymmetries due to *systematic* and *stable cross-competitive effects*. Fortunately, this can be accomplished with relative ease within the framework of attraction models as shown below.

$$\mathcal{A}_i = \exp(\alpha_i + \epsilon_i) \prod_{k=1}^{K} \prod_{j=1}^{m} f_k(X_{kj})^{\beta_{kij}} \tag{3.4}$$

$$s_i = \mathcal{A}_i \Big/ \sum_{j=1}^{m} \mathcal{A}_j$$

where β_{kij} is the parameter for the cross-competitive effect of variable X_{kj} on brand i.

Equation (3.4) is called an attraction model with differential cross-competitive effects or a *fully extended* attraction model to distinguish it from a differential-effects attraction model (3.1). The most important feature of the fully extended model is that the attraction for brand i is now a function not only of the firm's own actions (variables X_{ki}'s, $k = 1, 2, \ldots, m$) but also of all other brands' actions (variables X_{kj}'s, $k = 1, 2, \ldots, K; j = 1, 2, \ldots, m$). The β_{kij}'s for which i is different from j are the *cross-competitive effects* parameters, which partly determine cross elasticities. The β_{kij}'s for which j equals i (i.e., β_{kii}) are *direct-effects* parameters and are equivalent to the β_{ki}'s in the differential-effects model (3.1). This notation is cumbersome, but it is necessary to keep track of who is influencing whom. Note that the fully extended model has many more parameters (with $m \times 2 \times K$ β_{kij}'s and m α_i's) than the original attraction model (with $K + m$ parameters) and the differential-effects model (with $mK + m$ parameters). We will take up the issues related to estimating β_{kij}'s in Chapter 5.

3.5   Properties of Fully Extended Models

In order to see what market and competitive structures implied by the fully extended model (3.4) , let us look at the direct and cross elasticities for this model.

MCI Model:

$$e_{s_i.j} = \beta_{kij} - \sum_{h=1}^{m} s_h \beta_{khj}$$

MNL Model:

$$e_{s_i.j} = (\beta_{kij} - \sum_{h=1}^{m} s_h \beta_{khj}) X_{kj}$$

These formulas are common for both direct and cross elasticities; if i is equal to j, the above formulas give direct elasticities for brand i, otherwise they give cross elasticities.[2] $e_{s_i.j}$ is the elasticity of market share for brand i with respect to changes in marketing variable X_{kj} for

---

[2]The elasticity formulas may be more succinctly written in matrix notation.
MCI Model:
$$E = (I - JD_s)B$$

MNL Model:
$$E = (I - JD_s)BD_X$$

where:

brand j, and it is given by β_{kij} minus the weighted average of β_{khj}'s over h, where the weights are the market shares of respective brands (s_h). Figure 3.1 illustrates the competitive pattern implied by the elasticity formulas.

Figure 3.1: Cross Elasticities in the Fully Extended Model

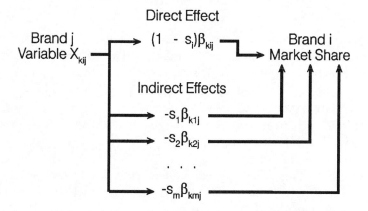

Let's assume that variable X_{kj} in this case is the price for brand j. Then parameter β_{kij} for which i is not equal to j tends to take a positive value. In other words, when brand j reduces its price the share of brand i tends to decrease. This effect of brand j's price change on brand i's share is depicted as the *direct effect* in Figure 3.1. Note that the direct effect is modified by the size of brand i's share. When brand i's share is nearly one, brand i is little affected directly by the moves by brand j.[3] The influence of brand j's price change is not limited to the direct effect to brand i, however. When brand j reduces its price, its own share should increase. Furthermore, the market shares of brand 1 through m

$E = m \times m$ matrix with elements $\{e_{s_i.j}\}$

$I = m \times m$ identity matrix

$J = m \times m$ matrix of all 1's

$D_s = m \times m$ diagonal matrix of market shares $\{s_1, s_2, \ldots, s_m\}$

$B = m \times m$ matrix with elements $\{\beta_{kij}\}$

$D_X = m \times m$ diagonal matrix of variables $\{X_{k1}, X_{k2}, \ldots, X_{km}\}$.

---

[3]This statement is true for the relative changes ($\partial s_i / s_i$) in brand i's share. In terms of absolute sales volume, the impact of brand j's price change may be substantial.

(other than brand i and j) will also receive a negative effect, which in turn should have a positive effect on brand i's share. *Indirect effects* in Figure 3.1 depict influences of those kinds.

In order to examine formally the points raised above, rewrite the cross-elasticity formula for MCI models as follows.

$$e_{s_i \cdot j} = (1 - s_i)\beta_{kij} - s_j\beta_{kjj} - \sum_{h \neq i,j}^{m} s_h\beta_{khj} \ .$$

The first term, of course, represents the direct effects. The second term shows the indirect effects through brand j. The last term consists of indirect effects through all other brands. If X_{kj} is brand j's price, one expects that $\beta_{kjj} < 0$ and $\beta_{kij} > 0$ (for $i \neq j$). Since the first and last terms are expected to be positive and the second term negative, the sign of $e_{s_i \cdot j}$ is indeterminate, and dependent on the relative size of $(1 - s_i)\beta_{kij} - s_j\beta_{kjj}$ and $\sum_{h \neq i,j}^{m} s_h\beta_{khj}$.

Consider the following special cases.

Case 1: All cross-elasticity parameters $(\beta_{kij}, \ i \neq j)$ are zero. In this case, $e_{s_i \cdot j} = -s_j\beta_{kjj}$, This is the same as the cross-elasticity formula for the differential-effects MCI models.

Case 2: All cross-elasticity parameters $(\beta_{kij}, \ i \neq j)$ are approximately equal. In this case,

$$\sum_{h \neq i,j}^{m} s_h\beta_{khj} \approx (1 - s_i - s_j)\beta_{kij} \ .$$

Then

$$e_{s_i \cdot j} \approx s_j(\beta_{kij} - \beta_{kjj}) \ .$$

This suggests that $e_{s_i \cdot j}$ has the same sign as β_{kij}.

Case 3: β_{kij} is nearly zero, but

$$\sum_{h \neq i,j}^{m} s_h\beta_{khj} > s_j\beta_{kjj} \ .$$

In this case $e_{s_i \cdot j}$ may have a sign different from β_{kij}.

Case 3 is an interesting situation because, in this case, it is possible that brand i even gain a share when brand j reduces its price. For case 3 to occur brand j's share should be relatively small, but the impact of its actions on brands other than i must be large. (This brings to our mind an image of an aggressive small brand j which is frequently engaged in guerilla price-wars.) In addition, brand i must be reasonably isolated from the rest of the market, implying that it is a *niche*-er. This case illustrates the richness of the description of market and competitive structures offered by the fully extended attraction models.

It may be added that if $i = j$, we may write

$$e_{s_i.i} = (1 - s_i)\beta_{kii} - \sum_{h \neq i}^{m} s_h \beta_{khi} \ .$$

The first term represents the direct effect of X_{ki} on brand i's share; the second term gives the sum of all indirect effects on brand i's share through influences on all other brands. This formula suggests a possibility that, even if the direct effect is negligible (e.g., β_{kii} is small), direct elasticity, $e_{s_i.i}$, may be sizeable due to the combination of indirect effects. In other words, a brand may be able to increase its share merely by reducing other brands' shares. The reader should note that simple-effects or differential-effects attraction models do not allow such a possibility. This is another indication of descriptive richness of the fully extended attraction models.

To summarize, the fully extended (i.e., differential cross elasticity) attraction models offer an enormous advantage over many market-share models in that it is capable of describing the complexity of market and competitive structures with relative ease. Since the simple-effects and differential-effects models may be considered as the special cases of the fully extended models,[4] we will adopt the latter models as the basic models of market shares in this book.

3.6 Determining Competitive Structures

Once cross-elasticity parameters are introduced in market-share models, it becomes possible to specify market and competitive structures on the basis of cross elasticities among brands. An example will serve to illustrate this concept. Suppose that the marketing variable in question is price. One may estimate share elasticities with respect to price using a differential cross-elasticities market-share model. Table 3.2 shows the matrix of direct and cross elasticities among seven brands in a hypothetical industry.

---

[4]In technical jargon, we say that the simple-effects and differential-effects models are *nested* within the fully extended models.

Table 3.2: Direct and Cross Elasticities for Seven Brands

(a) Original Order

Brand	1	2	3	4	5	6	7
1	−1.5	1.8	0.5	0.0	0.1	0.9	0.7
2	1.6	−3.7	0.3	0.4	0.1	1.3	1.2
3	0.3	0.2	−0.2	0.6	0.2	0.2	0.4
4	0.3	0.5	0.0	−0.8	0.9	0.4	0.2
5	0.3	0.6	0.4	1.1	−1.2	0.3	0.3
6	0.6	1.3	0.4	0.3	0.5	−1.4	0.5
7	0.2	0.8	0.2	0.1	0.2	0.4	−1.5

(b) Reordered

Brand	1	2	6	7	4	5	3
1	−1.5	1.8	0.9	0.7	0.0	0.1	0.5
2	1.6	−3.7	1.3	1.2	0.4	0.1	0.3
6	0.6	1.3	−1.4	0.5	0.3	0.5	0.4
7	0.2	0.8	0.4	−1.5	0.1	0.2	0.2
4	0.3	0.5	0.4	0.2	−0.8	0.9	0.0
5	0.3	0.6	0.3	0.3	1.1	−1.2	0.4
3	0.3	0.2	0.2	0.4	0.6	0.2	−0.2

At the first glance, the existence of a market and competitive structure may not be apparent from Table 3.2(a). However, if we rearrange the table both row- and column-wise, we obtain Table 3.2(b), in which the existence of submarkets or brand groups is more apparent. Because of mutually large cross elasticities, brands 1, 2, 6 and 7 form a group. Brands 4 and 5 form another. Brand 3 is more or less isolated. In this example the groups are rather distinct in that the cross elasticities between the brands in the first group and those in the second and third groups are small. Though the brands in each group are highly interdependent, price competition between the first group and the second and third groups is expected to be moderate or virtually nonexistent.

It would be too hasty for one to say that this industry consists of three brand groups on the basis of Table 3.2 alone, since we have no knowledge of what market structure(s) may be suggested with respect to other marketing variables. It may turn out that another structure is suggested by share elasticities with respect to product quality or promotional outlays. It is necessary to look at the whole complex pattern of interdependencies between brands before one is able to say how submarkets are formed. But the principle which we will follow in determining market structures in the remaining part of this book will be the same as the illustrative example: we will look at the tables of direct and cross elasticities for relevant marketing variables and reorganize them in such a manner that brands which have mutually large cross elasticities are collected in a group. In this task multivariate techniques based on factor analysis will be employed. We will turn to the procedures actually used in determining market structures in Chapter 6.

A word of caution is in order. Analyzing tables of share elasticities may not yield a clear-cut pattern of brand grouping in some situations. Brand groups may be partially interlocked. Or groups may be *nested* (or contained) within larger groups. Table 3.3 gives an example of interlocking brand groups.

Table 3.3: Interlocking and Nested Brand Groups

Brand	1	2	3	4	5	6	7
1	−2.1	0.8	0.9	0.5	*	*	*
2	0.6	−1.9	0.7	0.8	*	*	*
3	1.1	0.9	−1.2	0.6	1.0	*	*
4	0.8	0.7	0.7	−1.8	0.6	*	*
5	*	*	0.4	0.9	−2.2	0.8	0.7
6	*	*	*	*	0.5	−1.5	0.8
7	*	*	*	*	0.9	0.6	−0.7

For the sake of clarity the entries which have insignificant cross elasticities are not shown. In this example, group 2 (brands 3, 4, and 5) is interlocked with group 1 (brands 1 through 4) and groups 3 (brands 5, 6, and 7). In this situation one may interpret that elasticities in the table are produced by three distinct buyer segments, each of which perceives a different set of brands as relevant alternatives. But it is also plausible to think that there are only two segments in the market, and that price changes by brand 5 for some reasons affect only brands 3 and 4 in the first group. Those two interpretations are not separable from the table.

3.7   Hierarchies of Market Segments

Ambiguities in interpreting the nature of competition from the tables of elasticities are often caused by the aggregation, that is, by not explicitly recognizing segments of buyers in the market. As was already pointed out, the overt pattern of brand grouping does not necessarily give hints about the underlying patterns of buyer demand.

There are two possible interpretations on the nature of brand groups in Table 3.2, for example. One interpretation is that there exist three distinct market segments and the cross elasticities reflect the difference in product perception among segments. The buyers who belong to the first segment may consider brands 1, 2, 6, and 7 as relevant alternatives either because of their product attributes or their collective availability at the retail level; those who belong to the second segment may consider only brands 4 and 5 as relevant alternatives; and so forth. In this interpretation brand groups correspond one to one with market segments of buyers.

The second interpretation of brand groups is that brands tend to be grouped in accordance with different types of buyer needs they serve. Suppose that the consumer uses regular and instant coffee for different occasions (e.g., regular coffee with meals, but instant coffee for other occasions). This will cause the coffee market to be divided into the regular and instant brand groups, and minor price differences between the two groups will not affect demands of either. This type of segmentation on the basis of needs, or a *benefit* segmentation, does not produce distinct buyer segments in the market. Of course if two brand groups serve two entirely isolated buyer needs, they should be treated as two distinct industries rather than one. But if the price of regular coffee is drastically reduced, the demand for instant coffee may be affected. A regular brand with an aggressive price policy may have some cross elasticities with instant brands, or vice versa. Moderate cross elasticities between groups would force one to treat them as a single industry.

As in the above example, if the elasticities are measured only for the entire market, it will be impossible to establish the propriety of the above two interpretations solely on the basis of tables such as Table 3.2. In order to evaluate the correctness of these two interpretations, one will need data sets such as consumer panels (either diary or scanner panels). Moreover, it is desirable to have accompanying data on the buyer perception of alternative brands. Lacking such detailed data sets, however, one should at least understand well the aggregate implications of variabilities in elasticities among buyer segments. We will first look at the nature of elasticities in a multisegmented market.

Suppose that there are two segments in the market, containing N_1 and N_2 buyers, respectively. We will use the notation $q_{i(l)}$ and $s_{i(l)}$ to indicate, respectively, the sales volume and market share of brand i in the lth segment. Since

$$s_i = [q_{(1)}s_{i(1)} + q_{(2)}s_{i(2)}]/q$$

where:

$q_{(l)}$ = sales volume in segment l ($l = 1, 2$)

q = total sales volume $(q_{(1)} + q_{(2)})$.

The point share elasticity of brand i with respect to X_{kj} is given by

$$e_{s_i.j} = [(q_{(1)}/q)(\partial s_{i(1)}/\partial X_{kj}) + (q_{(2)}/q)(\partial s_{i(2)}/\partial X_{kj})](X_{kj}/s_i) \ .$$

This shows that an overall elasticity is the weighted average of corresponding segment elasticities, weights being the relative sales volumes for respective segments. If we write the segment elasticity as $e_{s_i.j(l)}$, then the general expression for $e_{s_i.j}$ is given by

$$e_{s_i.j} = \sum_{l=1}^{L}(q_{i(l)}/q_i)e_{s_i.j(l)}$$

where L is the number of segments and q_i is the sales volume for brand i for the entire market. This expression gives one the means to compute the overall elasticity matrix from matrices for segments.

3.8 Distinctiveness of Marketing Activities

Fully extended attraction models have advanced our ability to deal with the complexity of market and competitive structures, but there are other aspects of competition which have not been properly dealt with even in the fully extended models. We will turn to the some of the more critical issues in this section and the next one. Here we will take up the issue of *distinctiveness* of marketing activities by competing brands.

The main thesis of this section is that a brand's marketing actions may or may not influence the behavior of buyers depending on the degree to which its actions are distinguishable from the actions of its competitors. This issue is very much related to the distinction between importance and salience of product attributes in buyers' choice. For example, any consumer will say that being nutritious is one of the important attributes in his/her choice of bread. But, if all brands of bread available in the market have the same nutritional value (or at least are perceived so by consumers), being nutritious will not affect the consumer's choice of brands of bread. Instead consumers may decide on the basis of the color of package, position of store shelf, or likes and dislikes of the persons who appeared in television commercials. In a fiercely competitive industry the pressure of competition usually works to equalize the products offered by firms with respect to those attributes which buyers perceive important. Thus, as an economist put it, consumers tend to make their choice on the basis of the least important (yet salient) attributes of the product.

This phenomenon is not limited to product attributes. The authors posit that the effectiveness of any marketing activity would be dependent on the degree that it is distinct from those of competitors. Even casual observations bear out this proposition. Price reduction by a firm would have more effects on market shares when other brands' prices are kept high than it would when all competitors also reduce their prices. The market-share impact of one firm's promotion would be significantly greater when the firm is alone in promotion than it would when all firms engage in promotional activities. Advertising activities by firms competing in an oligopolistic industry tend to cancel out each other's effect, so much so that they have little influence on market shares. (When the Surgeon General of the United States prohibited cigarette commercials on television, it was rumored that the parties who were most pleased by the decree were the competing cigarette manufacturers.)

If we take the position that it is the differences between brands, rather than the absolute levels of marketing activities that materially affect buyers' preference, then we will have to devise a scheme to bring the distinctiveness of marketing activities among brands into market-share analysis. Luckily, attraction models handle the distinctiveness issue quite naturally. Consider the general form of attraction models.

$$\mathcal{A}_i = \exp(\alpha_i + \epsilon_i) \prod_{k=1}^{K} f_k(X_{ki})^{\beta_k}$$

$$s_i = \mathcal{A}_i / \sum_{j=1}^{m} \mathcal{A}_j \ .$$

It is obvious that the value of market share for brand i, s_i, will not change if we divide the numerator and denominator of the second equation above by a constant. Specifically, if we divide each $\mathcal{A}_i$ by the geometric mean of $\mathcal{A}_i$ over i, $\tilde{\mathcal{A}}$, namely

$$\tilde{\mathcal{A}} = \sqrt[m]{\prod_{j=1}^{m} \mathcal{A}_j}$$

the operation will not affect the value of s_i, since

$$(\mathcal{A}_i/\tilde{\mathcal{A}})/ \sum_{j=1}^{m} (\mathcal{A}_j/\tilde{\mathcal{A}}) = \mathcal{A}_i / \sum_{j=1}^{m} \mathcal{A}_j = s_i \ .$$

Let us look at the specific forms of $\tilde{\mathcal{A}}$ for MCI and MNL models.
MCI Model:

$$\tilde{\mathcal{A}} = \exp(\bar{\alpha} + \bar{\epsilon}) \prod_{k=1}^{K} \tilde{X}_k^{\beta_k}$$

MNL Model:

$$\tilde{\mathcal{A}} = \exp(\bar{\alpha} + \bar{\epsilon}) \prod_{k=1}^{K} \exp(\beta_k \bar{X}_k)$$

where:

$\bar{\alpha} = $ the arithmetic mean of α_i over i $(i = 1, 2, \ldots, m)$

$\bar{\epsilon} = $ the arithmetic mean of ϵ_i over i

$\tilde{X}_k = $ the geometric mean of X_{ki} over i

$\bar{X}_k = $ the arithmetic mean of X_{ki} over i.

Using the above results we may write MCI and MNL models as follows.
MCI Model:

$$\mathcal{A}_i^* = \exp[(\alpha_i - \bar{\alpha}) + (\epsilon_i - \bar{\epsilon})] \prod_{k=1}^{K} (X_{ki}/\tilde{X}_k)^{\beta_k}$$

MNL Model:

$$\mathcal{A}_i^* = \exp[(\alpha_i - \bar{\alpha}) + (\epsilon_i - \bar{\epsilon})] \prod_{k=1}^{K} \exp[\beta_k(X_{ki} - \bar{X}_k)]$$

and for both models[5]

$$s_i = \mathcal{A}_i^* / \sum_{j=1}^{m} \mathcal{A}_j^* \ .$$

Consider the implication of the foregoing analysis. One may express the variables in MCI and MNL models in a *deviation* form without changing the properties of the models. In other words, we may express a variable either as

$$X_{ki}^* = X_{ki} / \tilde{X}_k$$

or

$$X_{ki}^* = X_{ki} - \bar{X}_k$$

and substitute X_{ki}^* for X_{ki} in MCI or MNL models, respectively. This property of attraction models does not change if we move from the simple-effects form to differential-effects models and fully extended models.[6] This shows that the variables in attraction models may be replaced by some equivalent form of deviations from the industry mean and that those models in essence operate on the principle of distinctiveness. Take an MCI model, for example. If X_k is price, each brand's price may be expressed as deviations from the average price for the industry. If all brands charge the same price, X_{ki}^* will be equal to one, and price will not affect the shares of brands. Only when the prices for some brands

---

[5]If one divides s_i by the geometric mean of s_i over i, the result would be equal to $\mathcal{A}_i^*$. In other words, if we let $\tilde{s}$ be the geometric mean of s_i over i, that is,

$$\tilde{s} = \sqrt[m]{\prod_{i=1}^{m} s_i}$$

then

$$s_i^* = s_i / \tilde{s} = \mathcal{A}_i^* \ .$$

This fact will be extensively utilized in the estimation procedure in Chapter 5.

[6]If monotone transformations (f_k) other than identity or exponential are used, substituting

$$f_k^*(X_{ki}) = f_k(X_{ki}) / \tilde{f}_k(X_k)$$

where $\tilde{f}_k(X_k)$ is the geometric mean of $f_k(X_{ki})$ over i, for $f_k(X_{ki})$ in an attraction model, will not change the nature of the model.

deviate from the industry mean do they influence market shares of themselves and others.

The handling of distinctiveness by attraction models becomes a technically difficult issue when the variable in question is a qualitative one. Product attributes are the example of variables of this type. A make of refrigerator may or may not have an ice-maker; an automobile model may or may not have an automatic transmission; a brand of toothpaste may or may not have tar-control ingredients, etc. Such a variable may take only two values, namely, one if the product (or brand) has an attribute and zero if it does not. Of course, one may compute the industry average for a binary (two-valued) variable (which is the same as the proportion of products or brands which have that attribute) and subtract it from the value for each product/brand. But by this operation the transformed variable may take either positive or negative values, and hence it may be used only with an MNL model (or some monotone transformation f which allows negative values). In order to incorporate binary variables in an MCI model a simple but effective transformation – the *index of distinctiveness* – was developed.[7]

Suppose that X_k is a variable associated with the possession or nonpossession of an attribute. Let the proportion of products (or brands) in this industry which have the attribute be r. If there are 10 brands and two brands have the attribute, r will be 0.2. The value of the index of distinctiveness for each brand is determined by the following simple operation.

If brand i has the attribute, $X_{ki} = 1/r$.

If brand i does not have the attribute, $X_{ki} = 1 - r$.

Thus if r equals 0.2, those brands with the attribute are given the value of 5 and those without the attribute will be given the value of 0.8. Note that the smaller r, the greater the value of X_k for those brands that have the attribute. This represents in essence the effect of the distinctiveness of a brand. If a brand is only one which has the attribute the index value $(1/r)$ becomes maximal.

It is interesting to note that this index has a rather convenient property that it is ratio-wise symmetrical to the reversal of coding a particular attribute. If we reversed the coding of possession and nonpossession of an attribute in the previous numerical example, r would be 0.8, and the value of X_k for those brands with the attribute would be 1.25 (= 1/0.8)

_____

[7]Nakanishi, Masao, Lee G. Cooper & Harold H. Kassarjian [1974], "Voting for a Political Candidate Under Conditions of Minimal Information," *Journal of Consumer Research*, 1 (September), 36–43.

and that for the brands without the attribute would be 0.2 (= 1/5). In other words, those brands without the attribute become distinctive in the reverse direction.

The index of distinctiveness shown above transforms a binary variable such that it is usable in an MCI model. Cooper and Nakanishi[8] found that this index is a special case of a more general transformation applicable not only for qualitative variables but also for any quantitative variable. First, convert any variable X_{ki} to a standardized score by the usual formula.

$$z_{ki} = (X_{ki} - \bar{X}_k)/\sigma_k$$

where:

$\bar{X}_k$ = the arithmetic mean of X_{ki} over i

σ_k = the standard deviation of X_{ki} over i.

Since standardized z-scores (z_{ki}'s) may take both positive and negative values, they may be used in an MNL model in the form of $\exp(z_{ki})$, but cannot be used in an MCI model. To create a variable usable in the latter model transform z-scores in turn in the following manner.

$$
\begin{aligned}
\zeta_{ki} &= \quad (1 + z_{ki}^2)^{1/2}, \text{ if } z_{ki} \geq 0 \\
\zeta_{ki} &= \quad (1 + z_{ki}^2)^{-1/2}, \text{ if } z_{ki} \leq 0
\end{aligned}
\tag{3.5}
$$

This new transform, ζ_k, (to be called the *zeta-score* for X_k) takes only positive values and has a property that it is ratio-wise symmetrical when the positive and the negative directions of variable X_k are reversed. For example, let the value of ζ_{ki} be 2.5. If X_{ki} is multiplied by -1, ζ_{ki} will take a value of 0.4 (= 1/2.5). It may be easily shown that the zeta-score includes the index of distinctiveness as a special case for binary variables.[9]

---

[8]Cooper, Lee G. & Masao Nakanishi [1983], "Standardizing Variables in Multiplicative Choice Models," *Journal of Consumer Research*, 10 (June), 96–108.

[9]For a binary variable X_k, $\bar{X}_k = r$ and $\sigma_k = r(1 - r)$. Hence

$$
\begin{aligned}
z_{ki}^2 &= \quad (1 - r)/r \text{ if } X_{ki} = 1 \\
z_{ki}^2 &= \quad r/(1 - r) \text{ if } X_{ki} = 0.
\end{aligned}
$$

Substitution of the z_{ki}^2's in the zeta-score formula yields squared roots of distinctiveness indices.

The zeta-score is based on the ratio of the noncentral moment of inertia about brand i to the central moment of inertia on measure X_k (namely, the variance of X_k) — thus reflecting how an object stands out from a group relative to the variability of the group. This ratio is not affected by a general linear transformation of X_k, making it an appropriate transformation of interval-scale ratings — thus allowing interval-scale rating to be used in MCI as well as MNL models. The ratio has a minimum value of one for brands at the center (i.e., the mean of X_k), and increases as a particular brand gets farther away from the center. To translate this ratio into a usable index we invert it at the mean of the underlying variable. This allows us to tell if a brand is distinctively high or distinctively low in an attribute compared to the other brands in the competitive offering. Figure 3.2 gives the comparison of the zeta-score with the $\exp(z_{ki})$ transform.

Figure 3.2: Comparison of Zeta-Score and Exp(z-Score) Transforms

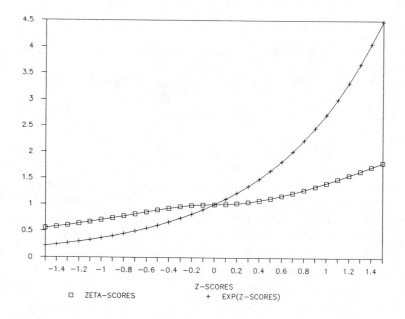

Although the shape of two transforms are quite similar, the choice between the two may be made by the form of the elasticities. The direct

and cross elasticities for the $\exp(z_{ki})$ transforms are given by

$$E = (I - JD_s)BSD_X$$

and those for the zeta-transforms are given by

$$E = (I - JD_s)BSD_z$$

where:

$S = $ the $m \times m$ matrix with elements $\{\partial z_{kj}/\partial X_{ki}\}$, i.e.,

$$S = \frac{1}{\sigma_k}[I - \frac{1}{m}J - \frac{1}{m}ZZ']$$

$D_s = $ an $m \times m$ diagonal matrix with the ith diagonal element s_i

$D_X = $ an $m \times m$ diagonal matrix with the ith diagonal element X_{ki}

$\sigma_k = $ the standard deviation of X_k over i

$J = $ an $m \times m$ matrix of 1's

$Z = $ an $m \times 1$ vector of standardized scores (i.e., $z_{ki} = (X_{ki} - \bar{X}_k)/\sigma_k$)

$D_z = $ an $m \times m$ diagonal matrix with the ith diagonal element

$$|z_{ki}|/(1 + z_{ki}^2) \ .$$

Figure 3.3 compares the elasticities of the zeta-score with the $\exp(z_{ki})$ transform.

The dip in the middle of the elasticity plot for zeta-scores corresponds to the flat portion of the zeta-score function depicted in Figure 3.2. With zeta-scores, change is always depicted as slower in the undifferentiated middle portion of the distribution. Consider what this might imply for a frequently purchased branded good ($FPBG$). If it establishes an initial *sale price* about one-half a standard deviation below the average price in the category, the price is distinctively low and market-share change is relatively rapid. If the price drops further from this point, market share increases, but at a slower and slower rate. Bargain-hunting brand switchers have already been attracted to the brand, and little more is to be gained from further price cuts. If the price increases from this initial sale price, market share drops rapidly at first, as the value of being

Figure 3.3: Comparison of Zeta-Score and Exp(z-Score) Elasticities

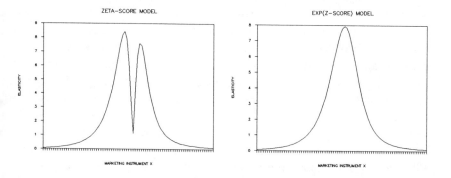

distinctively low priced is dissipated. At the undifferentiated position at the middle of the price distribution, market share is changing least rapidly as minor changes on either side of the average price go largely unnoticed. This indistinct region is similar to what DeSarbo, et al.[10] represent in their friction-pricing model and similar to what Gurumurthy and Little[11] discuss in their pricing model based on Helson's adaptation-level theory. On the high-priced side and analogous series of events happen. Small price increases around the average price are not noticed, but once the brand price is high enough to be distinguished from the mass, the loss of market share becomes more rapid. At some point, however, the change in market share must decline, as the brand looses all but its most loyal following.

In many categories of *FPBG*'s the brands pulse between a relatively high shelf price and a relatively low sale price. In such cases the middle of the elasticity curve is vacant and the values of the elasticities for zeta-scores and exp(z-scores) might be quite similar. The exp(z-score) elasticities might be most descriptive of the path of market-share change from aggregate advertising expenditures, with increasing market-share growth as the expenditures move from zero up to the industry average,

---

[10]DeSarbo, Wayne S., Vithala Rao, Joel H. Steckel, Yoram Wind & Richard Columbo [1987], "A Friction Model for Describing and Forecasting Price Changes," *Marketing Science*, 6, 4 (Fall), 299–319.

[11]Gurumurthy, K. & John D. C. Little [1986], "A Pricing Model Based on Perception Theories and Its Testing on Scanner Panel Data," Massachusetts Institute of Technology Working Paper Draft, May.

and diminishing growth rate for additional expenditures. If the analyst has reasons for preferring one form of elasticities to the other, he/she should choose the one which fits his/her needs best.

An advantage zeta-scores or exp(z-scores) have relative to raw scores is due to their role in separating the underlying importance of a feature from the particular pattern of shared features in any given choice context. If two brands are both on feature in a store they do not each get the same boost in market share as if they were featured alone. By specifically modeling such contextual effects we overcome the limitations imposed by the IIA (context-free) assumption of Luce choice models discussed in Chapter 2. The IIA assumption does not recognize that the value of a major promotion is somehow shared by all the brands on sale in that time period. The parameters of a raw-score (Luce-type) model will always reflect the underlying value of the feature commingled with the particular pattern of shared features in the contexts used for calibration. By explicitly modeling the pattern of feature sharing with a distinctiveness index, the parameters are free to reflect the underlying value of a feature. In forecasting, one again uses either zeta-scores or exp(z-scores) to help translate the underlying value of a feature to the particular pattern of shared features in new time periods. Whatever the value of a feature, we know that the per-brand worth is diluted as the number of brands on feature increases. When all brands are on sale, there will be no differential market-share benefit — just an increase in the cost of doing business. There are many situations in which marketing actions must be distinct to be effective.

Transformations such as exp(z-scores) and zeta-scores not only highlight the differences among brands but serve to standardize variables. This reduces the multicollinearity inherent in the differential-effects forms of market-response models as will be shown in Chapter 5.

3.9   Time-Series Issues

Up to this point we have discussed competition only in the *static* sense, in that brands are competing within a single period of time. Gains and losses of market shares for competing brands are viewed as the joint market responses to marketing activities among competitors in the same time period. But in the real world we shall have to be more concerned with the *dynamic* aspects of competition. A firm's marketing activities affect the performance of its product, as well as that of its competitors, not only in a single period but also over many periods. A new or improved product may not achieve immediate market acceptance; promotional activities may have delayed (or *lagged*) effects; efforts to secure channel cooperation may only bear fruit a long time afterwards, etc. Furthermore, there are seasonal and cyclical fluctuations in market demand which may have important competitive implications and affect the performance of all brands in an industry. If market-share analysis is to be meaningful, it is necessary to introduce elements in the analysis to account for those *dynamic* competitive phenomena.

The developments in data-gathering techniques (to be described in Chapter 4) in the recent years have given the analyst a new impetus to perform time-series analysis of market-share data. Store audits have been the traditional source of bi-monthly market-share data, but it would have taken too many periods for the analyst to obtain from this source a sufficient number of observations for standard time-series analysis, such as the Box-Jenkins procedure. But the introduction of optical scanners at the retail level has completely changed the picture. With proper care, the analyst will be able to obtain weekly, or even daily, market-share figures at some selected stores. This drastic improvement in data collection has opened a new avenue of time-series analysis for market-share data.

Major considerations about time-series analysis may be summarized in the following manner.

1. Seasonal and other regular fluctuations in industry sales.

2. Seasonal and other regular fluctuations in market shares.

3. Delayed effects of marketing variables.

Each will be discussed in turn.

First, the industry sales (i.e., *market demand*) for many products are clearly subject to seasonal and other types of regular or cyclical fluctuations over time. Ice cream in summer and toys in December are prime examples of highly seasonal concentrations in sales. For another example, some products might show a high rate of sales in the first week of the month, following the payday. This tends to produce a regular pattern of within-month cyclical fluctuations for weekly data. We will need to take account of regular fluctuations in the industry sales in order to be able to predict brand sales accurately. The theory in time-series analysis tells us to model regular fluctuations of this sort by the following form.

$$Q_{(t)} = f[w_1 Q_{(t)} + w_2 Q_{(t-1)} + \cdots + w_T Q_{(t-T)}]$$

where:

$Q_{(t)}$ = the industry sales in period t

w_τ = the weight attached to $Q_{(t-\tau)}$ $(\tau = 1, 2, \ldots, T)$.

Seasonal variations may be handled by a heavy weighting of w_τ for suitable months or weeks. The beginning-of-the-month surge in some brand shares due to paydays may be handled by heavy weighting of w_τ in weekly data.

Second, the market shares of a brand may also exhibit clear seasonal or cyclical fluctuations. Unlike the industry sales, market shares are expected to be less subject to seasonal variations. However, there still may be some situations in which relatively regular fluctuations in market shares appear. Suppose that the sales of a brand in a month were especially high because of a special promotional offer and that the average purchase cycle for the product class is three months. This brand's share may show a peak in every third month after that, creating a pattern resembling a seasonal fluctuation, provided that the initial offer created a loyal group of customers. For whatever the real reasons, relatively regular fluctuations in market shares may be expressed as a function of weighted averages of past market shares, that is,

$$s_{i(t)} = f[\phi_1 s_{i(t-1)} + \phi_2 s_{i(t-2)} + \cdots + \phi_p s_{i(t-p)}]$$

where $s_{i(t)}$ is the market share of brand i in period t and ϕ_τ's $(\tau = 1, 2, \ldots, p)$ are weights attached to past shares.

Third, we need to recognize the delayed effects of marketing variables on market shares of competing brands. Much evidence has been accumulated regarding the fact that advertising and other promotional effects tend to be felt not only in the period of execution but also in the subsequent periods. Such delayed effects may be expressed as the functional relationships between past marketing activities and the current market shares. Mathematically stated, those relationships may be written as:

$$s_{i(t)} = f[X_{(t)}, X_{(t-1)}, \ldots, X_{(t-r)}]$$

where $X_{(t)}$ is the vector of marketing variables in period t for all brands in the industry, that is,

$$X_{(t)} = \left(X_{11(t)} \cdots X_{1m(t)}; X_{21(t)} \cdots X_{2m(t)}; \ldots; X_{K1(t)} \cdots X_{Km(t)} \right)$$

where m is the number of brands in the industry and K is the number of relevant marketing variables.

If we combine the last two formulations, we obtain the following dynamic market-share model.

$$s_{i(t)} = f[\phi_1 s_{i(t-1)} + \phi_2 s_{i(t-2)} + \ldots + \phi_p s_{i(t-p)}, X_{(t)}, X_{(t-1)}, \ldots, X_{(t-r)}] \; .$$

The main question is how to specify the function f in the above equation. One may, of course, think of using a linear formulation such as

$$
\begin{aligned}
s_{i(t)} \;=\; & \phi_1 s_{i(t-1)} + \phi_2 s_{i(t-2)} + \ldots + \phi_p s_{i(t-p)} + \\
& \alpha + \beta_{i0} X'_{(t)} + \beta_{i1} X'_{(t-1)} + \ldots + \beta_{ir} X'_{(t-r)} + \epsilon_{(t)} \quad (3.6)
\end{aligned}
$$

where $\alpha, \beta_{i0}, \ldots, \beta_{ir}$ are parameters and $\epsilon_{(t)}$ is the error term. Note that β_{iv} $(v = 0, 1, 2, \ldots, r)$ is a row vector of $(K \times m)$ parameters $\{\beta_{kijv}\}$, each of which shows the effect of $X_{kj(t-v)}$ on $s_{i(t)}$ and that the symbol "$\prime$" indicates the transpose of a row vector to a column vector.

Unfortunately, this formulation does not do because it does not satisfy the logical-consistency conditions discussed in Chapter 2. In other words, there is no guarantee that the values of $s_{i(t)}$ estimated by this model will be contained in the range between zero and one and the sum of market shares will be equal to one. There may be other formulations which satisfy the logical-consistency conditions, but in this book we will propose a special form that is based on the log-centering transform discussed in Chapter 2.

Let us redefine variables as follows.

$s^*_{i(t)}$ = the log-centered market-share for brand i in period t i.e.,

$$\log(s_{i(t)}/\tilde{s}_{(t)})$$

$\tilde{s}_{(t)}$ = the geometric mean of $s_{i(t)}$ over i in period t

$X^*_{(t)}$ = a vector with elements $\{\log(X_{ki(t)}/\tilde{X}_{k(t)})\}$ $(k = 1, 2, \ldots, K;$ $i = 1, 2, \ldots, m)$

$\tilde{X}_{k(t)}$ = the geometric mean of $X_{ki(t)}$ over i for period t.

The proposed time-series model is expressed as

$$
\begin{aligned}
s^*_{i(t)} \;=\; & \phi_1 s^*_{i(t-1)} + \phi_2 s^*_{i(t-2)} + \ldots + \phi_p s^*_{i(t-p)} + \\
& \beta_{i0} X^{*\prime}_{(t)} + \beta_{i1} X^{*\prime}_{(t-1)} + \ldots + \beta_{ir} X^{*\prime}_{(t-r)} + \epsilon_{(t)} \; . \quad (3.7)
\end{aligned}
$$

The reader will note that equations (3.6) and (3.7) are remarkably similar, except that in (3.7) log-centered variables are used. Yet equation (3.7) is based on the attraction models of market share, namely, MCI and MNL models, and yields logically consistent estimates of market shares. Furthermore (3.7) is linear in its (log-centered) variables, and therefore its time-series characteristics are well known. For those reasons time-series analysis may be performed using log-centered variables. The future values of the $s^*_{i(t)}$'s may be computed from (3.7) and then transformed back to the $s_{i(t)}$'s. For a further justification of equation (3.7), see Appendix 3.10.1.

There are some more issues which must be discussed before we close this section. In proposing equation (3.7) we did not touch on the property of the error term, $\epsilon_{(t)}$. One of the major issues in time-series analysis is the handling of the error term which may be correlated with its own past values. In particular, it has been suggested to define $\epsilon_{(t)}$ as a weighted average of present and past values of another variable, $u_{(t)}$, a white-noise error term which has zero mean and variance σ^2.

$$\epsilon_{(t)} = u_{(t)} + \theta_1 u_{(t-1)} + \ldots + \theta_q u_{(t-q)}$$

where $\theta_1, \ldots, \theta_q$ are parameters. In this specification it is clear that $\epsilon_{(t)}$ is correlated with $\epsilon_{(t-1)}, \epsilon_{(t-2)}, \ldots, \epsilon_{(t-q)}$ because they share common terms in variable u. If we combine this specification of the error term with equation (3.7), we will have a time-series model known as an ARMAX(p, q) model.[12]

Another issue that must be taken into account is the obvious fact that market shares of different brands are not independent of each other. The joint determination of market shares may be modeled by the following scheme. Let

$$s^*_{(t)} = \left(s^*_{1(t)} s^*_{2(t)} \cdots s^*_{m(t)} \right)'$$

be the column vector of log-centered values of market shares for period t, and

$$X^{**}_{(t)} = \begin{pmatrix} X^*_{(t)} \\ X^*_{(t)} \\ \cdots \\ X^*_{(t)} \end{pmatrix}$$

---

[12]If we assume that $\epsilon_{(t)}$ are independently distributed with zero mean and a constant variance, (3.7) is called an ARX(p) model.

be the $m \times (m \times K)$ matrix with each row identical to $X^*_{(t)}$. Using this notation the ARMAX model is written as

$$
\begin{aligned}
s^*_{(t)} = \quad & \Phi_1 s^*_{(t-1)} + \Phi_2 s^*_{(t-2)} + \ldots + \Phi_p s^*_{(t-p)} + \\
& X^{**}_{(t)} B'_0 + X^{**}_{(t-1)} B'_1 + \ldots + X^{**}_{(t-r)} B'_r + E_{(t)}
\end{aligned} \qquad (3.8)
$$

where:

Φ_l = the $m \times m$ matrix with elements $\{ \phi_{lij} \}$

ϕ_{lij} = the parameter for the effect of $s^*_{j(t-l)}$ on $s^*_{i(t)}$

B_v = the $m \times (m \times K)$ matrix with elements $\{ \beta_{kijv} \}$

$E_{(t)} = (\epsilon_{1(t)} \epsilon_{2(t)} \ldots \epsilon_{m(t)})'$

$\epsilon_{i(t)}$ = the error term for $s^*_{i(t)}$.

The model specified by equation (3.8) is known as a vector-valued ARMAX model in the literature of time-series analysis. In the theoretical sense it is a most comprehensive formulation of time-series properties associated with market-share analysis. In the practical sense, however, it is too unwieldy for the analyst to utilize. For one thing, it is extremely difficult to specify the model correctly in terms of the lag structure in the model. Unless there are some a priori grounds that give the number of lags, such as p, q, r, those numbers will have to be specified by a tedious trial-and-error process. For another thing, even if the model is correctly specified in terms of the lag structure, the model has been known to pose serious estimation problems, especially when many parameters are involved. With relatively moderate numbers of brands, variables and/or the lags, the total number of parameters which must be estimated will become large. For example, if $m = 5$, $K = 3$, $p = 2$, $r = 2$, and $q = 1$, the total number of parameters (θ's, β's and ϕ's) to be estimated is

$$
(m \times m) \times p + m \times (m \times K) \times r + m \times q = 205
$$

excluding the number of variance components for $E_{(t)}$. It can be seen that even a reasonable attempt for realistic modeling based on the vector-valued ARMAX model is bound to be frustrated for those reasons.

In the remaining part of this book we will take a pragmatic stance in that the auto-correlations of the error term $\epsilon_{i(t)}$ are negligible except for perhaps the first-order correlations (i.e., corr$[\epsilon_{i(t)}, \epsilon_{i(t-1)}]$). Furthermore, by adopting a simplifying assumption that u_i and u_j are uncorrelated within a period as well as over periods, we introduce a model called a seemingly uncorrelated ARMAX model whose parameters may be more easily estimated. This model seems to capture the basic properties of over-time competition between the brands without unduly complicating the analysis.

3.10   Appendix for Chapter 3

3.10.1   *Log-Linear Time-Series Model

In the last section for time-series issues, we proposed the following log-linear model of time-series analysis in lieu of a linear model.

$$
\begin{aligned}
s^*_{i(t)} \;=\; & \phi_1 s^*_{i(t-1)} + \phi_2 s^*_{i(t-2)} + \ldots + \phi_p s^*_{i(t-p)} + \\
& \beta_{i0} X^{*\prime}_{(t)} + \beta_{i1} X^{*\prime}_{(t-1)} + \ldots + \beta_{ir} X^{*\prime}_{(t-r)} + \epsilon_{(t)} \ .
\end{aligned} \tag{3.9}
$$

To convince the reader of the compatibility of this time-series model with the market-share models in this book, the MCI and MNL models in particular, we first begin with the following specification of attraction for brand i in period t.

$$
\mathcal{A}_{i(t)} = \mathcal{A}^{\phi_1}_{i(t-1)} \mathcal{A}^{\phi_2}_{i(t-2)} \cdots \mathcal{A}^{\phi_p}_{i(t-p)} \exp(\alpha_i + \epsilon_{i(t)}) \prod_{k=1}^{K} \prod_{v=0}^{r} \prod_{j=1}^{m} X^{\beta_{kijv}}_{kij(t-v)} \ .
$$

This is a straightforward extension of the cross-effects model in (3.4). One may apply the log-centering transformation to the above model to obtain

$$
\begin{aligned}
\mathcal{A}^*_{i(t)} \;=\; & \alpha_i + \phi_1 \mathcal{A}^*_{i(t-1)} + \phi_2 \mathcal{A}^*_{i(t-2)} + \ldots + \phi_p \mathcal{A}^*_{i(t-p)} + \\
& \beta_0 X^*_{(t)} + \beta_1 X^*_{(t-1)} + \ldots + \beta_r X^*_{(t-r)} + \epsilon^*_{i(t)}
\end{aligned} \tag{3.10}
$$

where:

$\mathcal{A}^*_{i(t)}$ = the log-centered attraction for brand i in period t
   i.e., $\log(\mathcal{A}_{i(t)} / \tilde{\mathcal{A}}_{(t)})$

$\tilde{\mathcal{A}}_{(t)}$ = the geometric mean of $\mathcal{A}_{i(t)}$ over i in period t

$X^*_{(t)}$ = a vector with elements $\{\log(X_{ki(t)} / \tilde{X}_{k(t)})\}$ ($k = 1, 2, \ldots, K; i = 1, 2, \ldots, m$)

$\tilde{X}_{k(t)}$ = the geometric mean of $X_{ki(t)}$ over i for period t

$\epsilon^*_{i(t)}$ = the log-centered value of $\epsilon_{i(t)}$

$\beta_0, \beta_1, \ldots, \beta_r$ are parameters vectors.

The above equation looks much the same as equation (3.7) except that the latter is defined for the log-centered values of $s_{i(t)}$ rather than those of $\mathcal{A}_{i(t)}$.

Fortunately, it may be easily proved that $s^*_{i(t)}$ is equal to $\mathcal{A}^*_{i(t)}$. Since $s_{i(t)}$ is proportional to $\mathcal{A}_{i(t)}$, one may write $s_{i(t)} = c\mathcal{A}_{i(t)}$, the constant of proportionality, c, being the sum of $\mathcal{A}_{j(t)}$ over j. Applying the log-centering transformation to $s_{i(t)}$ we have

$$s^*_{i(t)} = \log(s_{i(t)}/\tilde{s}_{(t)}) \ .$$

But since $s_{i(t)} = c\mathcal{A}_{i(t)}$ and hence $\tilde{s}_{(t)} = c\tilde{\mathcal{A}}_{(t)}$, implying $s^*_{i(t)} = \mathcal{A}^*_{i(t)}$. Substituting $s^*_{i(t)}$ for $\mathcal{A}^*_{i(t)}$ in equation (3.10), we obtain equation (3.7). Note that model (3.8) is a multivariate extension of model (3.7) and no additional justification is necessary. Thus we have shown that the log-linear time-series models (3.7) and (3.8) are logical extensions of the attraction models of this book.

Chapter 4

Data Collection

The goal of market-share analysis is to assess the effectiveness of marketing actions in competitive environments. The data-collection principle which derives from this goal is to measure the *causal variables* and *performance indicators* so as to give as clear a view of marketing effectiveness as possible. There are two main threats to achieving clarity. The first threat comes from inaccuracies in the record of transactions and market conditions. The second threat comes from problems in aggregating even accurate records over time, space, and transaction units. We will discuss these threats in the next two sections. Then we will review the kind of data currently being collected by national tracking services and discuss how these data can be combined into a *market information systems*.

4.1   The Accuracy of Scanner Data

A data feast has been laid on the table for market researchers to enjoy.[1] It all arrives on the analyst's plate so well prepared and presented that it is easy to forget that the ingredients may be less than perfect to begin with.

In optically scanned, point-of-sale systems the shopping basket is the basic transaction unit. If the focus of a competitive analysis or a marketing-effectiveness study is on a single category such as margarine or coffee, then only a component of the basic transaction is of primary interest. This component gets recorded in two ways. First, it is posted to an accumulating record of sales for that particular stock-keeping unit (SKU). And second, if the customer is part of an ongoing scanner panel,

---

[1]We wish to acknowledge Penny Baron for showing us how this feast is prepared.

the whole transaction is posted to a longitudinal (over time and stores) record of this member's purchases.

For the data to be accurately recorded the many components in the management system (of which the POS system is only a part) all have to work properly. The current advertised specials have to be properly entered into the central price file. When advertised specials involve multiple like items, such as brand sizes, colors, or special packs, the proper parent-child relations need to be recorded for each different Uniform-Product-Code (UPC) description included in the advertised special. In multiple-store retail chains the updated price file has to be properly downloaded to the store controller at each retail location. There has to be integrity in the communications between the store controller and each register. Price is advertised in multiple ways. The price tags on items, shelf markings, in-store displays, newspaper or magazine features, home mailers, television and radio spots all have to report prices which are consistent among themselves and with the central price file. And, of course, the item has to scan properly. If an item does not scan, the cashier is likely to record the price manually without the UPC codes needed to post this part of the transaction to the proper files. The scan rate has a very important effect on the utility of the data.

Store managers are granted varying degrees of autonomy by their respective chains, but many have the flexibility to alter prices in their store's controller in order to meet competitive pressures in the immediate locale, or to substitute *like items* for out-of-stock advertised specials. There is cause for concern about how these special items are recorded in the local system during a promotion period and what happens to these records when the promotion is concluded. A single program normally reverses all the special prices at the end of a promotional period. It is a complex matter to deal with the general rule and all the exception.

While in most data collection efforts the *research staff* is responsible for data integrity, with scanner data *management* is responsible. The buyer/merchandiser function, the store-operations function and the informations-systems function of the firm must all work together to insure the accuracy of scanner data. It is an issue of major importance not only to the utility of the data for further research but also to customer satisfaction and to the firm's compliance with business and professional codes. Fortunately, scanner-based systems provide the records that allow management to trace back to the source of an inaccuracy. Error tracking is an important feedback mechanism — helping to insure price integrity, and thereby insuring the utility of the data for kinds of analyses discussed in this book.

4.2   Issues in Aggregation

Before the advent of optical scanners, we had a different view of marketing performance. One could plot quarterly or annual sales versus marketing expenditures and get the naive view that more successful companies
spent more on their advertising and promotional efforts. This would be
a particularly naive view if this year's marketing budget is based on last
year's revenues or profits. During sustained periods of growth, this leads
to expanding budgets and sometimes a corporate sense of invulnerability
as expanding markets lead to sales growth almost regardless of competitive activity. During recessionary times, the macro-economic conditions
provide a ready scapegoat for corporate performance. Gross aggregation
of this sort masks the victories and defeats in each competitive arena
which, in sum, constitute firm performance.

The basic analytical principles involved here are similar to those discussed in section 2.8 on the relation between market share and choice
probabilities. The issue there concerned whether individual choice probabilities are accurately reflected in aggregated market shares. There
we saw that special attention is needed only when choice probabilities
are heterogeneous and purchase frequencies are heterogeneous and correlated with choice probabilities — Case 4(b). In the present context
we are collecting data to reflect how the causal conditions of the marketplace relate to market shares. Causal condition are most likely to
be the elements of the marketing mix such as prices and promotion but
also could include regional or seasonal differences, or differences among
consumer segments. Table 4.1 displays the four cases.

The analogy to Case 1 would be when the market shares are homogeneous and the causal conditions are homogeneous. This might be the
case when multiple stores in a retail chain offer the same promotion in a
particular week and get essentially the same market response in different
areas. Then no insight will be lost through aggregation. Case 2 refers to
when market shares are heterogeneous, but causal conditions are homogeneous. This is a situation in which essentially identical stores (perhaps
stores in a chain), in essentially identical areas and time periods, offer
the same promotional package, and get different market responses. It
sounds like a missing-variables problem (i.e., there is something we could
measure which could explain the differences). If one can find the missing

Table 4.1: Aggregating Market Shares and Causal Conditions

Market Shares	Causal Conditions	
	Homogeneous	Heterogeneous
Homogeneous	Case 1: $E(s_i) = \pi_i$ $\overline{f(X_k)} = f(\bar{X}_k)$	Case 3: $E(s_i) = \pi_i$ $\overline{f(X_k)} \neq f(\bar{X}_k)$
Heterogeneous	Case 2: $E(s_i) = \bar{\pi}_i$ $\overline{f(X_k)} = f(\bar{X}_k)$	Case 4 (a) Uncorrelated: $E(s_i) = \bar{\pi}_i$ $\overline{f(X_k)} \neq f(\bar{X}_k)$ Case 4 (b) Correlated: $E(s_i) = \bar{\pi}_i + cov(\mu, \pi_i)/\bar{\mu}$ $\overline{f(X_k)} \neq f(\bar{X}_k)$

variable then the causal conditions would no longer be homogeneous and Case 2 is no longer relevant. But if Case 2 describes the situation, investigating the average market shares (or other performance measures) will not distort the known relations to the causal conditions. The primary loss will be degrees of freedom. In Case 3 the market shares are homogeneous and the casual conditions are heterogeneous. Promotions differ over stores but the market shares do not change. While this might seem unlikely, it can happen. Marketing efforts can be ineffective. Case 3 is like Case 4(a) because if market shares do not change they can not be correlated with changes in casual conditions. Here the concerns involve how the aggregation over causal conditions is achieved. Any variable, X_k, we measure as an indicator of a causal condition will be represented in the models as $f(X_k)$. Whenever causal conditions are heterogeneous it is probably true that the function of the average measure (i.e., $f(\bar{X}_k)$) is not equal to the average of the functions (i.e., $\overline{f(X_k)}$). Given a choice, it should be the function values which are aggregated rather than the original variables.[2] Since there is no variation in the market shares, the variation lost through aggregation of the causal conditions is unexplainable, and probably therefore not a major loss to our understanding.

---

[2]Often the log-centered form of the variable is a proper and convenient form to aggregate.

In Case 4(a) there is heterogeneity in both causal conditions and market shares, but there is no correlation between the variability in market shares and the variability in causal conditions. This is like Case 3, in that aggregation should be done carefully, but there will be little, if any, loss in explanatory power. Finally, in Case 4(b), we have the heterogeneity in market share being correlated with heterogeneity in causal conditions. If differences across regions are correlated with differences in market shares, then the model should be expanded to reflect the role of regions. Similarly, seasonal effects could be incorporated into the model, if they were correlated with differences in market shares. Explanatory power will be lost if cases of these types are aggregated.

While market-share analysis is applicable in broader arenas, the packaged-goods industry will be used as the basis around which the general principles of data collection and aggregation will be discussed. The diffusion of scanner technology has had its greatest impact on the packaged-goods industry. In our estimation it is no accident that the growth in promotion budgets relative to advertising budgets in packaged-good firms has coincided with the availability of data showing the surges in sales which correspond to short-term promotions. But to assess if these promotional expenditures are worthwhile, we need data which are aggregated to correspond to the promotional event. This is a classic Case 4(b) situation. There are huge swings (heterogeneity) in market shares which are correlated with the changes (heterogeneity) in causal conditions (the promotional environment). Aggregation that combines promotion and nonpromotion periods can obscure the relations we wish to study.

The basic time unit of a promotion is a week. This does not mean that promotions only last one week. But in any given week a promotion could begin or end. Temporal aggregation beyond a week would virtually assure that the onset or termination of a promotion would be averaged in with nonpromotion sales, as was the case with Nielsen's bimonthly store-audit data. One could argue for representing each day, but since the promotional conditions are essentially homogeneous over days in a week, we have either Case 1 or 2 and sacrifice at most degrees of freedom rather than explanatory power with such aggregation.[3]

The basic spatial unit is either the grocery chain in a trading area or the stores within a grocery chain. A trading area is conveniently defined by the local newspapers. Newspaper features announcing a promotion

---

[3]One problem is that promotions could begin on different weekdays in different trading areas. This will create at least a small aggregation bias in a weekly database.

on a brand for all the local stores of a particular grocery chain help specify the boundaries of a trading area. In each trading area one day has typically evolved as *Food Day* (i.e., the day on which the special food ads are printed reporting the promotions which are available for the coming week). The basic principle is to capture the events as close to the place of occurrence as possible. Retail scanner data record the events as they occur, whereas warehouse-withdrawal data capture events further from the place of transaction. If we decide to aggregate over stores within a grocery chain, we are averaging possibly heterogeneous market shares over a homogeneous promotional environment — a Case 2 situation, losing degrees of freedom, but not explanatory power.

The basic transaction unit is the brand. Brands come in different sizes (or weights) and versions (e.g., conditioners for dry, normal, or oily hair, coffee ground for drip, electric or regular percolators or automatic coffee makers). With every variation in size, version, special pack, etc., there is a unique UPC code. This can translate into dozens of separate UPC codes for a single brand — typically far too much detail to utilize in market-share analysis. At the other extreme, national advertising typically lumps all the versions and sizes under a single brand banner. The best level of aggregation lies somewhere between these two extremes. But exactly where is difficult to judge. It depends on the business decisions being studied, on practical matters such as computer capacity, and on experience issues such as how familiar one is with this style of analysis. For scanner data one guideline comes from the causal data. If separate sizes or versions of a brand are promoted together, they probably can be lumped together in the data set. As with the matter of industry definition discussed in Chapter 2, we can make a tentative definition, perform the analysis and see if the competitive map portrays substantively different roles to the different sizes or versions of a brand. Our experience in the coffee market led to aggregating all sizes together, but distinguishing between ground and soluble, and between caffeinated and noncaffeinated versions of a brand. In an Australian household-products category (Carpenter, Cooper, Hanssens & Midgley [1988]) various sizes of a brand were aggregated into an 11-competitor market. In a proprietary study of another household-products category the various sizes of each brand were also differentiated, leading to a 66-competitor market — too unwieldy for most purposes.

Aggregating minor brands is also a very judgmental issue. In the Australian household-products study all the wet versions of minor brands were aggregated into AW4 and all the dry versions of minor brands were aggregated into AD4. There were so many minor brands in the market that these aggregates became the largest brands in the study. Since combining small brands together is always a Case 4(b) aggregation, creating large-seeming competitors out of many tiny brands is to be avoided whenever possible. It is probably preferable to allow many more brands as separate units of observation, but restrict the variables which describe these brands to simple-effects, rather than differential effects or fully extended representations. This topic will be taken up in Chapter 5.

We now turn to a description of the kinds of data which are being collected from thousands of stores each week.

4.3 National Tracking Data

4.3.1 Store-Level Scanner Data

This section will describe the variables recorded in the major retail-scanner databases. The data are reported in each store in each week for each UPC code, so that aggregation into brands and grocery chains are separate issues. The prototypes are based on InfoScan/PromotionScan from Information Resources, Inc. (IRI), and a new database, Monitor, from A.C. Nielsen (a division of Dun & Bradstreet).[4]

The emphasis in these databases is on descriptive tracking — staying as close as possible to the data and using analytical modeling as little as possible, but creating a database which can be aggregated to fit the analytical needs of any client. In each store-week a core set of measures is reported.

Volume — which is either reported in units sold or equivalized volumes such as pounds, ounces, equivalized cases, or whatever the client wants. In carbonated beverages the standard reporting unit is 192 ounce equivalent cases. In toilet paper the standard reporting unit is sheets. It can be any unit which reflects the way business is done in the category. In most product categories one would prefer equivalized units because these will add up sensibly over UPCs. In a very few categories the reporting standard is equivalized servings. In powdered soft drinks this is done because the characteristics of

---

[4]In mid-1987 Dun & Bradstreet reached a tentative agreement to acquire IRI and form Nielsen Information Resources. This move was blocked in November 1987 by the unanimous vote of the SEC. The industry consequences of this blocked attempt are still being played out at the time of this writing. This chapter tries to reflect the types of data which will be available for market-share analysis regardless of the outcomes.

the weights are so different — considering sugar-added versions, plain versus artificial sweeteners such as aspartame, that any kind of a weight approach would not reflect a reasonable sense of comparable offerings. But the report of equivalized servings is needed in many more categories than it is offered. Wet and dry versions which can often compete with each other are made much more comparable when reported in equivalized servings.[5] The same is true for ground versus soluble coffee, freeze-dried versus canned goods, and others. It is up to individual firms to develop the equivalent servings for their product categories.

Dollars — the revenues received. Current price can be found by dividing Volume by Dollars.

Regular Price — an imputed shelf price. Since price in the current period could reflect promotional discounts one needs a small artificial-intelligence algorithm to impute a regular price from the prior stream of prices for this UPC item in this store. Such algorithms look for past maximum prices or find the median over the past five or seven periods. Difficulties arise in trying to differentiate a change in shelf price from a temporary promotion price, or in trying to differentiate a long series of temporary price reductions from a regular price.

ACV — All Commodity Volume of the store. This is reported either as an annual number which does not vary from week to week, or as a weekly number which is calibrated against total scanned dollars. One can figure out what percentage the scanned dollars are of total movement in the store and use this as an adjustment between stores. Monitor uses an ACV number which is a store characteristic. This number is adjusted only when there are serious basic changes in the store's volume.

ACV Selling — the ACV for that item or group of items reported only in stores where there was some movement of that item.

Baseline Sales — a straight time-series approach to assessing baseline sales. Since reporting in these databases is done at the UPC-store level, one can not reflect the influence of causal variables on baseline

---

[5]Wet and dry versions of some household products differ ten-to-one in price for equivalized servings.

sales. This must be done by separate analyses. In the databases themselves only a simple exponential smoothing is practical — using very few prior periods and weighting the most recent ones most heavily.[6] In Monitor, the baseline-sales figures are computed twice. The first estimate is used to find outliers in the data. Data which show huge sales spikes above the preliminary baseline despite the absence of promotions are tagged (and called *residual-causal observations*), as are observations where sales are precipitously below the preliminary baseline (called *short-sale observations*). These are possibly misunderstood data or weeks for which the store environment is not properly coded. The baseline-sales algorithm is run again without the tagged data.

Baseline Dollars — a combination of the baseline-sales estimate with the regular-price algorithm.

Along with codes for the geographic market area (e.g., the Chicago market) and the grocery chain (e.g., Jewel), these are the basic set of measures which can be gathered directly from POS systems. Note the emphasis on only those basic measures which will add together sensibly over related UPCs. One reports sales volumes, not market shares, until the question, "Shares of what?" can be answered.

4.3.2 Store Audits

Nielsen's Monitor is like the combination of IRI's InfoScan and PromotionScan. PromotionScan audits the stores and newspapers to record the promotional environment. Displays and features are separately collected as zero-one measures, gathered either by people in the stores or outside agents and then integrated into the store database each week. The Majer's classification of newspaper features (A – major ads, B – coupon-sized ads, C – line ads) is becoming the standard. A measure reflecting in-ad coupon should be included, rather than merely being reflected as an A- or B-feature in Majer's terms. The displays are sometimes broken down into big displays, little displays (such as shelf talkers), end-of-aisle (gondola-end) displays, or dump bins in products categories such as bar soap.

When display, store-coupon, and feature measures are incorporated with the data from the POS system, it becomes straightforward to track

---

[6]Both InfoScan and Monitor use an Erlang (1,1) model. InfoScan has some additional terms in its baseline-sales measure for weather or seasonality.

indices such as volume sold on feature, display or any trade deal, or average price or price discount on any style promotion. Over weeks we can track duration of promotions to investigate stores' promotion policies or promotional wearout.

Manufacturers' coupons have been the slowest to be integrated into tracking services. While the purchase price is reported net of coupons redeemed, a simple zero-one measure for the redemption of a manufacturers' coupons is not very helpful. The volume sold on manufacturers' coupons is not reported in either InfoScan or Monitor, but is recorded in the BehaviorScan panels mentioned below. In BehaviorScan panels the coupons used in each transaction of a panelist are put in a separate plastic bag at the check stand, then hand-keyed into the panelist's computer file each week. Given the effort involved, it is not surprising that recording of manufacturers' coupons has lagged behind other developments.

4.3.3   Household Scanner Panels

A member of a household scanner panel does little that is conspicuously different from any other shopper. When purchases are made the cashier scans the panel member's bar-coded card. Thus, regardless of the store in which the purchases were made, the organization maintaining the panel can accumulate a comprehensive record of transactions for the household. The panel members are offered minor appliances or similar gifts, and lotteries for more major gifts, such as vacations. Demographic information is collected at the time of recruitment. Very little in the way of traditional survey-research questioning is conducted on panel members. It is generally felt that the more you question these people the less typical their shopping behavior becomes.

The role of household scanner panels in tracking databases such as InfoScan is partly different than the role of IRI's BehaviorScan, Nielsen's Erim or SAMI/Burke's Adtel panels which were organized to support controlled market tests for new products or advertising campaigns. BehaviorScan panels consist of up to 3,000 households in each of 10 midsized, media-isolated markets. The media isolation is needed for control in advertising tests. To do national tracking requires that panels to be organized in major urban markets. Major urban markets such as New York, Chicago, and Los Angeles are not conducive to controlled store tests because the geographically broad shopping patterns make it organizationally difficult to capture all purchases of a household, and because the market-research organization lacks the ability to control exposure to advertising. Both kinds of panels must reflect the total purchase profile of the market area. But the BehaviorScan panels must also be partitionable into a number of parallel subgroups for various test and control conditions. BehaviorScan panels help assess new-product sales potential, media weight, media copy, price and promotions, and shelf location. The primary focus of a panel for a national tracking service is simply on providing nationally representative data which help to explain the store-level performance. On a store-week level household scanner panels readily provide penetration measures such as the percent of households using the category or brand (down to the UPC level). Over time one can observe the aggregate path of brand diffusion. Average interpurchase time and average purchase quantity can be reported for the category or the brand. These could be combined to reflect the aggregate household inventory of each brand, leading to interesting studies of how household inventories interact with the promotional environment. One can also report aggregate demographic characterization of the purchasers of different brands.

Panels for market-share analysis must provide the necessary data to address the heterogeneity issue discussed in Chapter 2, "Is there a correlation between brand-choice probabilities and usage frequency?" This suggests partitioning the panel into heavy users and light users, and looking for any systematic differences in choice probabilities across brands. If systematic differences appear, a segmentation is indicated as is discussed later in this chapter.

4.3.4 Other Data Sources

Warehouse-withdrawal or bimonthly store-audit data used to be the primary methods for tracking sales. But for assessing marketing effectiveness these data have obvious shortcomings. We can know what is withdrawn, and can combine these data with the retail promotional environment. But the lag between withdrawal and sales has to be established and may vary over retail locations. There are also the potential for early withdrawal in anticipation of the retail promotion, transshipment of a good trade deal or stockpiling by the stores late in the trade deal to take advantage of discounted wholesale prices even after the retail promotion is over. While warehouse-withdrawal data are useful for understanding behavior in the channels of distribution, their utility for market-share analysis has diminished with the availability of data which track transactions at the retail outlet. Bimonthly store-audit data are temporally aggregated to an extent which masks the weekly pulsing of sales.

Diary panels have also waned in popularity with the emergence of scanner panels. Diary panels suffer from problems of the accuracy of recall and recording which are eliminated by scanner panels. Even when the accuracy issue is attacked by the use of in-home UPC readers, insuring that all transactions are scanned in-home is still problematic. Any in-home measurement or diary maintenance is more obtrusive than transaction scanning at the point of purchase. How long panelists are unaffected by their special status is a concern in any panel, but the more obtrusive the panel measurement, the more of a problem this becomes.

Some of the data which now flow from controlled test-market scanner panels (e.g., BehaviorScan, Erim, or Adtel), should become available for tracking services. The television-exposure data now collected from panel slices in BehaviorScan contain important information for evaluating the effectiveness of media campaigns. Some BehaviorScan households electronically collect viewing data every five seconds and dump the record automatically via an early morning telephone call which is answered just before the bell rings. If a store-level solution to the problem of recording manufacturers' coupons is not found, scanner panels can provide estimates. Subpartitions of panels have also been made available for more traditional market-research surveys of brand perceptions and preferences, as well as attitudes, opinions, and interests. Using standardizations such as zeta-scores or $\exp(z\text{-scores})$ makes it straightforward to integrate interval-scale consumer ratings into market-share analysis.

4.4 Market Information Systems

The idea that we can relate all of the measures described above to market performance, and do so in a way that allows us to assess the unique marketing effectiveness of each brand, is a captivating challenge to market analysts and a unique opportunity for managers. While the models are oriented to relating the partial impact of each marketing instrument on volume sold (and the consequent revenues), the costs associated with the marketing effort of the firm and the retailer are also obtainable (or estimable). The models serve as an inference engine, which, combined with data and decision-support software, become an information system capable of simulating the profit consequences of any competitive scenario. The market-wide coverage of the data and the models is why we term these *market information systems.*

The models which form the inference engine collectively constitute the system of models for competitive analysis depicted in Figure 4.1. The "Competitive Structure Information (Longitudinal)" refers to a database of the style developed in this chapter, where the focus is on market-share data for each store each week and the causal variables presumed to influence the transactions. Note that the "Standardized Data" feed into the market-share model while the "Raw Data" feed the category-volume model. While the modeling can be done in other ways, we feel the raw prices and promotion levels drive the total size of the pie, while the distinctiveness of marketing efforts reflected in the standardized data influences how the pie is shared. The "Segment Structure Information" which also feeds these two models refers to the data from household panels which provide for additional understanding of store-level results and also indicate if segmentation of the store-level data is advisable. If a partition of heavy users versus light users is indicated, the panel provides estimates of the population market shares for each segment and the store sales provide sum constraints which should be useful in developing good estimates.

The products of the market-shares times category-volume estimates are sales forecasts for each brand in the market. These forecasts must be diagnostically rich to fulfill their role in this system. The diagnostic value of the sales models comes primarily from the elasticities. We know from equation (2.19) that the sum of the market-share elasticity and the category-volume estimates is the sales elasticity.[7] A univariate time-series approach to forecasting category volume will not provide the required elasticities. We need to know how the internal conditions of the market affect total category volume. Basically this means we need terms in the category-volume model which correspond to the differential effects in the market-share model. With such variables in a sales model we can run any kind of simulations required for brand planning, and obtain the elasticities needed for investigating competitive structure and for feeding the strategic-analysis model.

The main method for investigating market structure is through competitive maps. The procedures, described fully in Chapter 6, look at the structure underlying the asymmetric, brand-by-brand arrays of cross elasticities over store-weeks, and highlight the events which produce sys-

---

[7]The equation assumes no systematic competitive reaction, but this assumption is relaxed in Chapter 6.

tematic changes in competitive structure. A map corresponding to each structural change can be constructed to assess the threats and opportunities associated with market events. Chapter 6 will also introduce the "Logit Ideal-Point Model"[8] which can localize the most preferred regions in the competitive maps. Competitive maps can help direct the inquiry into the market which is essential to brand planning.

Firms have data on their own costs and should be able to provide estimates of competitors' costs as well as the costs borne by the retailers for features, displays, and store coupons. The close tying of forecasted revenues with estimated costs enables managers to assess the effectiveness of marketing actions and facilitates brand planning. With panel data on media exposure, one can see how advertising expenditures translate into exposures and how exposures translate into sales. When cost data are combined with the elasticities from the sales model the basic ingredients are present for a strategic-analysis model. Carpenter, Cooper, Hanssens, and Midgley [1988] show how elasticities from attraction models can be used to investigate optimal price and advertising policies under the boundary conditions of no competitive reaction and optimal competitive reaction. The role of these kinds of analyses is discussed in Chapter 7.

Brand planning, in general, and promotion planning, in particular, are directly affected by such a market information system. While management is required to be explicit about the competitive environment it expects to face, plans can be tested for both their profits and robustness to competitive efforts. Chapter 7 presents a brand-planning exercise which uses such a system.

---

[8]Cooper, Lee G. & Masao Nakanishi [1983b], "Two Logit Models for External Analysis of Preferences," *Psychometrika*, 48, 4 (December), 607–20.

Figure 4.1: A System of Models for Competitive Analysis

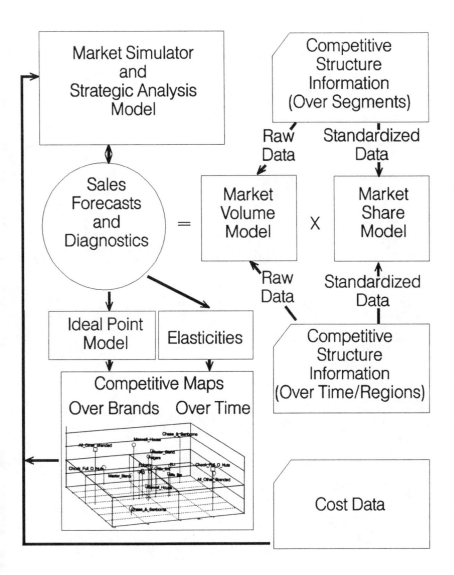

Chapter 5

Parameter Estimation

5.1 Calibrating Attraction Models

In Chapter 3 we presented market-share attraction models in detail. As we tried to describe realistically the market and competitive structures, more and more complex models had to be introduced — ending at a cross-effects model which has a unique role for each piece of information (e.g., each price or each feature) on the brand to which it refers as well as on every other competitor. From the practical point of view, however, these complex models are not useful unless it is possible for one to calibrate them from the actual market performance of brands. Calibration establishes the *value* or *importance* of each of these roles in determining the market performance of each brand. In this chapter we will review the techniques to estimate the parameters of attraction models. We will begin with the most basic models, i.e., the simple-effects form of MCI and MNL models, and then proceed to more complex models such as differential-effects and cross-effects models. To remind the reader, the general specification of simple-effects attraction models is given below.

$$\mathcal{A}_i = \exp(\alpha_i + \epsilon_i) \prod_{k=1}^{K} f_k(X_{ki})^{\beta_k} \tag{5.1}$$

$$s_i = \mathcal{A}_i / \sum_{j=1}^{m} \mathcal{A}_j$$

where:

s_i = the market share of brand i

103

$\mathcal{A}_i$ = the attraction of brand i

m = the number of brands

X_{ki} = the value of the kth explanatory variable (X_k) for brand i (e.g., prices, product attributes, expenditures for advertising, distribution, sales force)

K = the number of explanatory variables

f_k = a positive, monotone transformation of X_k

ϵ_i = the specification-error term

α_i, β_k $(i = 1, 2, \ldots, m; k = 1, 2, \ldots, K)$ = parameters to be estimated.

We may choose either MCI or MNL models, depending on whether f_k is an identity transformation or an exponential transformation. We will often use the MNL model below in order to simplify our presentation, but the corresponding derivations for the MCI model would be straightforward. Before presenting the use of regression analysis, we will first discuss other estimation techniques applicable to model (5.1).

5.1.1 Maximum-Likelihood Estimation

The maximum-likelihood approach to parameter estimation assumes that the data are obtained from a random sample (sample size n) of individuals who are asked to choose one brand from a set of brands (i.e., *choice set*).[1] The resultant data consist of the number of individuals who selected object i, n_i $(i = 1, 2, \ldots, m)$. This describes a typical multinomial choice process. In order for us to use this type of data, we must modify the definition of the model (5.1) slightly. We assume that the probability, π_i, rather than the market share s_i, that an individual chooses brand i, is specified as[2]

$$\pi_i = \mathcal{A}_i / \sum_{j=1}^{m} \mathcal{A}_j \ .$$

---

[1]See Haines, George, H., Jr., Leonard S. Simon & Marcus Alexis [1972], "Maximum Likelihood Estimation of Central-City Food Trading Areas," *Journal of Marketing Research*, IX (May), 154–59. Also see McFadden [1974].

[2]See sections 2.8 and 4.1 for discussions of when market shares and choice probabilities are interchangeable.

Clearly π_i is a function of the parameters of the model, that is, the α's and β's. We may write the likelihood for a set of observed choices $n_1, n_2, \ldots, n_m$ as

$$L(\alpha_1, \alpha_2, \ldots, \alpha_m; \beta_1, \beta_2, \ldots, \beta_K) = \prod_{i=1}^{m} \pi_i^{n_i} \qquad (5.2)$$

and the logarithm of the likelihood function as

$$\log L(\alpha_1, \alpha_2, \ldots, \alpha_m; \beta_1, \beta_2, \ldots, \beta_K) = \sum_{i=1}^{m} n_i \log \pi_i \ .$$

By maximizing L or $\log L$ with respect to the parameters of the model, we obtain the maximum-likelihood estimates of them. The maximum-likelihood technique may be extended to the cases where observations are taken at more than one *choice situation* (multiple time periods, locations, customer groups, etc.) provided that an independent sample of individuals is drawn at each choice situation. For example, if a series of independent samples is drawn over time, the log-likelihood function may be written as

$$\log L(\alpha_1, \alpha_2, \ldots, \alpha_m; \beta_1, \beta_2, \ldots, \beta_K) = \sum_{t=1}^{T} \sum_{i=1}^{m} n_{it} \log \pi_{it}$$

where n_{it} and π_{it} are the number of individuals who chose brand i in period t and the probability that an individual chooses brand i in period t, respectively, and T is the number of periods under observation.

The maximum-likelihood procedure is a useful technique for parameter estimation in that the properties of estimated parameters are well known,[3] but we choose not to use it in this book for several reasons. First, since the likelihood and log-likelihood functions are nonlinear in parameters α's and β's, the maximum-likelihood procedure requires a nonlinear mathematical-programming algorithm to obtain parameter estimates. Besides being cumbersome to use, such an algorithm does not ensure that the global maximum for the likelihood function is always found. Second, we will be using POS data primarily in calibrating the model. Since POS data generated at a store include multiple purchases in a period made by the same customers, the observed n_i's may not follow the assumptions of a multinomial distribution which underlie the

---

[3] See Haines, et al. [1972].

likelihood function. Third, we will be in most cases using observed market shares, that is, the proportions of purchases of brand i, p_i, based on an unknown but large total number of purchases.[4] The regression techniques developed in the next section are more easily adaptable to this type of data than the maximum-likelihood procedure.

5.1.2 Log-Linear Estimation

We will be presenting estimation procedures based on regression analysis in the next section, but the fact that logit models could be estimated by first applying a log-linear transformation and then applying a regression procedure has been known for a long time. We will review some of these procedures before we turn to the approach which we believe is the most convenient.

Over thirty-five years ago Berkson[5] showed that a logistic model of binary choice becomes linear in parameters by the so-called *logit transformation*. Suppose that each individual in a sample (of size n) independently chooses object 1 with probability π_1, given by

$$\pi_1 = \frac{1}{1 + \beta_0 \exp(-\sum_{k=1}^{K} \beta_k X_{k1})}$$

where:

$\pi_1 = $ the probability that object 1 is chosen in a binary choice

$X_{k1} = $ the kth characteristic of object 1

$\beta_0, \beta_1, \ldots, \beta_K = $ the parameters to be estimated.

If the logit transformation is applied to the above model, we have

$$\log\left(\frac{\pi_1}{1 - \pi_1}\right) = -\log \beta_0 + \sum_{k=1}^{K} \beta_k X_{k1} \qquad (5.3)$$

---

[4] Neither multiple purchases in a single shopping trip, nor purchases of a brand on each of multiple shopping trips within a single reporting period (e.g., a week), fit well with the multinomial-sampling assumptions. Yet both such occurrences can be common in POS data. When analyzing POS data at the store-week level the market shares are not subject to the sampling variation with which maximum-likelihood procedures deal so well. Only the specification error requires special treatment. Section 5.4 presents generalized least-squares (GLS) procedures to cope with the issues.

[5] Berkson, Joseph [1953], "A Statistically Precise and Relatively Simple Method of Estimating the Bioassay with Quantal Response, Based on the Logistic Function," *Journal of the American Statistical Association*, 48 (September), 565–99.

That equation (5.3) is linear in parameters $\log \beta_0$ and β_k $(k = 1, 2, \ldots, K)$ suggests the use of regression analysis. But, since the probability π_1 is unobservable, it must be replaced in the left-hand side of (5.3) by p_1 which is the proportion of individuals in the sample who selected object 1. The final estimating equation is in the following form.

$$\log \left(\frac{p_{1t}}{1 - p_{1t}} \right) = -\log \beta_0 + \sum_{k=1}^{K} \beta_k X_{k1t} + \epsilon_t . \tag{5.4}$$

The subscript t indicates the tth subgroup from which the p_1's are calculated. The error term ϵ_t is the difference between logit transforms of π_1 and p_1, and known to be a function of π_1 and the sample size per subgroup from which p_1 is calculated.[6]

Berkson's method has been extended to the estimation of parameters of multinomial logit (MNL) models by Theil.[7] Assume a multinomial choice process in which each individual independently selects object i with probability π_i from a set of m objects in a single trial, and let π_i be specified by an MNL model

$$\mathcal{A}_i = \exp(\alpha + \sum_{k=1}^{K} \beta_k X_{ki} + \epsilon_i)$$

$$\pi_i = \mathcal{A}_i / \sum_{j=1}^{m} \mathcal{A}_j$$

This model differs from (5.1) in that a single parameter α is specified instead of m parameters, $\alpha_1, \alpha_2, \ldots, \alpha_m$. Theil noted that

$$\log \left(\frac{\pi_i}{\pi_1} \right) = \log \left(\frac{\mathcal{A}_i}{\mathcal{A}_1} \right) = \sum_{k=1}^{K} \beta_k (X_{ki} - X_{k1}) + (\epsilon_i - \epsilon_1)$$

---

[6]To examine the property of the error term, first expand the left-hand side of (5.4) by the Taylor expansion, keep the first two terms, and apply the mean-value theorem to obtain

$$\epsilon = \log \left(\frac{p_1}{1 - p_1} \right) - \log \left(\frac{\pi_1}{1 - \pi_1} \right) = \left(\frac{\pi_1^*}{1 - \pi_1^*} \right) (p_1 - \pi_1)$$

where π_1^* is a value between π_1 and p_1 . The error term is clearly a function of π_1 and therefore heteroscedastic (i.e. unequal variance). If we assume a simple binomial process for each individual selecting object 1 and a reasonably large sample size ($n >$ 100, say), the variance of ϵ is approximately equal to $1/n\pi_1(1 - \pi_1)$. The use of a generalized least-squares procedure is called for.

[7]Theil, Henri [1969], "A Multinomial Extension of the Linear Logit Model," *International Economics Review*, 10 (October), 251–59.

where 1 is an arbitrarily chosen object, and suggested the following estimation equation which is linear in parameters $\beta_1, \beta_2, \ldots, \beta_K$.

$$\log\left(\frac{p_{it}}{p_{1t}}\right) = \sum_{k=1}^{K} \beta_k (X_{kit} - X_{k1t}) + \epsilon_{it}^* \tag{5.5}$$

where p_i is the proportion of individuals who chose object i in sample, and ϵ_{it}^* is the combined error term. Subscript t indicates the tth subsample. It is obvious that equation (5.4) is a special case of (5.5) for which the number of objects in the choice set, m, equals 2. The total degrees of freedom for this estimation equation is $(m-1)T$ where T is the number of subsamples. It is known that the variances of ϵ_{it}^*'s are unequal, and McFadden [1974] studied a method for correcting for this problem. The estimation technique which we will propose in the next section is a variant of Theil's method. It is true that both Theil's method and our method yield identical estimates of parameters and their properties are also identical, but we believe that our method has an advantage in its ease of interpretation.

5.2   Log-Linear Regression Techniques

As we have noted in Chapter 2, model (5.1) becomes linear in its parameters by applying the log-centering transformation. Take the MNL model, for example. First, take the logarithm of both sides of (5.1).

$$\log s_i = \ \alpha_i + \sum_{k=1}^{K} \beta_k X_{ki} + \epsilon_i$$
$$- \log[\sum_{j=1}^{m} \exp(\alpha_j + \sum_{k=1}^{K} \beta_k X_{kj} + \epsilon_j)] \ .$$

If we sum the above equation over i ($i = 1, 2, \ldots, m$) and divide by m, we have

$$\log \tilde{s} = \ \bar{\alpha} + \sum_{k=1}^{K} \beta_k \bar{X}_k + \bar{\epsilon}$$
$$- \log[\sum_{j=1}^{m} \exp(\alpha_j + \sum_{k=1}^{K} \beta_k X_{kj} + \epsilon_j)]$$

where $\tilde{s}$ is the geometric mean of s_i and $\bar{\alpha}, \bar{X}_k$ and $\bar{\epsilon}$ are the arithmetic means of α_i, X_{ki} and ϵ_i, respectively, over i. Subtracting the above equation from the preceding one, we obtain the following form which is linear in its parameters.

$$\log\left(\frac{s_i}{\tilde{s}}\right) = (\alpha_i - \bar{\alpha}) + \sum_{k=1}^{K} \beta_k (X_{ki} - \bar{X}_k) + (\epsilon_i - \bar{\epsilon}) \ .$$

Similarly, the application of the log-centering transformation to the MCI model results in

$$\log\left(\frac{s_i}{\tilde{s}}\right) = (\alpha_i - \bar{\alpha}) + \sum_{k=1}^{K} \beta_k \log(X_{ki}/\tilde{X}_k) + (\epsilon_i - \bar{\epsilon})$$

where $\tilde{X}_k$ is the geometric mean of X_{ki}. Since those two equations are linear in parameters $\alpha_i^* = (\alpha_i - \bar{\alpha})$ $(i = 1, 2, \ldots, m)$ and β_k $(k = 1, 2, \ldots, K)$, one may estimate those parameters by regression analysis.

Suppose that we obtain market-share data for T *choice situations*. In the following, we often let subscript t indicate the observations in period t, but this is simply an example. Needless to say, the data do not have to be limited to time-series data, and choice situations may be stores, areas, customer groups, or combinations such as store-weeks. Applying the log-centering transformation to the market shares and the marketing variables for each situation t creates the following variables:

$s_{it}^* = \log(s_{it}/\tilde{s}_t)$ $(i = 1, 2, \ldots, m)$

$\tilde{s}_t = $ the geometric mean of s_{it}

$X_{kit}^* = \log(X_{kit}/\tilde{X}_{kt})$ $(i = 1, 2, \ldots, m; k = 1, 2, \ldots, K)$

$\tilde{X}_{kt} = $ the geometric mean of X_{kit}.

Using the above notation, the regression models actually used to estimate the parameters are specified as follows.

MNL Model:

$$s_{it}^* = \alpha_1 + \sum_{j=2}^{m} \alpha_j' d_j + \sum_{k=1}^{K} \beta_k(X_{kit} - \bar{X}_{kt}) + \epsilon_{it}^* \tag{5.6}$$

MCI Model:

$$s_{it}^* = \alpha_1 + \sum_{j=2}^{m} \alpha_j' d_j + \sum_{k=1}^{K} \beta_k X_{kit}^* + \epsilon_{it}^* \tag{5.7}$$

where $\epsilon_{it}^* = (\epsilon_{it} - \bar{\epsilon}_t)$ and $\bar{\epsilon}_t$ is the arithmetic mean of ϵ_{it} over i in period t. Variable d_j is a dummy (binary-valued) variable which takes value of 1 if $j = i$ and 0 otherwise. Note that estimated values of α_i' $(i = 2, 3, \ldots, m)$ from (5.6 – 5.7) are not the estimates of original parameters α_i, but the estimates of difference $(\alpha_i - \alpha_1)$ where brand 1 is an arbitrarily chosen brand. Thus we have shown that the parameters of attraction model (5.1) are estimable by simple log-linear regression models (5.6 – 5.7). However, as was surmised from the discussion of Berkson's and Theil's methods, the error term ϵ_{it}^* in those regression models may not have an equal variance for all i and t. We will turn to this problem in a later section.

In earlier work[8] we showed that the regression models (5.6 – 5.7) are in turn equivalent to the following regression models.

MNL Model:

$$\log s_{it} = \alpha_1 + \sum_{j=2}^{m} \alpha_j' d_j + \sum_{u=2}^{T} \gamma_u D_u + \sum_{k=1}^{K} \beta_k X_{kit} + \epsilon_{it} \qquad (5.8)$$

MCI Model:

$$\log s_{it} = \alpha_1 + \sum_{j=2}^{m} \alpha_j' d_j + \sum_{u=2}^{T} \gamma_u D_u + \sum_{k=1}^{K} \beta_k \log X_{kit} + \epsilon_{it} \qquad (5.9)$$

Variable D_u is another dummy variable which takes value of 1 if $u = t$ and 0 otherwise. The corresponding models (5.6 – 5.7) and (5.8 – 5.9) yield an identical set of estimates of α_i''s and β_k's , and in this sense they are redundant. But one of the advantages of (5.8 – 5.9) is that it is not necessary to apply the log-centering transformation to market shares and marketing variables before regression analysis can be performed, and therefore reduces the need for pre-processing of data. If the number of choice situations, T, is reasonably small, it is perhaps easier to use (5.8 – 5.9). If T is so large that the specification of dummy variables D_u $(u = 2, 3, \ldots, T)$ becomes cumbersome, then the use of (5.6 – 5.7) is recommended. In addition, the properties of the error term ϵ_{it} in (5.8 – 5.9) are easier to analyze than those of ϵ_{it}^* in (5.6 – 5.7).

5.2.1   Organization of Data for Estimation

Leaving theoretical issues aside for a while, let us look at the actual procedures one must follow for parameter estimation. Given a standardized statistical-program package, such as SAS$^{(R)}$, the first thing one must do is to arrange the data so that the regression analysis program in such a package may handle regression models (5.6 – 5.7) and (5.8 – 5.9).

---

[8]Nakanishi, Masao & Lee G. Cooper [1982], "Simplified Estimation Procedures for MCI Models," *Marketing Science*, 1, 3 (Summer), 314-22.

Suppose that we have market-share data for m brands in T *choice situations* (periods, areas, customer groups, etc.), and accompanying marketing activities data. Market-share data may be in the form of percentages (or proportions) or in absolute units. If one ignores for the moment the heteroscedasticity (i.e., unequal variances and nonzero covariances) problems associated with the error terms in regression models (5.6 – 5.9), whether the market-share data are in absolute units or in percentages is immaterial, because the log-centering transformation yields identical parameter estimates regardless of whether it is applied to proportions or the actual numbers of units sold.[9] Table 5.1 is an example of market-share data generated by a POS system.

These data were actually obtained at a single store in 14 weeks (i.e., $T = 14$). There are five national and two regional brands of margarine ($m = 7$). Brand 2 is the same as brand 1 and brand 4 is the same as brand 3, but in larger packages. All brands are half-pound (225g) packages except brands 2 and 4 which are one-pound (450g) packages. The market shares do not sum to one presumably due to private-label brands not listed here. Market shares are *volume shares* computed by first converting the numbers of units sold to weight volumes and then computing the weight-volume share of each brand. Inspection of the table will show that the market is obviously very price-sensitive.

We will now try to estimate the price elasticity of market shares based on attraction model (5.1). Also given are average daily sales volumes of margarine in this store expressed in units of half-pound package equivalents. The first step in estimation is to create a data set which includes dummy variables d_j ($j = 2, 3, \ldots, m$) and D_u ($u = 2, 3, \ldots, T$) so that regression model (5.8 – 5.9) may be used. We chose (5.8 – 5.9) because the number of periods T is reasonably small ($= 14$). Table 5.2 shows a partial listing of the data set arranged for estimation with the REG procedure in the SAS[(R)] statistical package.

Market share and price data are taken from Table 5.1, and the logarithms of shares and prices are added. In addition two sets of dummy variables — week dummies and brand dummies — are put in the data set. The dummy variables (D1–D5) for only the first five weeks are reported to save space. If the reader examines the pattern of two sets of dummy variables, their meaning should be self-explanatory. The dummy

---

[9]This property of log-centering is called the homogeneity of the 0th degree. The estimated values of α_1 in (5.8 – 5.9) are the only terms affected by the choice between proportions and actual numbers, but it does not influence the values of market shares estimated by the inverse log-centering transformation.

Table 5.1: POS Data Example (Margarine)

Weeks	1	2[a]	3	Brands 4[b]	5	6	7	Ave. Daily Vol.
1 share[c]	4	51	3	3	0	1	9	83
price[d]	192	139.5	158	146	163	128	148	
2 share	2	75	2	1	0	0	5	103
price	192	140	158	170	163	128	148	
3 share	3	48	1	1	21	0	13	98
price	192	138.5	158	170	100	138	133	
4 share	4	44	24	-	0	0	11	72
price	192	139	139	170	163	148	128	
5 share	5	23	10	1	-	26	7	84
price	192	139	141	170	163	128	128	
6 share	6	6	3	2	0	36	13	61
price	192	176	158	170	163	128	128	
7 share	4	5	5	3	-	12	20	74
price	192	179	163	170	163	128	128	
8 share	3	2	2	2	41	8	11	107
price	192	169	185	161	100	134	128	
9 share	8	5	3	10	-	21	17	57
price	192	168	188	129.5	163	138	128	
10 share	19	3	1	47	-	5	8	77
price	178	179	188	120	163	138	128	
11 share	12	2	2	19	0	18	15	65
price	178	179	188	136.5	163	138	128	
12 share	6	47	1	5	0	10	9	87
price	180	139.5	188	149	163	141	128	
13 share	2	23	1	13	26	6	5	120
price	192	139	188	137	100	138	128	
14 share	28	15	10	19	3	3	6	107
price	132	139	144	134	109	143	128	

[a] Brand 2 is the 1 lb. package of brand 1.
[b] Brand 4 is the 1 lb. package of brand 3.
[c] Market Share in %.
[d] Price per 1/2 pound in Yen.

Table 5.2: Data Set for Estimation

Week	Brand	Share	Log Share	Price	Log Price	Week Dummies					Brand Dummies						
						D1	D2	D3	D4	D5	d1	d2	d3	d4	d5	d6	d7
1	1	4	1.38629	192	5.25750	1	0	0	0	0	1	0	0	0	0	0	0
1	2	51	3.93183	139	4.93806	1	0	0	0	0	0	1	0	0	0	0	0
1	3	3	1.09861	158	5.06260	1	0	0	0	0	0	0	1	0	0	0	0
1	4	3	1.09861	146	4.98361	1	0	0	0	0	0	0	0	1	0	0	0
1	5	0	.	163	5.09375	1	0	0	0	0	0	0	0	0	1	0	0
1	6	1	0.00000	128	4.85203	1	0	0	0	0	0	0	0	0	0	1	0
1	7	9	2.19722	148	4.99721	1	0	0	0	0	0	0	0	0	0	0	1
2	1	2	0.69315	192	5.25750	0	1	0	0	0	1	0	0	0	0	0	0
2	2	75	4.31749	140	4.94164	0	1	0	0	0	0	1	0	0	0	0	0
2	3	2	0.69315	158	5.06260	0	1	0	0	0	0	0	1	0	0	0	0
2	4	1	0.00000	170	5.13580	0	1	0	0	0	0	0	0	1	0	0	0
2	5	0	.	163	5.09375	0	1	0	0	0	0	0	0	0	1	0	0
2	6	0	.	128	4.85203	0	1	0	0	0	0	0	0	0	0	1	0
2	7	5	1.60944	148	4.99721	0	1	0	0	0	0	0	0	0	0	0	1
3	1	3	1.09861	192	5.25750	0	0	1	0	0	1	0	0	0	0	0	0
3	2	48	3.87120	138	4.93087	0	0	1	0	0	0	1	0	0	0	0	0
3	3	1	0.00000	158	5.06260	0	0	1	0	0	0	0	1	0	0	0	0
3	4	1	0.00000	170	5.13580	0	0	1	0	0	0	0	0	1	0	0	0
3	5	21	3.04452	100	4.60517	0	0	1	0	0	0	0	0	0	1	0	0
3	6	0	.	138	4.92725	0	0	1	0	0	0	0	0	0	0	1	0
3	7	13	2.56495	133	4.89035	0	0	1	0	0	0	0	0	0	0	0	1
4	1	4	1.38629	192	5.25750	0	0	0	1	0	1	0	0	0	0	0	0
4	2	44	3.78419	139	4.93447	0	0	0	1	0	0	1	0	0	0	0	0
4	3	24	3.17805	139	4.93447	0	0	0	1	0	0	0	1	0	0	0	0
4	4	.	.	170	5.13580	0	0	0	1	0	0	0	0	1	0	0	0
4	5	0	.	163	5.09375	0	0	0	1	0	0	0	0	0	1	0	0
4	6	0	.	148	4.99721	0	0	0	1	0	0	0	0	0	0	1	0
4	7	11	.39790	128	4.85203	0	0	0	1	0	0	0	0	0	0	0	1
5	1	5	.60944	192	5.25750	0	0	0	0	1	1	0	0	0	0	0	0
5	2	23	.13549	139	4.93447	0	0	0	0	1	0	1	0	0	0	0	0
5	3	10	.30259	141	4.94876	0	0	0	0	1	0	0	1	0	0	0	0
5	4	1	0.00000	170	5.13580	0	0	0	0	1	0	0	0	1	0	0	0
5	5	.	.	163	5.09375	0	0	0	0	1	0	0	0	0	1	0	0
5	6	26	3.25810	128	4.85203	0	0	0	0	1	0	0	0	0	0	1	0
5	7	7	1.94591	128	4.85203	0	0	0	0	1	0	0	0	0	0	0	1

variables for weeks graphically reflect that the influence of a particular
week is constant over brands. The dummy variables for brands graphically reflect that the baseline level of attraction for each brand is constant
over weeks, and thus independent of variations in market conditions.

5.2.2 Reading Regression-Analysis Outputs

Now we are in a position to estimate the parameters of attraction model
(5.1), in which the only marketing variable is price. Letting P_{it} be the
price of brand i in week t, there is only one attraction component for the
MCI version of (5.1) which may be written as

$$\mathcal{A}_{it} = \exp(\alpha_i + \epsilon_{it}) P_{it}^{\beta_p}$$

which in turn shows that the regression model (5.8) is applicable here.

$$\log s_{it} = \alpha_1 + \sum_{j=2}^{m} \alpha_j' d_j + \sum_{u=2}^{T} \gamma_u D_u + \beta_p \log P_{it} + \epsilon_{it} \ .$$

Table 5.3 gives the estimation results from the SAS$^{(R)}$ REG procedure.
The dependent variable is, of course, the logarithm of market share. The
first part of the output gives the analysis of variance results. The
most important summary statistic for us is, of course, the R^2 figure of
0.735 (or the adjusted R^2 value of 0.65) which suggests that almost 75%
of the total variance in the dependent variable (log of share) has been
explained by the independent (=exploratory) variables (log of price, in
this case) and dummy variables d_2 through d_7 and D_2 through D_{14}. The
F-test with the "Prob>F" figure of 0.0001 shows that the R^2 value is high
enough for us to put our reliance on the regression results.[10] Note that
the total degrees of freedom (i.e., the available number of observations –
1) is not 97 but 83. This is because there are *observations* in the data set
(see Table 5.2) for which the market share is zero. Since one cannot take
the logarithm of zero, the program treats those observations as missing,
decreasing the total degrees of freedom. The problems associated with
zero market shares will be discussed in section 5.11.

The second part of the output gives the parameter estimates; the
intercept gives the estimate of α_1; D2 through D7 give estimates of

---

[10]This test is really against a null hypothesis that all the parameters are zero. There
is less than a one-in-ten-thousand chance that this null hypothesis is true. So we can
be confident that something systematic is going on, but it takes a much closer look to
understand the sources and meaning of these systematic influences.

Table 5.3: Regression Results for MCI Equation (5.8)

Model: MODEL1					
Dep Variable: LSHARE					
		Analysis of Variance			
		Sum of	Mean		
Source	DF	Squares	Square	F Value	Prob>F
Model	20	77.33391	3.86670	8.765	0.0001
Error	63	27.79373	0.44117		
C Total	83	105.12764			
Root MSE		0.66421	R-Square	0.7356	
Dep Mean		1.92529	Adj R-Sq	0.6517	
C.V.		34.49902			
Parameter Estimates					
		Parameter	Standard	T for H_0	
Variable	DF	Estimate	Error	Parm=0	Prob> $|T|$
INTRCPT	1	44.798271	4.25812533	10.521	0.0001
D2	1	−0.623847	0.29148977	−2.140	0.0362
D3	1	−1.485840	0.26424009	−5.623	0.0001
D4	1	−1.866469	0.30893368	−6.042	0.0001
D5	1	−3.550847	0.61502980	−5.773	0.0001
D6	1	−1.971343	0.36375236	−5.419	0.0001
D7	1	−2.253214	0.37405428	−6.024	0.0001
DD2	1	0.254732	0.40530020	0.629	0.5319
DD3	1	0.117670	0.38957828	0.302	0.7636
DD4	1	0.620464	0.43444539	1.428	0.1582
DD5	1	0.269731	0.38377375	0.703	0.4847
DD6	1	0.634560	0.38485999	1.649	0.1042
DD7	1	0.644783	0.38546807	1.673	0.0993
DD8	1	0.243568	0.37504599	0.649	0.5184
DD9	1	0.778571	0.38417509	2.027	0.0469
DD10	1	0.424670	0.38363952	1.107	0.2725
DD11	1	0.742352	0.38454418	1.930	0.0581
DD12	1	0.547800	0.38402005	1.426	0.1587
DD13	1	0.274498	0.37351312	0.735	0.4651
DD14	1	−0.214251	0.37808396	−0.567	0.5729
LPRICE	1	−8.337254	0.81605692	−10.217	0.0001

$\alpha'_2, \ldots, \alpha'_7$; DD2 through DD14 give the estimates of $\gamma_2, \gamma_3, \ldots, \gamma_{14}$; the value next to LPRICE gives the estimate of β_p, and so forth. From this table several important facts concerning the competitive structure of margarine in this store are learned.

First, the estimated price parameter is a large negative value, -8.34, indicating that the customers of this store are highly price-sensitive. The statistical significance for the estimate is shown by the T-value and "Prob> $|T|$" column, both of which show that the estimate is highly significant.[11] Recall from Chapter 2 that the parameter value is not the same as the share elasticity for a specific brand. In the case of an MCI model, the latter is given by $\beta_p(1 - s_{it})$. For example, if a brand has a 20% share, its share elasticity with respect to price is approximately $-8.34 \times (1 - 0.2) = -6.67$, indicating a 10% price cut should lead to a 66.7% increase in share (from 20% to 33%).

Second, the estimates of brand specific parameters, $\alpha'_2, \ldots, \alpha'_m$, are all negative and statistically significant. The true values of $\alpha'_2, \ldots, \alpha'_m$ are estimated by adding the corresponding regression estimates to the estimated value of α_1. Since α_1 is estimated at 44.8, we know that brand 1 has the strongest attraction if other things are equal. Brand 5 has the weakest attraction with $\alpha_1 + \alpha_5 = (44.8 - 3.55) = 41.25$. This implies that, other things being equal, brand 1 is 35 times ($= \exp 3.55$) as attractive as brand 5. It is rather interesting to note that brand 2 (which is one-pound package of brand 1) has approximately one-half the attraction ($\exp -.62 \approx 0.54$) of brand 1. Even within a brand a weaker size has to resort to lower unit prices than the stronger size to gain a larger share .

Third, the estimates of $\gamma_2, \gamma_3, \ldots, \gamma_T$ are with few exceptions (weeks 6, 7, and 11) statistically insignificant. This normally suggests that dummy variables $D_2, D_3, \ldots, D_T$ may be deleted from the regression model, which in turn suggests that a multiplicative model of market share (discussed in Chapter 2) probably would have done as well as the attraction (MCI) model in analyzing the data in Table 5.1. However, we chose an attraction model not only because of how well it fits the data but because it represents a more logically consistent view of the market

---

[11]To be precise it is significantly different from zero. It should also be noted that the reported probability levels are for two-tailed tests. While nondirectional hypotheses are appropriate for time-period and brand dummy variables, we often have directional hypotheses about the influences of prices or other marketing instruments. The reported probabilities should be cut in half to assess the level of significance of one-sided tests.

Table 5.4: Regression Results for MNL Equation (5.9)

Model: MODEL1
Dep Variable: LSHARE

Analysis of Variance

Source	DF	Sum of Squares	Mean Square	F Value	Prob>F
Model	20	77.22749	3.86137	8.719	0.0001
Error	63	27.90015	0.44286		
C Total	83	105.12764			

Root MSE	0.66548	R-Square	0.7346
Dep Mean	1.92529	Adj R-Sq	0.6504
C.V.	34.56501		

Parameter Estimates

Variable	DF	Parameter Estimate	Standard Error	T for H_0 Parm=0	Prob> $|T|$
INTRCPT	1	11.250720	1.01638598	11.069	0.0001
D2	1	−0.743850	0.29829963	−2.494	0.0153
D3	1	−1.582301	0.26788475	−5.907	0.0001
D4	1	−1.980421	0.31598491	−6.267	0.0001
D5	1	−3.087742	0.58245966	−5.301	0.0001
D6	1	−2.074613	0.37148467	−5.585	0.0001
D7	1	−2.309865	0.37915203	−6.092	0.0001
DD2	1	0.240284	0.40596127	0.592	0.5560
DD3	1	0.133747	0.39036655	0.343	0.7330
DD4	1	0.648161	0.43501731	1.490	0.1412
DD5	1	0.301956	0.38439750	0.786	0.4351
DD6	1	0.665472	0.38586824	1.725	0.0895
DD7	1	0.680742	0.38658443	1.761	0.0831
DD8	1	0.282518	0.37617724	0.751	0.4554
DD9	1	0.829837	0.38524729	2.154	0.0351
DD10	1	0.486656	0.38459756	1.265	0.2104
DD11	1	0.773457	0.38552149	2.006	0.0491
DD12	1	0.555236	0.38479525	1.443	0.1540
DD13	1	0.315302	0.37443996	0.842	0.4029
DD14	1	−0.236656	0.37918145	−0.624	0.5348
PRICE	1	−0.053868	0.00528884	−10.185	0.0001

and competition.[12] Since our purpose is to estimate the parameters of an attraction model correctly, it is not justified for us to drop those dummy variables from the regression equation.

Table 5.4 gives the estimation results by equation (5.8) of the MNL version of attraction model (5.1). The independent variables are the same as those of (5.9), except that price itself is used instead of the logarithm of price. The overall pattern of estimated parameters is very similar to those from (5.9). The estimated value of the price elasticity parameter, β_p, is -0.054. Recall that the share elasticity with respect to a marketing variable (price in this case) is given by $\beta_p P_{it}(1 - s_{it})$. If s_{it} is 0.2 and price is 150 yen for a brand, the price elasticity is approximately -6.5, which agrees well with the estimated elasticity value from equation (5.9).

5.2.3   The Analysis-of-Covariance Representation

It may added that regression models (5.8 – 5.9) are equivalent to an analysis-of-covariance (ANCOVA) model of the following form.

MNL Model:

$$\log(s_{it}) = \mu + \mu_i + \mu_t + \sum_{k=1}^{K} \beta_k X_{kit} + \epsilon_{it}$$

or

MCI Model:

$$\log(s_{it}) = \mu + \mu_i + \mu_t + \sum_{k=1}^{K} \beta_k \log(X_{kit}) + \epsilon_{it}$$

where:

μ = the grand mean

μ_i = the brand main effects $(i = 1, 2, \ldots, m)$

μ_t = the period main effects $(t = 1, 2, \ldots, T)$.

---

[12]The parameters for the time periods merely serve the role of insuring that the other parameters are identical to those of the original nonlinear model. This structure guarantees that the model will produce market-share estimates which are always non-negative and always sum to one over estimates for all alternatives in a choice situation.

There is no brand-by-period interaction term because there is one *observation* per brand-period combination. The ANCOVA models yield parameter estimates that are identical to those obtained from models (5.8 – 5.9). This ANCOVA representation clarifies the characteristics of (5.8); an attraction model requires that the period main effects be taken out before the parameters of marketing variables are to be estimated. If we ignore the properties of the error term (discussed in the next section), the ANCOVA model may be convenient to use in practice since it does not require cumbersome specification of brand and period dummy variables.

5.3   Properties of the Error Term

We have deferred the discussion of the analysis of the error term up to this point, though it has been suggested that the error terms in regression models (5.6 – 5.7) and (5.8 – 5.9) are known to have unequal variances and non-zero covariances in some cases and may require special care in estimation. Before we show this, we will have to make some assumptions as to the composition of the error term with respect to the sources of error.

It is important to recognize two sources of errors inherent in the estimation of market-share models. The variability due to sampling is clearly one source of error, but there is another source of error we must consider. Recall that attraction model (5.1) includes an error term, ϵ_i, which arises due to the omission of some relatively minor factors from its specification of explanatory variables, the X_{kit}'s, in (5.1). We will call this source of error the *specification error*. Considering those sources of error, the error terms in regression models (5.8 – 5.9) may be expressed as

$$\epsilon_{it} = \epsilon_{1it} + \epsilon_{2it}$$

where ϵ_{i1t} is the specification-error term and ϵ_{2it} is the sampling-error term.[13] The error term in regression model (5.6) is given by subtracting $\bar{\epsilon}_t$, the means of ϵ_{it} over i in period t, from ϵ_{it}. Hence we may write

$$\epsilon_{it}^* = \epsilon_{1it}^* + \epsilon_{2it}^* = (\epsilon_{1it} - \bar{\epsilon}_{1t}) + (\epsilon_{2it} - \bar{\epsilon}_{2t})$$

where $\bar{\epsilon}_{1t}$ and $\bar{\epsilon}_{2t}$ are respective means of ϵ_{1it} and ϵ_{2it} over i in period t.

---

[13]To be precise, the error term in attraction model (5.1) should be written as ϵ_{1it}, but we will not change the notation at this point for the reasons that will become apparent later.

5.3.1 Assumptions on the Specification-Error Term

We will make the following assumptions regarding the specification-error term, ϵ_{1it}, throughout the remainder of this book.

1. ϵ_{1it} is normally distributed with mean 0 and variance σ_i^2 ,

2. the covariance between ϵ_{1it} and ϵ_{1jt} is σ_{ij} for all t,

3. there is no correlation between ϵ_{1it} and ϵ_{1ju} if $u \neq t$,

4. ϵ_{1it} is uncorrelated with the sampling-error term, ϵ_{2it}.

We have so far made no assumption about the sampling-error term (except that it is uncorrelated with the specification-error term) because the method of data collection greatly affects the properties of sampling errors. Two basic methods of data collection will be distinguished.

One is the survey method in which a sample is randomly drawn from a universe of consumers/buyers. In this case the unit of analysis is the individuals in the sample. One may ask the respondent which brand he/she selected or how many times he/she purchased each brand in a period. Individual selections or purchases are then aggregated over the sample to yield market-share estimates. It may be noted that the so-called consumer panels — diary or optical-scanner — share essentially the same characteristics as the survey method as a data collection technique because the unit of analysis is an individual consumer or household.

Another basic method concerns data gathered from POS system. It should be emphasized that POS-generated market-share data are based on *all* purchases made in a store in a period and not on the responses obtained from a sample of customers to the store. This means that we need not be concerned with the normal sources of sampling variations (i.e., sampling variations among customers within a store). Our only concern is with sampling variations between stores, since POS data currently available to syndicated users are usually based on a sample of stores. We will deal with each type of data collection method in turn.

5.3.2 Survey Data

Let us assume that a series of samples of consumers or buyers is obtained by a simple random sampling. We assume that an independent sample is drawn for each period (or choice situation). Since the following analysis is limited within a period, time subscript t is dropped for simplicity.

As noted above, one may ask the respondent either which brand he/she chose or how many times he/she bought each brand in a period. We will have to treat those two questioning techniques separately.

First consider the case in which each respondent is asked which single brand he/she chose from a set of available brands (= choice set). In this case we may assume that the aggregated responses to the question follow a multinomial choice process. Formally stated, given a sample size n and the probability that a respondent chose brand i is π_i $(i = 1, 2, \ldots, m)$ (m is the number of available brands), the joint probability that brand i is chosen by n_i individuals $(i = 1, 2, \ldots, m)$ is given by

$$P(n_1, n_2, \ldots, n_m) = \frac{n!}{n_1! n_2! \ldots n_m!} \prod_{i=1}^{m} \pi_i^{n_i} \ .$$

The market-share estimates are $p_i = n_i/n$ $(i = 1, 2, \ldots, m)$. These estimates are subject to sampling variations.

Let us now turn to the properties of the sampling-error term

$$\epsilon_{2i} = \log p_i - \log \pi_i \quad (i = 1, 2, \ldots, m)$$

when market-share estimates, the p_i's, are generated by the multinomial process described above. It is well known that for a reasonably large sample size ($n > 30$, say), p_i is approximately normally distributed with mean π_i and variance $\pi_i(1 - \pi_i)/n$. Given this approximate distribution, we want to know how ϵ_{2i} is distributed. We will use the same technique as that used by Berkson. First, expand $\log p_i$ by the Taylor expansion around $\log \pi_i$ and retain only the first two terms. Then apply the mean-value theorem to obtain

$$\log p_i = \log \pi_i + \left(\frac{p_i - \pi_i}{\pi_i^*} \right)$$

where π_i^* is a value between p_i and π_i. This shows that for a reasonably large sample size, $\log p_i$ is approximately normally distributed with mean $\log \pi_i$ and variance $\pi_i(1 - \pi_i)/n\pi_i^{*2}$. The approximation will improve with the increase in sample size, n. Thus the sampling error is also approximately normally distributed with mean zero and variance $\pi_i(1 - \pi_i)/n\pi_i^{*2}$. Furthermore, due to the nature of a multinomial process, it is known that ϵ_{2i} and ϵ_{2j} $(j \neq i)$ in the same period are correlated and have an approximate covariance$-\pi_i\pi_j/n\pi_i^*\pi_j^*$ where π_j^* is a value between p_j and π_j. For a reasonably large sample size, we may take

$$\begin{aligned} \mathrm{Var}(\epsilon_{2i}) &= (1 - \pi_i)/n\pi_i & (i = 1, 2, \ldots, m) \quad (5.10) \\ \mathrm{Cov}(\epsilon_{2i}, \epsilon_{2j}) &= -1/n & (j \neq i) \ . \end{aligned}$$

Clearly the variance of the error term is a function in π_i and takes a minimum value $1/n$ for $\pi_i = 0.5$ and a large value for very small values of π_i. For example, if $\pi_i = 0.01$, the variance of ϵ_{2i} is approximately equal to $99/n$. This phenomenon is called *heteroscedasticity* in the variance of ϵ_{2i}. But we must also be concerned with the covariance between ϵ_{2i} and ϵ_{2j} to the extent $1/n$ is not negligible.

The above properties of the error term are based on the assumptions that each respondent is asked which brand he/she chose in a given choice situation. The properties change considerably if the respondent is asked how many units of each brand he/she purchased in a period. The individual responses are aggregated over the sample to yield the number of units of brand i bought by the entire sample, x_i $(i = 1, 2, \ldots, m)$. The estimate of market share of brand i is given by $\hat{s}_i = x_i/x$ where x is the sum of the x_i's over i. What are the properties of the error term when the logarithm of $\hat{s}_i$ is used as the dependent variable in regression model (5.8 – 5.9) or the log-centered value of $\hat{s}_i$ is used in (5.6 – 5.7)? The answer depends on the assumption we make on the process which generates the x_i's. In general the derivation of the properties of the error term is a complicated task since $\hat{s}_i$ is a ratio of two random variables x_i and x, the latter including the former as a part of it. Luckily for us, however, the estimated value of parameters of (5.6 – 5.7) will not change if we used the log-centered value of $\bar{x}_i$, the mean of x_i, in place of the log-centered value of $\hat{s}_i$ in (5.6 – 5.7), since

$$\log\left(\frac{\bar{x}_i}{\tilde{x}}\right) = \log\left(\frac{\hat{s}_i}{\tilde{\hat{s}}}\right)$$

where $\tilde{x}$ and $\tilde{\hat{s}}$ are the geometric means of x_i and $\hat{s}_i$ over i in a given period. This in turn suggests that in regression model (5.8 – 5.9) we may use $\log(x_i)$ as the dependent variable without changing the estimated values of parameters other than α_1. This reduces our task in analyzing the properties of the error term considerably.

Suppose that the x_i's are generated by an arbitrary multivariate process with means $\mu_1, \mu_2, \ldots, \mu_m$ and covariance matrix Θ with elements $\{\theta_{ij}\}$. Note that the true market share is given by $s_i = \mu_i/\mu$ where μ is the sum of the μ_i's over i. The sample mean of x_i, $\bar{x}_i$, is an estimate of μ_i. We obtain the linear approximation of $\log x_i$ by the usual method, that is,

$$\log \bar{x}_i = \log \mu_i + \frac{1}{x_i^*}(\bar{x}_i - \mu_i)$$

where x_i^* is a value between $\bar{x}_i$ and μ_i. If we replace $\log(\hat{s}_i)$ in the equations leading to (5.8 – 5.9) by $\log \bar{x}_i$, the sampling-error term becomes

$$\epsilon_{2i} = \log \bar{x}_i - \log \mu_i \ .$$

When the sample size is reasonably large, the approximate variances and covariances among the ϵ_{2i}'s are given by

$$\begin{aligned} \text{Var}(\epsilon_{2i}) &= \theta_{ii}/n\mu_i^2 \quad (i = 1, 2, \ldots, m) \\ \text{Cov}(\epsilon_{2i}, \epsilon_{2j}) &= \theta_{ij}/n\mu_i\mu_j \quad (j \neq i) \ . \end{aligned}$$

These results agree with those for the multinomial process, if we note that $\mu_i = \pi_i$ and $\bar{x}_i = p_i$ in the latter process. The variance and covariances of the sampling error term are clearly functions of μ_i and may take a large value if μ_i or μ_j are near zero. The existence of heteroscedasticity is obvious.

We now combine the above results with our assumptions on the specification-error term. Under the assumptions of a multinomial choice process and a single choice per individual, the approximate variances and covariances among the ϵ_i's in a same period are given by

$$\begin{aligned} \text{Var}(\epsilon_i) &= \sigma_i^2 + \text{Var}(\epsilon_{2i}) \quad (i = 1, 2, \ldots, m) \\ \text{Cov}(\epsilon_i, \epsilon_j) &= \sigma_{ij} + \text{Cov}(\epsilon_{2i}, \epsilon_{2j}) \quad (j \neq i) \end{aligned}$$

where $\text{Var}(\epsilon_{2i})$ and $\text{Cov}(\epsilon_{2i}, \epsilon_{2j})$ are given either by (5.10). Because of the heteroscedasticity of the error term, it is known that the estimated parameters of regression models (5.6 – 5.9) based on the ordinary least-squares (OLS) procedure do not have the smallest variance among the class of linear regression estimators. Nakanishi and Cooper [1974] suggested the use of a two-stage generalized least-squares (GLS) procedure in the case of a multinomial choice situation to reduce the estimation errors associated with regression models (5.6 – 5.9). The interested reader is referred to Appendix 5.14 for more details of this GLS procedure.

5.3.3 POS Data

When the market-share estimates are obtained from POS systems, it is not necessary for us to consider the sampling errors within a store, but, if our market-share data are obtained by aggregating market-share figures for a number of stores, we should expect that there are variations between stores. This presents us the heteroscedasticity problem similar to what we encountered with survey data. But there are additional problems as well. Each store tends to offer its customers a uniquely packaged marketing activities. If we aggregate market-share figures from several stores, we will somehow have to aggregate marketing variables over the stores. As discussed in Chapter 4, aggregation is safe if the causal condition (i.e., promotional variables) are homogeneous over the stores – as might be the case when stores within a grocery chain are combined. One should avoid the ambiguity which results from aggregation, either by explicitly recognizing each individual store or by aggregating only over stores (within grocery chains) with relatively homogeneous promotion policies. We will take this approach in the remainder of this book.

Stated more formally, let s_{iht} be the market share of brand i in store h in period t, and X_{kiht} be the value of the kth marketing variable in store h in period t. Regression model (5.6 – 5.7) may be rewritten with the new notation as

MNL Model:

$$s_{iht}^* = \alpha_1 + \sum_{j=2}^{m} \alpha_j' d_j + \sum_{k=1}^{K} \beta_k (X_{kiht} - \bar{X}_{kht}) + \epsilon_{iht}^* \qquad (5.11)$$

MCI Model:

$$s_{iht}^* = \alpha_1 + \sum_{j=2}^{m} \alpha_j' d_j + \sum_{k=1}^{K} \beta_k \log(X_{kiht}/\tilde{X}_{kht}) + \epsilon_{iht}^* \qquad (5.12)$$

where s_{iht}^* is the log-centered value of s_{iht} in store h in period t, and $\bar{X}_{kht}$ and $\tilde{X}_{kht}$ are the arithmetic mean and geometric mean of X_{kiht} over i in store h in period t.

The main advantage of a disaggregated model such as (5.11 – 5.12) is that we do not have to deal with sampling errors in estimation. Similar expressions may be obtained for (5.7) or (5.9), but in actual applications there will be too many dummy variables which have to be included in the model. It will be necessary to specify $(H \times T - 1)$ dummy variables, where H is the number of stores, which replaces the $(T - 1)$ period dummy variables in (5.8 – 5.9). With only a moderate number of stores and periods it may become impractical to try to include all necessary dummy variables for estimation, in which case the use of models (5.11 – 5.12) is recommended.

5.4 *Generalized Least-Squares Estimation

In the preceding section we noted that the error terms in regression models for estimating parameters of market-share models tend to be heteroscedastic, i.e., have unequal variances and nonzero covariances. If market-share figures are computed from POS data, the error terms in regression models (5.6 – 5.12) involve only what we call *specification errors*. Let Σ be the variance-covariance matrix of specification errors with variances σ_i^2 ($i = 1, 2, \ldots, m$) on the main diagonal and covariances σ_{ij} ($j \neq i$) as off-diagonal elements. Because matrix Σ is heteroscedastic, Bultez and Naert[14] proposed an iterative GLS procedure. The steps of an iterative GLS procedure are as follows.

1. The OLS procedure is used to estimate the parameters in one of the regression models (5.6 – 5.12), and Σ is estimated from the residual errors.[15]

2. The data for each period are re-weighted by the estimated $\widehat{\Sigma}^{-\frac{1}{2}}$.

3. The first two steps are repeated until the estimated values of the regression parameters converge.

There is one minor problem in applying this iterative procedure. It may be remembered that, in regression model (5.6), the log-centering transformation is applied to the dependent variable, the variance-covariance matrix for the ϵ_{it}^*'s is given by

$$\Sigma^* = (I - J/m)\Sigma(I - J/m)$$

where I is an identity matrix and J is a matrix, all elements of which are equal to 1. The dimensions of both I and J is $m \times m$, where m is the number of available brands. $\widehat{\Sigma}^*$ computed from OLS residuals is therefore singular and not invertible. Since regression models (5.8 – 5.9) are equivalent to (5.6 – 5.7), the residuals estimated from the former are identical to those estimated from the latter, and hence the estimated covariance matrices are also identical. In general, if both brand-dummy variables and period- (or store-) dummy variables are inserted in a regression model, the estimated residual covariance matrix becomes singular.

---

[14] Bultez, Alain V. & Philippe A. Naert [1975], "Consistent Sum-Constrained Models," *Journal of the American Statistical Association*, 70, 351 (September) 529–35.

[15] One can simply sort the OLS residuals by brand and time period, compute the variance of each brand's residuals and compute the covariance between ordered residuals for each pair of brands.

This certainly is an impediment to the GLS estimation procedure which requires the inverses of estimated covariance matrices.

There are three methods of circumventing this problem. One is to delete one row and corresponding column from $\widehat{\Sigma}^*$ and invert it. One observation (which corresponds to the deleted row/column of $\widehat{\Sigma}^*$) per period is deleted and the parameters are estimated on the remaining data. The drawback of this technique is that estimated parameters will be transformations of original parameters, and hence will have to be transformed back to the original, a process which is rather cumbersome. A second method is to set to zero those off-diagonal elements of an estimated residual covariance matrix which are nearly zero. Though theoretically less justifiable, it has its merit in simplicity. Usually it is sufficient to set just a few elements to zero before the inverse may be obtained.[16] The third method is to find the generalized inverse of $\widehat{\Sigma}^*$.

5.4.1   Application of GLS to the Margarine Data

As an illustration of the GLS technique consider the data set given in Table 5.1. The OLS estimation technique applied to regression model (5.8) yielded the parameter estimates in Table 5.3. Residual errors were then computed from the above OLS results and Σ was estimated. The estimated Σ and its inverse are shown below. Those elements of the estimated Σ which were less than 0.3 were set to zero before the matrix was inverted.

Covariance Matrix

Brand	1	2	3	4	5	6	7
1	0.183164	−.050222	−.009048	−.063581	0.102546	−.142236	0.020543
2	−.050222	0.386247	−.233128	−.057280	−.156411	−.261190	0.186987
3	−.009048	−.233128	0.302828	0.062024	−.066156	−.020426	−.086928
4	−.063581	−.057280	0.062024	0.234230	−.304044	−.024887	−.078644
5	0.102546	−.156411	−.066156	−.304044	0.359436	0.074360	0.020021
6	−.142236	−.261190	−.020426	−.024887	0.074360	0.880167	−.444807
7	0.020543	0.186987	−.086928	−.078644	0.020021	−.444807	0.289530

---

[16]If

one wishes to be more formal in this method, one may set to zero those elements which are not significantly different from zero statistically. On the other hand, by setting *all* off-diagonal elements to zero we obtain an easily implemented, weighted least-squares (WLS) procedures which compensates only for differences the variance of specification errors between brands.

Inverse Covariance Matrix

Brand	1	2	3	4	5	6	7
1	−62.656	13.7604	−13.3493	14.4918	47.1276	−65.075	−108.934
2	13.760	−0.4766	3.5862	−8.6329	−13.2922	12.164	17.728
3	−13.349	3.5862	1.5801	−2.0956	6.5368	−12.807	−22.087
4	14.492	−8.6329	−2.0956	−4.2420	−14.5748	13.098	23.917
5	47.128	−13.2922	6.5368	−14.5748	−36.9378	45.266	76.131
6	−65.075	12.1642	−12.8072	13.0983	45.2664	−61.315	−102.342
7	−108.934	17.7275	−22.0868	23.9170	76.1315	−102.342	−165.360

The square-root of the above inverse matrix was pre-multiplied by the data matrix for each week, and the estimates of the following form are obtained.

$$(\alpha_1, \alpha_2, \ldots, \alpha_m, \beta_p)' = [\sum_{t=1}^{T}(X_t'\widehat{\Sigma}^{-1}X_t)]^{-1}[\sum_{t=1}^{T}(X_t'\widehat{\Sigma}^{-1}y_t)]$$

where X_t is the independent variable matrix and y_t is the vector of the dependent variable for period t. The re-estimated parameter values are shown in Table 5.5.

Table 5.5: GLS Estimates for Table 5.3

Variable	Parameter Estimate	Variable	Parameter Estimate
Intercept	45.4977		
D2	−0.6529	DD6	0.4764
D3	−1.505	DD7	0.4892
D4	−1.8942	DD8	0.0709
D5	−3.4476	DD9	0.6449
D6	−2.0313	DD10	0.5546
D7	−2.2964	DD11	0.6610
DD2	−0.1283	DD12	0.2626
DD3	−0.1412	DD13	0.0022
DD4	0.4260	DD14	−0.3082
DD5	0.1464	LOG(PRICE)	−8.4395

Table 5.5 gives the so-called two-stage GLS estimates. If necessary, residual errors and Σ may be computed from the above results again and another GLS estimates may be obtained. But, since the parameter estimates in Table 5.3 are extremely close to those in Table 5.5, further

iterations seem unnecessary. In fact it has been our experience that OLS
and GLS estimates are very similar in many cases. The OLS procedure
appears satisfactory in many applications.

So far we have reviewed estimation techniques applicable to relatively
simple attraction models (5.1). We have shown in Chapter 3 that attraction models may be extended to include differential effects and cross
effects between brands. In the following sections we will discuss more
advanced issues related to the parameter estimation of differential-effects
and cross-effects (*fully extended*) models.

5.5   Estimation of Differential-Effects Models

The differential-effects version of attraction model (5.1) is expressed as
follows.

$$\mathcal{A}_i = \exp(\alpha_i + \epsilon_i) \prod_{k=1}^{K} f_k(X_{ki})^{\beta_{ki}} \qquad (5.13)$$

$$s_i = \mathcal{A}_i / \sum_{j=1}^{m} \mathcal{A}_j$$

where either an identity or exponential transformation may be chosen for
f_k, depending on whether an MCI or MNL model is desired. The chief
difference between (5.1) and (5.13) is the fact that parameter β_{ki} has
an additional subscript i, suggesting that the effectiveness (and hence
the elasticity) of a marketing variable may differ from one brand to the
next. This is certainly a plausible model in some situations and worth
calibrating.

The estimation of parameters β_{ki} $(i = 1, 2, \ldots, m)$ is not extremely
complicated. Only a slight modification of regression models (5.6 – 5.9)
achieves the result. Using the previous definitions for dummy variables
d_j and D_u, the differential-effects versions of regression models (5.6 – 5.7)
are given by

   MNL Model:

$$s_{it}^* = \sum_{j=2}^{m} \alpha_j (d_j - \frac{1}{m}) + \sum_{k=1}^{K} \sum_{j=1}^{m} \beta_{ki}(d_j - \frac{1}{m}) X_{kit} + \epsilon_{it}^* \qquad (5.14)$$

   MCI Model:

$$s_{it}^* = \sum_{j=2}^{m} \alpha_j (d_j - \frac{1}{m}) + \sum_{k=1}^{K} \sum_{j=1}^{m} \beta_{ki}(d_j - \frac{1}{m}) \log X_{kit} + \epsilon_{it}^* \ . \qquad (5.15)$$

In regression models (5.14 – 5.15) the independent variables are replaced by each variable multiplied by $(d_j - 1/m)$, which equals $(1 - 1/m)$ if $j = i$, and $-1/m$ otherwise. Thus the number of independent variables is $(m \times K) + m - 1$. Note that regression models (5.14 – 5.15) will have to be estimated without the intercept term. Most regression programs provide us with this option.[17] We cannot obtain the estimate of α_1 from (5.14) or (5.15), but this poses no problem in computing market shares since the estimated value of α_i is actually the difference between true α_i and α_1.[18] Similarly regression models (5.8 and 5.9) may be modified as follows for their respective differential-effect versions.

MNL Model:

$$\log s_{it} = \alpha_1 + \sum_{j=2}^{m} \alpha'_j d_j + \sum_{u=2}^{T} \gamma_u D_u + \sum_{k=1}^{K} \sum_{j=1}^{m} \beta_{ki} d_j X_{kit} + \epsilon_{it} \qquad (5.16)$$

MCI Model:

$$\log s_{it} = \alpha_1 + \sum_{j=2}^{m} \alpha'_j d_j + \sum_{u=2}^{T} \gamma_u D_u + \sum_{k=1}^{K} \sum_{j=1}^{m} \beta_{ki} d_j \log X_{kit} + \epsilon_{it} \qquad (5.17)$$

Regression models (5.14 – 5.15) and (5.16 – 5.17) yield identical estimates of parameters α's (except α_1) and β's. If the number of periods (or choice situations) is large, (5.14 – 5.15) will be preferred.

The reader may feel that the following regression models are more straightforward modifications of (5.6 – 5.7), but it is *not* the case.

MNL Model:

$$s_{it}^* = \alpha_1 + \sum_{j=2}^{m} \alpha'_j d_j + \sum_{k=1}^{K} \sum_{j=1}^{m} \beta_{ki} d_j (X_{kit} - \bar{X}_{kt}) + \epsilon_{it}^* \qquad (5.18)$$

MCI Model:

$$s_{it}^* = \alpha_1 + \sum_{j=2}^{m} \alpha'_j d_j + \sum_{k=1}^{K} \sum_{j=1}^{m} \beta_{ki} d_j X_{kit}^* + \epsilon_{it}^* \qquad (5.19)$$

Models (5.18 – 5.19) do not represent an attraction model, but a log-linear market-share model in which the share of brand i is specified

---

[17]If an intercept term is included, its estimated value will be zero.
[18]Rather than automatically assigning α_1 as the brand intercept to drop, one can run the regression with all brand intercepts (which will be a singular model) and find the intercept closest to zero as the one to drop.

as

$$s_i = \exp(\alpha_i + \epsilon_i) \prod_{k=1}^{K} f_k(X_{ki}^*)^{\beta_{ki}}$$

where X_{ki}^* is a centered value of X_{ki}, that is, $(X_{kit} - \bar{X}_{kt})$ if f_k is an exponential transformation and $(X_{kit}/\tilde{X}_{kt})$ if f_k is an identity transformation. While these models themselves may have desirable features as market-share models, models (5.18 – 5.19) are not the estimating equations for (5.13).[19]

Let us see what those modifications mean from the illustrative data of Table 5.1. The independent variable in this case is price. In order to estimate regression model (5.17) (for an MCI version), data must be arranged as in Table 5.6. Only the dependent variable and a part of explanatory variables (log(price) × brand dummy variables) are shown. The week and brand dummy variables are the same style as in Table 5.2.

The estimation results are shown in Table 5.7. The fit of model, as measured by R^2, improved from 0.736 to 0.826. The gain from adding six more independent variables (LPD1 through LPD7 instead of LOG(PRICE)) may be measured by the incremental F-ratio 4.9386 $(= (86.8406 - 77.3339)/(6\times .32083))$, which is significant at the .99 level (df = 6, 57). This shows that the differential-effect model is a significant improvement over the explanatory power of the simple-effects model. The estimated parameter values are markedly different from one brand to the next. Looking at the price-parameter estimates, we note that a larger size tends to be more price sensitive than a smaller size even within a brand. Brands 2 and 4 have greater (in absolute values) values than brands 1 and 2. Brand 5 is most price sensitive with the estimated value of -24.08, but this may reflect the fact that this brand's share was zero and hence not available for estimation for 10 weeks out of 14. We shall discuss this issue in a later section. Two brands, 6 and 7, are not price sensitive. Their price parameters are not statistically different from zero as indicated by their respective "Prob.> $|T|$" values. As to the estimates of α's, we may note that they are negatively correlated with price-parameter estimates over brands, but we will not attempt to make generalizations on the basis of this single example.

The arrangement of data for estimating model (5.15) is given in Table 5.8. Only the dependent variable and the price × brand dummy

---

[19]The difference here is that (5.14 – 5.15) log-center the differential-effect variable, while (5.18 – 5.19) log-center the simple-effect variable and then multiply these log-centered variables by the brand-specific dummy variables.

Table 5.6: Data Set for Differential-Effects Model

Week	Brnd	Log Share	LPD1	LPD2	LPD3	LPD4	LPD5	LPD6	LPD7
1	1	1.38629	5.2575	0.0000	0.0000	0.0000	0.0000	0.0000	0.0000
1	2	3.93183	0.0000	4.9381	0.0000	0.0000	0.0000	0.0000	0.0000
1	3	1.09861	0.0000	0.0000	5.0626	0.0000	0.0000	0.0000	0.0000
1	4	1.09861	0.0000	0.0000	0.0000	4.9836	0.0000	0.0000	0.0000
1	5	.	0.0000	0.0000	0.0000	0.0000	5.0938	0.0000	0.0000
1	6	0.00000	0.0000	0.0000	0.0000	0.0000	0.0000	4.8520	0.0000
1	7	2.19722	0.0000	0.0000	0.0000	0.0000	0.0000	0.0000	4.9972
2	1	0.69315	5.2575	0.0000	0.0000	0.0000	0.0000	0.0000	0.0000
2	2	4.31749	0.0000	4.9416	0.0000	0.0000	0.0000	0.0000	0.0000
2	3	0.69315	0.0000	0.0000	5.0626	0.0000	0.0000	0.0000	0.0000
2	4	0.00000	0.0000	0.0000	0.0000	5.1358	0.0000	0.0000	0.0000
2	5	.	0.0000	0.0000	0.0000	0.0000	5.0938	0.0000	0.0000
2	6	.	0.0000	0.0000	0.0000	0.0000	0.0000	4.8520	0.0000
2	7	1.60944	0.0000	0.0000	0.0000	0.0000	0.0000	0.0000	4.9972
3	1	1.09861	5.2575	0.0000	0.0000	0.0000	0.0000	0.0000	0.0000
3	2	3.87120	0.0000	4.9309	0.0000	0.0000	0.0000	0.0000	0.0000
3	3	0.00000	0.0000	0.0000	5.0626	0.0000	0.0000	0.0000	0.0000
3	4	0.00000	0.0000	0.0000	0.0000	5.1358	0.0000	0.0000	0.0000
3	5	3.04452	0.0000	0.0000	0.0000	0.0000	4.6052	0.0000	0.0000
3	6	.	0.0000	0.0000	0.0000	0.0000	0.0000	4.9273	0.0000
3	7	2.56495	0.0000	0.0000	0.0000	0.0000	0.0000	0.0000	4.8904
4	1	1.38629	5.2575	0.0000	0.0000	0.0000	0.0000	0.0000	0.0000
4	2	3.78419	0.0000	4.9345	0.0000	0.0000	0.0000	0.0000	0.0000
4	3	3.17805	0.0000	0.0000	4.9345	0.0000	0.0000	0.0000	0.0000
4	4	.	0.0000	0.0000	0.0000	5.1358	0.0000	0.0000	0.0000
4	5	.	0.0000	0.0000	0.0000	0.0000	5.0938	0.0000	0.0000
4	6	.	0.0000	0.0000	0.0000	0.0000	0.0000	4.9972	0.0000
4	7	2.39790	0.0000	0.0000	0.0000	0.0000	0.0000	0.0000	4.8520
5	1	1.60944	5.2575	0.0000	0.0000	0.0000	0.0000	0.0000	0.0000
5	2	3.13549	0.0000	4.9345	0.0000	0.0000	0.0000	0.0000	0.0000
5	3	2.30259	0.0000	0.0000	4.9488	0.0000	0.0000	0.0000	0.0000
5	4	0.00000	0.0000	0.0000	0.0000	5.1358	0.0000	0.0000	0.0000
5	5	.	0.0000	0.0000	0.0000	0.0000	5.0938	0.0000	0.0000
5	6	3.25810	0.0000	0.0000	0.0000	0.0000	0.0000	4.8520	0.0000
5	7	1.94591	0.0000	0.0000	0.0000	0.0000	0.0000	0.0000	4.8520
6	1	1.79176	5.2575	0.0000	0.0000	0.0000	0.0000	0.0000	0.0000
6	2	1.79176	0.0000	5.1705	0.0000	0.0000	0.0000	0.0000	0.0000
6	3	1.09861	0.0000	0.0000	5.0626	0.0000	0.0000	0.0000	0.0000
6	4	0.69315	0.0000	0.0000	0.0000	5.1358	0.0000	0.0000	0.0000
6	5	.	0.0000	0.0000	0.0000	0.0000	5.0938	0.0000	0.0000
6	6	3.58352	0.0000	0.0000	0.0000	0.0000	0.0000	4.8520	0.0000
6	7	2.56495	0.0000	0.0000	0.0000	0.0000	0.0000	0.0000	4.8520

Table 5.7: Regression Results for Differential-Effects Model (MCI)

Model: MODEL1					
Dep Variable: LSHARE					
		Analysis of Variance			
		Sum of	Mean		
Source	DF	Squares	Square	F Value	Prob>F
Model	26	86.84061	3.34002	10.411	0.0001
Error	57	18.28703	0.32083		
C Total	83	105.12764			
Root MSE		0.56641	R-Square	0.8260	
Dep Mean		1.92529	Adj R-Sq	0.7467	
C.V.		29.41967			

		Parameter Estimates			
		Parameter	Standard	T for H_0	
Variable	DF	Estimate	Error	Parm=0	Prob> $|T|$
INTRCPT	1	36.797056	9.03858643	4.071	0.0001
D2	1	28.212012	11.56852482	2.439	0.0179
D3	1	1.325003	11.79902587	0.112	0.9110
D4	1	12.426886	11.09247984	1.120	0.2673
D5	1	77.155688	41.01572380	1.881	0.0651
D6	1	−32.861595	16.87525706	−1.947	0.0564
D7	1	−43.161568	18.20494075	−2.371	0.0211
DD2	1	0.144666	0.34886522	0.415	0.6799
DD3	1	0.160885	0.34227101	0.470	0.6401
DD4	1	0.783674	0.38370743	2.042	0.0458
DD5	1	0.560437	0.33938645	1.651	0.1042
DD6	1	1.070890	0.34384160	3.114	0.0029
DD7	1	1.087786	0.34488085	3.154	0.0026
DD8	1	0.479316	0.33693519	1.423	0.1603
DD9	1	0.997026	0.34999923	2.849	0.0061
DD10	1	0.689770	0.35708659	1.932	0.0584
DD11	1	1.035196	0.35245369	2.937	0.0048
DD12	1	0.565334	0.35135768	1.609	0.1131
DD13	1	0.176690	0.34733555	0.509	0.6129
DD14	1	0.107222	0.36223872	0.296	0.7683
LPD1	1	−6.837585	1.72929552	−3.954	0.0002
LPD2	1	−12.511968	1.47178224	−8.501	0.0001
LPD3	1	−7.357565	1.51269846	−4.864	0.0001
LPD4	1	−9.629287	1.46960177	−6.552	0.0001
LPD5	1	−24.078656	8.34529863	−2.885	0.0055
LPD6	1	−0.478779	2.78016380	−0.172	0.8639
LPD7	1	1.657518	3.33624420	0.497	0.6212

Table 5.8: Log-Centered Differential-Effects Data

Week	Brand	Log-Centered Share	Centered Log(Price)× Brand Dummy Variables						
			LPD1	LPD2	LPD3	LPD4	LPD5	LPD6	LPD7
1	1	−0.232	4.381	−0.823	−0.844	−0.831	0.000	−0.809	−0.833
1	2	2.313	−0.876	4.115	−0.844	−0.831	0.000	−0.809	−0.833
1	3	−0.520	−0.876	−0.823	4.219	−0.831	0.000	−0.809	−0.833
1	4	−0.520	−0.876	−0.823	−0.844	4.153	0.000	−0.809	−0.833
1	6	−1.619	−0.876	−0.823	−0.844	−0.831	0.000	4.043	−0.833
1	7	0.578	−0.876	−0.823	−0.844	−0.831	0.000	−0.809	4.164
2	1	−0.769	4.206	−0.988	−1.013	−1.027	0.000	0.000	−0.999
2	2	2.855	−1.052	3.953	−1.013	−1.027	0.000	0.000	−0.999
2	3	−0.769	−1.052	−0.988	4.050	−1.027	0.000	0.000	−0.999
2	4	−1.463	−1.052	−0.988	−1.013	4.109	0.000	0.000	−0.999
2	7	0.147	−1.052	−0.988	−1.013	−1.027	0.000	0.000	3.998
3	1	−0.665	4.381	−0.822	−0.844	−0.856	−0.768	0.000	−0.815
3	2	2.108	−0.876	4.109	−0.844	−0.856	−0.768	0.000	−0.815
3	3	−1.763	−0.876	−0.822	4.219	−0.856	−0.768	0.000	−0.815
3	4	−1.763	−0.876	−0.822	−0.844	4.280	−0.768	0.000	−0.815
3	5	1.281	−0.876	−0.822	−0.844	−0.856	3.838	0.000	−0.815
3	7	0.802	−0.876	−0.822	−0.844	−0.856	−0.768	0.000	4.075
4	1	−1.300	3.943	−1.234	−1.234	0.000	0.000	0.000	−1.213
4	2	1.098	−1.314	3.701	−1.234	0.000	0.000	0.000	−1.213
4	3	0.491	−1.314	−1.234	3.701	0.000	0.000	0.000	−1.213
4	7	−0.289	−1.314	−1.234	−1.234	0.000	0.000	0.000	3.639
5	1	−0.432	4.381	−0.822	−0.825	−0.856	0.000	−0.809	−0.809
5	2	1.094	−0.876	4.112	−0.825	−0.856	0.000	−0.809	−0.809
5	3	0.261	−0.876	−0.822	4.124	−0.856	0.000	−0.809	−0.809
5	4	−2.042	−0.876	−0.822	−0.825	4.280	0.000	−0.809	−0.809
5	6	1.216	−0.876	−0.822	−0.825	−0.856	0.000	4.043	−0.809
5	7	−0.096	−0.876	−0.822	−0.825	−0.856	0.000	−0.809	4.043
6	1	−0.129	4.381	−0.862	−0.844	−0.856	0.000	−0.809	−0.809
6	2	−0.129	−0.876	4.309	−0.844	−0.856	0.000	−0.809	−0.809
6	3	−0.822	−0.876	−0.862	4.219	−0.856	0.000	−0.809	−0.809
6	4	−1.227	−0.876	−0.862	−0.844	4.280	0.000	−0.809	−0.809
6	6	1.663	−0.876	−0.862	−0.844	−0.856	0.000	4.043	−0.809
6	7	0.644	−0.876	−0.862	−0.844	−0.856	0.000	−0.809	4.043

variables are shown. In addition, we need $(d_j - 1/m)$, where d_j is the usual brand dummy variable for each brand. Note that all variables sum to zero within each week. Note also that those observations for which log(share) is missing are deleted prior to centering. The estimated values of $\alpha_2, \alpha_3, \ldots, \alpha_m, \beta_{p1}, \beta_{p2}, \ldots, \beta_{pm}$ based on the data in Table 5.8 are identical to those given in Table 5.7.

5.6   Collinearity in Differential-Effects Models

Bultez and Naert [1975] reported that estimating the parameters of a differential-effects model by equations (5.14) and (5.15) was greatly inconvenienced by the existence of model-induced collinearity. To see their point, consider the data set shown in Table 5.9.

Table 5.9: Hypothetical Data for Differential-Effects Model

W e e k	B r a n d	log share	$X_1 \times$ Brand Dummies			$X_2 \times$ Brand Dummies		
			$X_1 D_1$	$X_1 D_2$	$X_1 D_3$	$X_2 D_1$	$X_2 D_2$	$X_2 D_3$
1	1	$\log(s_{11})$	X_{111}	0	0	X_{211}	0	0
1	2	$\log(s_{21})$	0	X_{121}	0	0	X_{221}	0
1	3	$\log(s_{31})$	0	0	X_{131}	0	0	X_{231}
2	1	$\log(s_{12})$	X_{112}	0	0	X_{212}	0	0
2	2	$\log(s_{22})$	0	X_{122}	0	0	X_{222}	0
2	3	$\log(s_{32})$	0	0	X_{132}	0	0	X_{232}
3	1	$\log(s_{13})$	X_{113}	0	0	X_{213}	0	0
3	2	$\log(s_{23})$	0	X_{123}	0	0	X_{223}	0
3	3	$\log(s_{33})$	0	0	X_{133}	0	0	X_{233}
.	.	.	.	.	.	.	.	.
.	.	.	.	.	.	.	.	.

This data set is for the estimation of regression model (5.16) in which three brands and two independent variables are assumed. (In actual estimation we will need brand and week dummy variables in addition to the variables above.) Collinearity (i.e., high correlations between two or more independent variables) is observed between independent variables for the same brand, e.g., between $X_1 D_1$ and $X_2 D_1$, between $X_1 D_2$ and $X_2 D_2$, between $X_1 D_3$ and $X_2 D_3$, and so forth. The reason for this phenomenon is demonstrated mathematically later in this section, but is easy to understand. Take variables called $X_1 D_1$ and $X_2 D_1$ for example. Those two variables have many zeroes in common for the same *observations* (weeks). When one takes the correlations between the two variables, those common zeroes artificially inflate the value of the correlation coefficient.

Because of the potential for artificially inflated correlations Bultez and Naert warned against careless usage of differential-effect models. Their warning was, however, somewhat premature. There are two aspects to the problem — the first concerning numerical analysis, and the second concerning the stability of parameters estimates.

Problems arise in numerical analysis when the crossproducts matrix for a regression model becomes singular or so nearly so that it cannot be inverted accurately. But, the crossproducts matrix for regression model (5.15) has a unique structure which is robust against high correlations induced by the model structure. (This is not to say that it is robust against any high correlations.) To simplify the discussion, assume that observations are taken only for three weeks. Then the number of independent variables in regression will be 11 (the intercept term, two week dummy variables, two brand dummy variables, and six variables $X_1 D_1$ through $X_2 D_3$). The crossproduct matrix for this set of variables will look as follows.

$$
\begin{pmatrix}
9 & 3 & 3 & 3 & 3 & \Sigma X_{11t} & \Sigma X_{12t} & \Sigma X_{13t} & \Sigma X_{21t} & \Sigma X_{22t} & \Sigma X_{23t} \\
3 & 3 & 0 & 1 & 1 & X_{112} & X_{122} & X_{132} & X_{212} & X_{222} & X_{232} \\
3 & 0 & 3 & 1 & 1 & X_{113} & X_{123} & X_{133} & X_{213} & X_{223} & X_{233} \\
3 & 1 & 1 & 3 & 0 & 0 & \Sigma X_{12t} & 0 & 0 & \Sigma X_{22t} & 0 \\
3 & 1 & 1 & 0 & 3 & 0 & 0 & \Sigma X_{13t} & 0 & 0 & \Sigma X_{23t} \\
\Sigma X_{11t} & X_{112} & X_{113} & 0 & 0 & \Sigma X_{11t}^2 & 0 & 0 & \Sigma X_{11t}X_{21t} & 0 & 0 \\
\Sigma X_{12t} & X_{122} & X_{123} & \Sigma X_{12t} & 0 & 0 & \Sigma X_{12t}^2 & 0 & 0 & \Sigma X_{12t}X_{22t} & 0 \\
\Sigma X_{13t} & X_{132} & X_{133} & 0 & \Sigma X_{13t} & 0 & 0 & \Sigma X_{13t}^2 & 0 & 0 & \Sigma X_{13t}X_{23t} \\
\Sigma X_{21t} & X_{212} & X_{213} & 0 & 0 & \Sigma X_{11t}X_{21t} & 0 & 0 & \Sigma X_{21t}^2 & 0 & 0 \\
\Sigma X_{22t} & X_{222} & X_{223} & \Sigma X_{22t} & 0 & 0 & \Sigma X_{12t}X_{22t} & 0 & 0 & \Sigma X_{22t}^2 & 0 \\
\Sigma X_{23t} & X_{232} & X_{233} & 0 & \Sigma X_{23t} & 0 & 0 & \Sigma X_{13t}X_{23t} & 0 & 0 & \Sigma X_{33t}^2
\end{pmatrix}
$$

In the above matrix summation is always over t (in this case over three weeks).

Collinearity in regression becomes a numerical-analysis problem when the crossproduct matrix such as above is nearly singular and thus the determinant is near zero. Since this matrix is in a block-matrix form, the critical issue is if sub-matrix

$$
\begin{pmatrix}
\Sigma X_{11t}^2 & 0 & 0 & \Sigma X_{11t} X_{21t} & 0 & 0 \\
0 & \Sigma X_{12t}^2 & 0 & 0 & \Sigma X_{12t} X_{22t} & 0 \\
0 & 0 & \Sigma X_{13t}^2 & 0 & 0 & \Sigma X_{13t} X_{23t} \\
\Sigma X_{11t} X_{21t} & 0 & 0 & \Sigma X_{21t}^2 & 0 & 0 \\
0 & \Sigma X_{12t} X_{22t} & 0 & 0 & \Sigma X_{22t}^2 & 0 \\
0 & 0 & \Sigma X_{13t} X_{23t} & 0 & 0 & \Sigma X_{33t}^2
\end{pmatrix}
$$

is invertible. This matrix may be put in the form of a block-diagonal matrix by simple row-column operations and thus is invertible, if each of the following three matrices is invertible.

$$
\begin{pmatrix}
\Sigma X_{11t}^2 & \Sigma X_{11t} X_{21t} \\
\Sigma X_{11t} X_{21t} & \Sigma X_{21t}^2
\end{pmatrix}
\begin{pmatrix}
\Sigma X_{12t}^2 & \Sigma X_{12t} X_{22t} \\
\Sigma X_{12t} X_{22t} & \Sigma X_{22t}^2
\end{pmatrix}
\begin{pmatrix}
\Sigma X_{13t}^2 & \Sigma X_{13t} X_{23t} \\
\Sigma X_{13t} X_{23t} & \Sigma X_{33t}^2
\end{pmatrix}
$$

This is to say that original correlations between X_{11} and X_{21}, X_{12} and X_{22}, and X_{13} and X_{23} over t are low. This is true even if the apparent (model-induced) correlations between them are high. The important condition for the invertibility of the cross-product matrix as a whole is that the correlations between original variables X_{kit} and X_{hit} ($h \neq k$) over t are not too high to begin with. (If the correlations between original variables are high, composite measures, such as those based on principal components, will have to be used for *any* differential-effects market-share model to be effective!) This conclusion does not change if the independent variables are the logarithms of original variables X_{ki}'s. Thus the numerical-analysis problems created by collinearity in the usual sense are not the real issues in this case.

Even though the matrix will usually be invertible, collinearity can still harm the regression estimates. A further look at the source and remedies for collinearity in these models is helpful. Since Bultez and Naert's [1975] discussion of the problem, their warning about collinearity in differential-effects attraction models has been echoed by Naert and Weverbergh and others.[20] While most of these articles also investigated

[20] Naert, Philippe A. & Marcel Weverbergh [1981], "On the Prediction Power of Market Share Attraction Models," *Journal of Marketing Research*, 18 (May), 146-153. Naert, Philippe A. & Marcel Weverbergh [1985], "Market Share Specification, Estimation and Validation: Toward Reconciling Seemingly Divergent Views," *Journal of Marketing Research*, 22 (November), 453–61. Brodie, Roderick & Cornelius A. de Kluyver [1984], "Attraction Versus Linear and Multiplicative Market Share Models:

differential-effects versions of multiplicative and linear-additive market-share models, no mention has been made in the marketing literature of possible collinearities in these model forms.

This section shows that the linear-additive and multiplicative versions of differential-effects market-share models suffer from the same sources of collinearities as the MCI and MNL versions. It is shown that the structural sources of collinearity are largely eliminated by two standardizing transformations — zeta-scores or the exponential transform of a standard z-score — discussed in section 3.8.

5.6.1 Three Differential-Effects Models

The three basic specifications of the differential-effects market-share models – linear-additive (LIN), multiplicative (MULT), and multiplicative competitive-interaction (MCI) or attraction versions – are given in equations (5.20 – 5.22) parallel to the definitions in Naert & Weverbergh's [1984] equations:

$$\text{LIN} \quad s_{it} = \alpha_i + \sum_{k=1}^{K} \beta_{ki} f_t(X_{kit}) + \epsilon_{it} \tag{5.20}$$

$$\text{MULT} \quad s_{it} = \mathcal{A}_{it} \tag{5.21}$$

$$\text{MCI} \quad s_{it} = \frac{\mathcal{A}_{it}}{\sum_{j=1}^{m} \mathcal{A}_{jt}} \tag{5.22}$$

where:[21]

$$\mathcal{A}_{it} = (\alpha_i + \epsilon_{it}) \prod_{k=1}^{K} [f_t(X_{kit})]^{\beta_{ki}} \; .$$

An Empirical Evaluation," *Journal of Marketing Research*, 21 (May), 194-201. Ghosh, Avijit, Scott Neslin & Robert Shoemaker [1984], "A Comparison of Market Share Models and Estimation Procedures," *Journal of Marketing Research*, 21 (May), 202-210. Leeflang, Peter S. H. & Jan C. Reuyl [1984a], "On the Predictive Power of Market Share Attraction Models," *Journal of Marketing Research* 21 (May), 211-215. Leeflang, Peter S. H. & Jan C. Reuyl [1984b], "Estimators of the Disturbances in Consistent Sum-Constrained Market Share Models," Working Paper, Faculty of Economics, University of Gronigen, P.O. Box 9700 AV Gronigen, The Netherlands.

[21] Note here we are focusing on f_t rather than f_k. We will assume we have agreed on the model type (MCI in this case, that is, f_k is the identity transformation) and our interest here is in the possible influence of transformations within a choice situation on collinearity.

All of these models are reduced to their corresponding simple-effects versions by assuming:

$$\beta_{ki} = \beta_{kj} = \beta_k \qquad \forall\, i,j \ .$$

The *reduced form*[22] resulting from this simplified estimation procedure allows us to see the similarities among all three specifications of the differential-effects model, as seen in Tables 5.2 and 5.9. Note in Table 5.9 that each differential effect has only one nonzero entry in each time period. The difference between LIN and MULT models is just that the MULT model uses the log of the variable as the nonzero entry and the LIN model uses the raw variable. The difference between the MULT and MCI models is basically that the MCI form incorporates a series of time-period dummy variables from Table 5.2 which insure that the estimated parameters are those of the original nonlinear model in equation (3.1). Another difference, of course, is that the estimates of market share in the MCI model come from *inverse log-centering*,[23] while in the MULT model the exponential transformation of the estimated dependent variable serves as the market-share estimate. *Inverse log-centering* and the time-period dummy variables guarantee that the MCI model will provide logically consistent market-share estimates (all estimates being between zero and one, and summing to one over all brands in each time period), while neither LIN or MULT provide logically consistent estimates.

The problem of collinearity can be traced to within-brand effects. There is zero correlation between a time-period dummy variable and a brand-specific dummy variable. Since the time-period dummy variables cannot be a major source of collinearity, then the MULT and MCI models do not differ substantially in their sources of collinearity. Nor do the correlations between effects for different brands contribute substantially to collinearity. For m brands the correlation between brand-specific dummy variables for different brands is $-1/(m-1)$. With even ten brands there is only 1% overlap in variance between intercepts for different brands. An analogous result holds for the correlations between dummy variables for different time periods. The within-brand effects are analyzed in the next section.

---

[22]The *reduced form* is simply the variables after they are transformed to be ready for input into a multiple-regression routine.

[23]Nakanishi & Cooper [1982].

5.6.2 Within-Brand Effects

The special problems of jointly longitudinal and cross-sectional analysis have been discussed in psychometrics, econometrics, as well as the quantitative-analysis areas in education, sociology, and geography. The earliest reference is to Robinson's[24] covariance theorem, which was presented by Alker[25] as:

$$r_{XY} = W R_{XY} \sqrt{1 - E_{YR}^2} \sqrt{1 - E_{XR}^2} + E R_{XY} E_{YR} E_{XR} \qquad (5.23)$$

where:

r_{XY} is the correlation between column X and column Y in the *reduced form* of the differential-effects model. In this application X and Y represent within-brand effects such as price and advertising for one brand.

$W R_{XY}$ is defined to be the pooled within-period correlation of X and Y. In our case this simplifies to a congruence coefficient, giving very high values under certain conditions discussed below.

$E R_{XY}$ is the between-period or ecological correlation. In our case this is the simple correlation between, say, the log of price and the log of advertising values for a single brand.

E_{YR} and E_{XR} are the correlation ratios (i.e., the proportions of variation in X and Y, respectively, that are attributable to between-period differences). In our case these values control how much weight is given to the congruence coefficient versus the simple correlation.

Looking again at Table 5.9 shows that for differential effects within a brand, all the nonzero entries are aligned and all the zero entries are aligned in the *reduced form*, and there is only one nonzero entry in each time period. This results in very simplified forms for the components of Robinson's covariance theorem. If we let x_t and y_t be the single nonzero

---

[24]Robinson, W. S. [1950], "Ecological Correlation and the Behavior of Individuals," *American Sociological Review*, 15, 351-357.

[25]Alker, Hayward R. Jr. [1969], "A Typology of Ecological Fallacies," in Mattei Dogan & Stein Rokkan (editors), *Quantitative Ecological Analysis in the Social Sciences*, Cambridge, MA: The M.I.T. Press, 69-86.

entries in period t for column X and Y, respectively, then for our special case:

$$WR_{XY} = \frac{\sum_{t=1}^{T} x_t y_t}{\sqrt{\sum_{t=1}^{T} x_t^2 \sum_{t=1}^{T} y_t^2}} \ .$$

This is a congruence coefficient, often used for assessing the agreement between ratio-scaled measures.[26] Because the mean levels of the variables influence the congruence, x and y of the same sign push WR_{XY} toward 1.0 much faster than the simple correlation. For prices (greater than \$1.00) and advertising expenditures the *reduced form* would have a series of positive log-values which might well have a very large value for WR_{XY}. For these same variables in share form (price-share or advertising-share), the *reduced form* would have matched negative numbers, which still could lead to large values for WR_{XY}. For variables of consistently opposite signs, WR_{XY} could push toward -1.0 even in cases of modest simple correlations.

For both raw variables (e.g., price and advertising) and for marketing variables in their share form (e.g., relative price and advertising share) the correlation ratios E_{XR}^2 and E_{YR}^2 have a *maximum* value of $\frac{1}{m}$.

$$E_{XR}^2 = \frac{\frac{1}{m^2}\left[\sum_{t=1}^{T} \frac{X_{jt}^2}{T} - \left(\frac{\sum_{t=1}^{T} X_{jt}}{T}\right)^2\right]}{\frac{1}{m}\left[\sum_{t=1}^{T} \frac{X_{jt}^2}{T} - \frac{1}{m}\left(\frac{\sum_{t=1}^{T} X_{jt}}{T}\right)^2\right]} \le \frac{1}{m} \ . \qquad (5.24)$$

So when correlating two effects within a brand we have at best:

$$r_{XY} = \left(\frac{m-1}{m}\right) WR_{XY} + \left(\frac{1}{m}\right) ER_{XY} \ . \qquad (5.25)$$

Thus the correlation r_{XY} is composed of two parts. A small part, at most $\frac{1}{m}$, is due to the simple correlation of the X and Y values for brand j over time periods. A very large part, at least $\frac{m-1}{m}$ is due to the congruence coefficient WR_{XY}. Thus, for raw-score or share-form marketing variables, pairwise collinearity is likely for any two effects within a brand in differential-effects models. But collinearity is not merely a pairwise

---

[26]Tucker, Ledyard R [1951], "A Method of Synthesis of Factor Analysis Studies," *Personnel Research Section Report*, No. 984, Washington, D.C., Department of the Army. Also see Korth, Bruce & Ledyard R Tucker [1975], "The Distribution of Chance Coefficients from Simulated Data," *Psychometrika*, 40, 3 (September), 361-372.

problem in these models.[27] Collective collinearity for all the within-brand effects is very likely indeed. This is true for the differential-effects versions of the linear-additive model, the multiplicative model as well as the MCI model. Fortunately there exist simple remedies which are the topic of the next section.

5.6.3 Remedies

The remedies for collinearity were hinted at in the Bultez and Naert [1975] article which first discussed the problem. They said, "... if the variables have zero means" the correlations in the extended model would be the same as the correlation in the simple model (p. 532). More precisely, it can be said that if the *reduced form* of the values for brand i for two different variables each have a mean of zero over time periods, then WR_{XY} is equal to ER_{XY}, and thus r_{XY} would be equal to the simple correlation of the *reduced forms* of the brand i values. This remedy is not a general solution for all variables in a differential-effects model because forming deviation scores within a brand over time ignores competitive effects. One case where this remedy might be appropriate, however, is for a variable reflecting the promotion price of a brand. This variable would reflect current price as a deviation from a brand's historic average price.

As potential remedies, consider zeta-scores and the exponential transformation of standard scores discussed in Chapter 3 (section 3.8). Both transformations standardize the explanatory variables, making the information relative to the competitive context in each time period. There are several advantages to standardizing measures of marketing instruments in each time period. First, one should remember that the dependent measures (share or choice probability) are expressed in a metric which, while normalized rather than standardized, is still focused on representing within time-period relations. Representations of the explanatory variables which have a have similar within time-period focus have the advantage of a compatible metric. In this respect, variables expressed in share form have as much of an advantage as zeta-scores or exp(z-scores). Any of the three would be superior to raw scores in reflecting the explanatory information in a way which aligns with the dependent variable.

---

[27]For further discussion see Mahajan, Vijay, Arun K. Jain & Michel Bergier [1977], "Parameter Estimation in Marketing Models in the Presence of Multicollinearity: An Application of Ridge Regression," *Journal of Marketing Research*, 14 (November), 586-591.

While raw prices might have a stronger relation with category volume or primary demand, relative prices could have more to do with how the total volume is shared among the competitors.

A second advantage applies to standardizations, rather than normalizations. In the *reduced form*, the means (of a brand over time periods) of a zeta-score or exp(z-score) are more likely to be closer to zero, than the corresponding means of the *reduced form* of a normalized variable. Thus WR_{XY} for a zeta-score or exp(z-score) would be less inflated (closer to the value of the simple correlation ER_{XY}) than would be the congruence coefficient for two within-brand effects represented in share form.

Table 5.10 provides an empirical demonstration of the effects on collinearity of zeta-scores and exp(z-scores), compared with the raw scores or the share scores. The data concern price and advertising measures representing competition among 11 brands in an Australian household-products category.[28] There are 11 differential-price effects, 10 differential-advertising effects, and 10 brand-specific intercepts in a differential-effects market-share model for this category. The tabled values are *condition indices* reflecting the extent of collinearity or near dependencies among the explanatory variables. A *condition index* is the ratio of the largest singular value (square root of the eigenvalue) to the smallest singular value of the *reduced form* of the explanatory variables in the market-share model.[29] The higher the *condition index* the worse the collinearity in the system of equations. Belsley, Kuh, and Welsch [1980] develop empirical evidence that weak dependencies are associated with *condition indices* between 5 and 10, moderate to strong relations are associated with indices of 30 to 100, and indices of 100 or more "appear to be large indeed, causing substantial variance inflation and great potential harm to regression estimates"(p. 153). Note in Table 5.10 for raw scores, X_{kit}, all three models (LIN, MULT, and MCI) reflect potential problems. These problems are not remedied when marketing instruments are expressed in share form. As a market-share model, which uses the share form of marketing instruments, becomes more comprehensive, by including more brands, the problems would worsen. This is because the price shares and advertising shares would, in general, become smaller, thus making the log of the shares negative numbers of larger and larger absolute value. This would press WR_{XY} closer to +1.0.

---

[28] Carpenter, Cooper, Hanssens, and Midgley [1988].

[29] Belsley, David A., Edwin Kuh & Roy E. Welsch [1980], *Regression Diagnostics: Identifying Influential Data and Sources of Collinearity*, New York: John Wiley & Sons, 103-4.

Table 5.10: Condition Indices Australian Household-Products Example

| Model | Raw Scores | Transformation of Raw Scores | | |
		Share Form	Zeta-Scores	Exp(Z-Scores)
LIN	3065	313	61	75
MULT	484	3320	22	17
MCI	627	3562	24	23

Standardizing within each competitive set using zeta-scores or exp(z-scores) has a dramatically favorable impact on the collinearity of the system of equations. The *condition indices* for the MULT and MCI models are less than 25. This is below the level indicating moderate collinearity, and far below the danger point.[30] Linear or nonlinear trends in the mean level of the raw variables are major contributors to collinearity. By removing the mean level of the raw variables in each time period, the two remedies illustrated in Table 5.10 both eliminate one major source contributing to high (positive or negative) values in WR_{XY}. By standardizing the variance over competitors in each time period, both remedies help keep the mean values for each brand over time nearer to zero.

These basic results mean that, if one standardizes variables in a manner appropriate for these multiplicative models, it is practical to use differential-effects market-share models.

5.7 Estimation of Cross-Effects Models

We now come to the estimation problems associated with the fully extended attraction (or cross-effects) model discussed in Chapter 3.

$$\mathcal{A}_i = \exp(\alpha_i + \epsilon_i) \prod_{k=1}^{K} \prod_{j=1}^{m} f_k(X_{kj})^{\beta_{kij}} \qquad (5.26)$$

$$s_i = \mathcal{A}_i / \sum_{j=1}^{m} \mathcal{A}_j$$

---

[30]The absolute standards given by Belsley Kuh and Welsh [1980] for condition indices are probably too conservative. As the number of variables and observations increases we can expect the ratio of the largest and smallest singular values to grow larger. Further study is needed to see what boundaries are acceptable for large data sets.

As before, the f_k in the above equation may be an identity (for an MCI model) or an exponential (for an MNL model) transformation. The most important property of the above model is, of course, the existence of cross-effect parameters, β_{kij} $(i, j = 1, 2, \ldots, m; k = 1, 2, \ldots, K)$. We are now faced with the seemingly insurmountable problem of estimating $(m \times m \times K) + m$ parameters.

Surprisingly, estimating parameters of a cross-effects model is not very difficult, and in some sense easier than estimating parameters of a differential-effects model. McGuire, Weiss, and Houston[31] showed that the following regression models estimate the parameters of (5.26).

MNL Model:

$$s_{it}^* = \alpha_1 + \sum_{j=2}^{m} \alpha_j' d_j + \sum_{j=1}^{m} \sum_{k=1}^{K} \sum_{h=1}^{m} \beta_{kij}^* d_h X_{kjt} + \epsilon_{it} \qquad (5.27)$$

MCI Model:

$$s_{it}^* = \alpha_1 + \sum_{j=2}^{m} \alpha_j' d_j + \sum_{j=1}^{m} \sum_{k=1}^{K} \sum_{h=1}^{m} \beta_{kij}^* d_h \log X_{kjt} + \epsilon_{it} \qquad (5.28)$$

where s_{it}^* is the log-centered value of s_{it}, the share of brand i in period t. Variable d_j is the usual brand dummy variable, but its value changes depending on where it is used in the above equation. In the first summation, $d_j = 1$ if $j = i$, and $d_j = 0$ otherwise; in the second summation, $d_h = 1$ if $h = j$, and $d_h = 0$ otherwise. It must be pointed out that β_{kij}^* in models (5.27 – 5.28) are not the same as parameter β_{kij} in model (5.26), but a deviation of the form

$$\beta_{kij}^* = \beta_{kij} - \bar{\beta}_{k.j}$$

where $\bar{\beta}_{k.j}$ is the arithmetic mean of β_{kij} over all brands $(i = 1, 2, \ldots, m)$. But it may be shown that the estimated values of β_{kij}^*'s are sufficient for computing the cross elasticities. Recall from Chapter 3 that the elasticities and cross elasticities of brand i's share with respect to a change in the kth variable for brand j is given by

MCI Model:

$$e_{s_{i.j}} = \beta_{kij} - \sum_{h=1}^{m} s_h \beta_{khj}$$

[31]McGuire, Timothy W., Doyle L. Weiss & Frank S. Houston [1977], "Consistent Multiplicative Market Share Models," in Barnett A. Greenberg & Danny N. Bellenger (editors), *Contemporary Marketing Thought. 1977 Educators Proceedings* (Series # 41), Chicago: American Marketing Association.

MNL Model:

$$e_{s_{i,j}} = (\beta_{kij} - \sum_{h=1}^{m} s_h \beta_{khj}) X_{kj} .$$

Take the MCI version, for example. Substitute β_{kij}^* for β_{kij} in the above equation.

$$
\begin{aligned}
\beta_{kij}^* - \sum_{h=1}^{m} s_h \beta_{khj}^* &= (\beta_{kij} - \bar{\beta}_{k.j}) - \sum_{h=1}^{m} s_h(\beta_{khj} - \bar{\beta}_{k.j}) \\
&= \beta_{kij} - \sum_{h=1}^{m} s_h \beta_{khj} - \bar{\beta}_{k.j} + \bar{\beta}_{k.j} \\
&= e_{s_{i,j}}
\end{aligned}
$$

since the sum of s_h over all brands is one. Thus the knowledge of the β_{kij}^*'s is sufficient to estimate $e_{s_{i,j}}$ for both the MCI-type and MNL-type cross-effects models.

Let us apply the regression model proposed by McGuire et al. to the illustrative data in Table 5.1. Since the data necessary for estimation involve 56 variables (including the intercept term), no table of data set-up is shown. Only the estimation results are given in Table 5.11. The model was estimated without the intercept. The notation for independent variables, LP$_i$D$_j$, where i and j are appropriate numbers, indicates the effect of log(price) of the ith brand on brand j's market share. There is a warning that the model is not *full rank*, because there are only four observations for brand 5 with a positive market share. Direct-effect parameters, LP$_i$D$_i$'s, for brand 1 through 4 are negative and statistically significant, and others are non-significant. Cross-effect parameters are mostly positive and/or statistically non-significant, but one of them, LP7D6, is negative and significant. Although we should refrain from making generalizations from this one set of data, it is perhaps justified to say that, as we move toward more complex models, the limitations of the test data set have become obvious. The number of observations is too small to provide one with stable parameter estimates. Furthermore, there seem to be other factors than price which affect market shares of margarine in this store. It is desirable then to obtain more data, especially from more than one store, along with the information on marketing variables other than price.

Table 5.11: Regression Results for Cross-Effects Model (MCI)

Model: MODEL1
Note : no intercept in model. R-square is redefined.
Dep Variable: LSHARE

Analysis of Variance

Source	DF	Sum of Squares	Mean Square	F Value	Prob>F
Model	52	92.58365	1.78045	8.451	0.0001
Error	32	6.74182	0.21068		
U Total	84	99.32547			

Root MSE	0.45900	R-Square	0.9321
Dep Mean	−0.00000	Adj R-Sq	0.8218
C.V.	−7.89278E+17		

NOTE : Model is not full rank. Least-squares solutions for the
parameters are not unique. Some statistics will be
misleading. A reported DF of 0 or B means that the
estimate is biased. The following parameters have been
set to 0, since the variables are a linear combination
of other variables as shown.

LP4D5 = +2.9223*D5 + 0.9531*LP1D5 + 0.7226*LP2D5 − 0.2564*LP3D5
LP5D5 = +5.8144*D5 − 0.2300*LP1D5
LP6D5 = +6.3121*D5 − 0.2992*LP1D5 − 0.7777*LP2D5 + 0.7946*LP3D5
LP7D5 = +5.2704*D5 + 0.1566*LP1D5 − 0.0181*LP2D5 − 0.2200*LP3D5

Parameter Estimates

Variable	DF	Parameter Estimate	Standard Error	T for H_0 Parm=0	Prob> $|T|$
D1	1	73.924694	46.10070856	1.604	0.1186
D2	1	−38.091548	46.10070856	−0.826	0.4148
D3	1	38.942488	46.10070856	0.845	0.4045
D4	1	−79.689368	64.73512217	−1.231	0.2273
D5	B	−52.022706	14.10815828	−3.687	0.0008
D6	1	59.130760	69.49275660	0.851	0.4012
D7	1	−17.793812	46.10070856	−0.386	0.7021
LP1D1	1	−5.096306	1.97465203	−2.581	0.0146
LP2D1	1	−0.365029	2.43911085	−0.150	0.8820
LP3D1	1	1.507052	2.27537629	0.662	0.5125
LP4D1	1	−2.353595	1.89200824	−1.244	0.2225
LP5D1	1	0.503063	0.70624068	0.712	0.4814
LP6D1	1	−6.100657	3.98554609	−1.531	0.1357
LP7D1	1	−2.894448	4.25472197	−0.680	0.5012
LP1D2	1	−0.252472	1.97465203	−0.128	0.8991

		Parameter Estimates			
Variable	DF	Parameter Estimate	Standard Error	T for H_0 Parm=0	Prob> $|T|$
LP2D2	1	−8.625451	2.43911085	−3.536	0.0013
LP3D2	1	2.107563	2.27537629	0.926	0.3613
LP4D2	1	3.041118	1.89200824	1.607	0.1178
LP5D2	1	0.800421	0.70624068	1.133	0.2655
LP6D2	1	1.336924	3.98554609	0.335	0.7395
LP7D2	1	9.615896	4.25472197	2.260	0.0308
LP1D3	1	−0.128008	1.97465203	−0.065	0.9487
LP2D3	1	1.150772	2.43911085	0.472	0.6403
LP3D3	1	−6.671369	2.27537629	−2.932	0.0062
LP4D3	1	−0.446255	1.89200824	−0.236	0.8150
LP5D3	1	0.378551	0.70624068	0.536	0.5957
LP6D3	1	−0.622859	3.98554609	−0.156	0.8768
LP7D3	1	−1.518813	4.25472197	−0.357	0.7235
LP1D4	1	−1.081137	2.35763232	−0.459	0.6496
LP2D4	1	6.997517	3.37627497	2.073	0.0463
LP3D4	1	−3.559763	3.99419070	−0.891	0.3795
LP4D4	1	−6.089339	1.89510791	−3.213	0.0030
LP5D4	1	0.194514	0.74768568	0.260	0.7964
LP6D4	1	12.210535	7.30809600	1.671	0.1045
LP7D4	1	7.680597	4.90866219	1.565	0.1275
LP1D5	B	6.205448	2.34288476	2.649	0.0124
LP2D5	B	3.608572	3.17368514	1.137	0.2640
LP3D5	B	0.569965	3.76236952	0.151	0.8805
LP4D5	0	0	0.00000000	.	.
LP5D5	0	0	0.00000000	.	.
LP6D5	0	0	0.00000000	.	.
LP7D5	0	0	0.00000000	.	.
LP1D6	1	3.523658	2.50575576	1.406	0.1693
LP2D6	1	0.112065	3.39656633	0.033	0.9739
LP3D6	1	−0.322265	4.07062686	−0.079	0.9374
LP4D6	1	1.837399	2.12068866	0.866	0.3927
LP5D6	1	1.098908	0.83529373	1.316	0.1977
LP6D6	1	−1.221249	7.39266721	−0.165	0.8698
LP7D6	1	−17.414894	5.82079344	−2.992	0.0053
LP1D7	1	0.104280	1.97465203	0.053	0.9582
LP2D7	1	1.630654	2.43911085	0.669	0.5086
LP3D7	1	2.086093	2.27537629	0.917	0.3661
LP4D7	1	1.615467	1.89200824	0.854	0.3995
LP5D7	1	−0.313301	0.70624068	−0.444	0.6603
LP6D7	1	−2.643566	3.98554609	−0.663	0.5119
LP7D7	1	1.060157	4.25472197	0.249	0.8048

5.8   A Multivariate MCI Regression Model

It should be pointed out that the parameter estimates of Table 5.11 may be obtained by applying a simple regression model of the following form to the data for each brand separately.

$$\log(s_{it}^*) = \alpha_i + \sum_{j=1}^{m} \beta_{pij} \log(P_{jt}) + \epsilon_{it} \ (i = 1, 2, \ldots, m) \tag{5.29}$$

In the above equation, α_i is simply the intercept term for brand i. The parameters thus estimated are identical to those in Table 5.11, although the significance level of each parameter is usually different from the one in Table 5.11, because the t-statistic and associated degrees of freedom are not the same. If one wishes only parameter estimates, model (5.26) is simpler to calibrate than model (5.13).[32]

The fact that (5.29) may be used to estimate the parameters of (5.26) has an extremely important implication. Note that, in estimating (5.29), the data for every brand involve the same set of independent variables, $\log(P_{1t}), \log(P_{2t}), \ldots, \log(P_{mt})$, plus an intercept term. One may summarize model (5.29) for m brands in the following multivariate regression model.

$$Y = XB + E \tag{5.30}$$

where:

Y = the $T \times m$ matrix with elements $\{\log(s_{it}^*)\}$ $(t = 1, 2, \ldots, T; i = 1, 2, \ldots, m)$

X = the $T \times (1 + m \times K)$ matrix $(J|X_1|X_2|\ldots|X_K)$

J = the $T \times 1$ vector $(111\ldots1)'$

X_k = the $T \times m$ matrix with elements $\{\log(X_{kit})\}$ $(t = 1, 2, \ldots, T; i = 1, 2, \ldots, m)$

B = the $(1 + m \times K) \times m$ matrix $(B_1|B_2|\ldots|B_m)$

$B_i = (\alpha_i|\beta_{1i1}\ldots\beta_{1im}|\beta_{2i1}\ldots\beta_{2im}|\ldots|\beta_{Ki1}\ldots\beta_{Kim})'$

E = the $T \times m$ matrix of elements $\{\epsilon_{it}\}$ $(t = 1, 2, \ldots, T; i = 1, 2, \ldots, m)$.

---

[32]If we replace $\log(P_{jt})$ with P_{jt}, the corresponding MNL model can be estimated.

Recall our assumptions for the specification-error term are still applicable to the error term, ϵ_{it}, in the above model. It is well known that under our assumptions on the error term, the OLS procedure, applied to each column of Y in (5.30) separately, yields the best linear-unbiased estimates (BLUE) of the parameters of B.[33] In other words, it is not necessary to resort to the GLS procedure to obtain minimum-variance estimates of a cross-effects model such as (5.27) or (5.28).

This fact, combined with the availability of equation (5.29) for brand-by-brand estimation, reduces the task of estimating the parameters of a cross-effects model and increases its usefulness as a market-diagnostic tool. When one has a sufficient number of observations (that is, $T > 1 + m \times K$), it is perhaps best to estimate a cross-effects model first, and then, after examining the pattern of estimated coefficients, determine if a simpler model, such as the simple attraction model or a differential-effects model, is adequate. When the number of observations is barely sufficient for a cross-effects model, one may decide to adopt a strategy to estimate a full cross-effects model first, and then decide to restrict some elements of the B matrix (the parameter matrix) to be zero (cf. Carpenter, Cooper, Hanssens, & Midgley [1988]). In this case, however, the OLS procedure is not applicable and a GLS procedure will have to be used.

5.9   Estimation of Category-Volume Models

So far we have considered the various techniques which may be used to estimate the parameters of market-share models, but the forecasting of brand sales volumes requires more than the knowledge of market shares. Because the sales volume of a given brand in a period is a product of the brand's share and (total) category sales volume for the period, one needs the forecast of category sales volumes.[34]

In this section we deal with the estimation of the parameters of category-volume models. Compared with the market-share estimation, the modeling for category sales volumes is a more straightforward application of econometric techniques. The illustrative data in Table 5.1 include the average daily sales volumes of margarine for this store. We will use these data to show some examples of category-volume models.

---

[33]See, for example, Finn, Jeremy D. [1974], *A General Model for Multivariate Analysis*, New York: Holt, Rinehart & Winston.

[34]Hereafter we will use *category volume* instead of *industry sales volume*, since the former fits better in the context of stores and market shares.

In this particular data set, brand price is the only marketing variable. We hypothesize that if the overall price level is low, the total volume will be high. We also hypothesize that if sales are extremely high in one week, the sales in the following weeks should be low because the store customers have not used up their stock. In order to represent those two hypotheses, we propose the following model.

$$Q_t = a + bQ_{t-1} + c \log \tilde{P}_t + u_t \qquad (5.31)$$

where:

Q_t = the category volume (in equivalent units) in period t

$\tilde{P}_t$ = the average price level in period t

u_t = an error term

a, b, c = parameters to be estimated.

We let the geometric mean of prices in a period be $\tilde{P}_t$. The following is the estimation result.

$$
\begin{array}{cccc}
Q_t & = & 508.8 & -0.4652 Q_{t-1} & -2.5116 \log \tilde{P}_t \\
    &   & (4.172) & (-1.681) & (-3.620) \\
    &   & \text{R-Square} & = 0.5764
\end{array}
$$

T-values are in the parentheses directly below the corresponding parameter estimates. The fit of the model is acceptable, judging from the R^2-value of 0.58 . The estimated parameters and their t-values bear out our initial guess that the average price level in the week and the sales volume in the preceding week are influential in determining the category volume.

There is another line of thought concerning the effect of price on category volumes that the prices of different brands have differential effects on category volumes. A brand's price reduction may increase its share, but may not affect category volumes, while another brand's price reduction may increase both its share and category volumes. To incorporate differential effects of brand price, we propose the following model.

$$Q_t = a + bQ_{t-1} + \sum_{i=1}^{m} c_i \log P_{it} + u_t \qquad (5.32)$$

where the c_i's are the differential price-effect parameters. The estimation results for this model are given below.

$$Q_t = 252.62 - 0.4947 Q_{t-1} - 0.1646 \log P_{1t} - 0.4799 \log P_{2t} - 0.06799 \log P_{3t}$$
$$(1.982)(-2.952) \qquad (-0.795) \qquad (-2.882) \qquad (-0.286)$$
$$- 0.1881 \log P_{4t} - 0.5646 \log P_{5t} - 0.2727 \log P_{6t} + 1.0631 \log P_{7t}$$
$$(-0.756) \qquad (-5.862) \qquad (-0.555) \qquad (2.218)$$

R-Square = 0.9581

The fit of the model is much improved. Brand 2 and 5 have significant effects on category volumes indicating that when those brands cut prices the customers to this store purchase more than their usual amounts, and that the following week's total volume suffers as a consequence. Note that the brand sales elasticity with respect to price, which measures the overall impact of brand i's price on its sales volume, is decomposed into two components:

$$e_{Q_i.P_i} = \text{Category-Volume Elasticity} + \text{Share Elasticity}.$$

For example, if we assume the differential-effects model, then

$$e_{Q_i.P_i} = c_i + \beta_{p_i}(1 - s_i)$$

where c_i is in model (5.32) and β_{p_i} is estimated by one of the models (5.14 – 5.17).

With the R^2-value of 0.96, equation (5.32) should give reasonably good estimates of category volumes. The positive sign of the estimated parameter for $\log P_{7t}$ poses a theoretical problem, but it probably reflects the effects of some marketing activities within the store which are not included in the model. As a forecasting model for category volume, this model should be used as it is.

Model (5.32) is in the form of a distributed-lag models. It is known that the ordinary-least squares procedure applied to (5.32) yields biased estimates of the model parameters. If there are an adequate number of observations, it is recommended to use time-series analysis procedures for parameter estimation. Weekly data produce a sufficient number of observations in two years for a time-series analysis model. If the number of observations is less than 50, however, it is perhaps best to use the OLS procedure.

These simplest category-volume models are linear in the effects of previous category volume while being linear in the logs of prices. As we incorporate marketing variables other than price, it is advisable to postulate more general, fully interactive models such as:

$$Q_t = \exp(a + u_t)Q_{t-1}^b \prod_{j=1}^m P_j^{c_j} \prod_{k=2}^K \exp(b_{kj}X_{kjt}) \ . \tag{5.33}$$

The *reduced form* of such a model may be characterized as being a log-log model in the effects of price and previous category volume, and log-linear in the other marketing variables (such as newspaper features, in-store displays and other marketing instruments which may be binary variables). This general form will be used with the coffee-market example developed in section 5.12.

5.10   Estimation of Share-Elasticities

In Chapter 6 we deal with the market-structure analysis based on the factor analysis of market-share elasticities. The reader may recall that there are two types of market-share elasticities, namely, point- and arc-share elasticities. Since the elasticities obtainable in practice are arc elasticities, one may think of factor-analyzing arc elasticities to investigate the structure of the market and competition. Unfortunately, this is not at all feasible.

Recall the definition of an arc elasticity for variable X_k.

$$e_{s_i} = \frac{\Delta s_i}{\Delta X_{ki}} \frac{x_{ki}}{s_i}$$

Δs_i in the above definition is not the total change in s_i, but the change corresponding to the change in X_{ki}, ΔX_{ki}. We have no means of separating the effects of various marketing variables on market shares, unless, of course, we apply some models to observed market shares. Indeed it is the main purpose of the models discussed in this book to identify the effects of marketing variables. Thus, in order to estimate share-elasticities specific to a marketing variable, we propose first to estimate the parameters of a market-share model from a data set (i.e., brand shares and marketing variables), and then use theoretical expressions for point elasticities (see Chapter 3) for the relevant model to obtain elasticities estimates.

A numerical example may clarify this procedure. When we applied the raw-score attraction model to the margarine data in Table 5.1, we have obtained a price-parameter estimate of -8.337. If a brand's share is 0.2, then the point-elasticity estimate is given by $-8.337 \times (1 - 0.2) = -6.67$. Although we are unable to estimate arc elasticities in this manner, point-elasticity estimates will serve as approximations for arc elasticities.

5.11 Problems with Zero Market Shares

Since the dependent variable in log-linear regression is the logarithm of either market shares or the numbers of units sold, it is impossible to compute the value of the dependent variable if observed market shares or numbers of units are zero. In any data collection procedure one may observe a zero market share or number of units sold for some brand-period combination. There are two procedures for handling those data sets which contain zero market shares.

The first is to assign some arbitrarily small values (0.001, say) to zero market shares. But this procedure amounts to assigning a large negative value to log 0, and tends to bias the estimated parameter values. (The smaller the assigned value, the greater the absolute values of estimated parameters.)

The second procedure is to delete from the data set those brand-period combinations for which observed market-shares are zero.[35] Though this procedure may seem arbitrary at first glance, it has some logic of its own. First, if a brand were not bought in a certain period, that would be sufficient basis to infer that the brand was not in the consumers' choice set. Second, since one is usually more interested in estimating accurately the behavior of those brands which command large shares, it may be argued that one need not bother with those brands which often take zero market shares. Third, that zero market shares are not usable for estimation is not a problem limited to log-linear regression procedures. Consider, for example, the case in which the share estimate for brand i in period t is based on the number of consumers who purchased that brand, n_{it} ($i = 1, 2, \ldots, m$). Assuming that numbers $\{n_{1t}, n_{2t}, \ldots, n_{mt}\}$ are generated by a multinomial process (see section 5.1.1 on maximum-likelihood estimation), one may wish to use a maximum-likelihood procedure for estimating parameters of attraction models. Note, however, that those observations for which $n_{it} = 0$ do not contribute at all to the likelihood function (5.2). In a sense, the maximum-likelihood procedure ignores all brand-period combinations for which $n_{it} = 0$.

There are two drawbacks to the deletion of zero market shares. One is the reduction of the degree of freedom due to the deletion. But this drawback may be compensated by a proper research design in that, if the number of brands per period is reduced by the deletion, the num-

[35]Young, Kan H. & Linds Y. Young [1975], "Estimation of Regressions Involving Logarithmic Transformations of Zero Values in the Dependent Variables," *The American Statistician*, 29 (August), 118–20.

ber of periods (or areas) may be increased to obtain an adequate degree of freedom. The second drawback is that the estimated parameters are somewhat biased (in the direction of smaller absolute values). But, we believe that the biases which are introduced by this procedure are far less than those which are introduced by replacing zero shares by an arbitrarily small constant. It may be added that we found in our simulation studies that the true parameter values lie between those estimated after deleting zero-share observations and those estimated after replacing zero shares by an arbitrary constant. This finding leads us to consider another somewhat arbitrary, and so far untested, procedure, which adds a small constant to all brand-period combinations, disregarding if they are zero share or not. In other words, we suggest that the dependent variable, $\log s_{it}$, is to be replaced by $\log(s_{it} + c)$, where s_{it} is the share of brand i in period t and c is the arbitrary constant. We found that, if one selects the value of c properly, the estimated parameters are free of biases which other two procedures tend to create. The appropriate value of c seems to vary from one data set to the next. So far we have been unable to find a logic to determining the correct value of c that is applicable to a particular data set. Here we only indicate that a fruitful course of research may lie in the direction of this estimation procedure.

Zero market shares create particularly difficult problems for the multivariate regression in (5.30). The missing market share for one brand may cause the observation to be deleted from all the regressions. In cases such as this, when it is particularly important to have all the dependent measures present, the EM algorithm discussed by Malhotra[36] could be useful.

When imputing values which are missing in the data one should always ask why are the data missing? The imputation literature[37] treats data missing-at-random (MAR), missing-completely-at-random (MCAR), and missing-by-unknown-mechanisms (MBUM), but rarely do these conditions fit the zero market shares in POS data. If a brand simply is not distributed in one or more of the retail outlets, neither MAR, MCAR, nor MBUM assumptions are appropriate. Even if the brand is distributed, it is not always possible to tell if the zero market share results from an out-of-stock condition or simply from no sales. But, in either case,

---

[36] Malhotra, Naresh [1987], "Analyzing Market Research Data with Incomplete Information on the Dependent Variable," *Journal of Marketing Research*, XXIV (February), 74–84.

[37] For an excellent recent treatment see Little, Roderick J. A. & Donald B. Rubin [1987], *Statistical Analysis with Missing Data*. New York: John Wiley & Sons, Inc.

these conditions are neither random or by unknown mechanisms. One clue comes from the other data associated with a brand. If price and promotional variables are present for the zero-market-share brand, one can assume the brand is distributed, but nothing more. The problem concerns only imputing the value of the dependent measure. If price and promotional measures are also missing, the imputation problem is more severe. Widely differing patterns of distribution would greatly complicate the multivariate regression in (5.30). In such cases it is probably simpler to delete the missing observations in the market-share model, and use the method discussed in section 5.12 for estimating cross effects.

While simply deleting the observation is an acceptable solution to the problem of differing patterns of distribution in market-share models, it is not an acceptable approach to this problem in category-volume models. Zero market share isn't the issue, since the dependent measure is the (log of) total sales volume. But missing values for prices are particularly worrisome, since we cannot take the log of a missing value. In the market-share model for POS data, there is an observation for each brand in each store in each week. For the corresponding category-volume model there is just an observation for each store in each week. The measures in an observation reflect the influence of each brand's prices and promotional activity on total volume. If we were to delete the whole observation whenever a single brand was not in distribution, widely differing distribution patterns over stores could result in the deletion of all observations. We wish to minimize the influence that the missing value has on the parameter corresponding to that measure, but allow the other measures in the observation to have their normal influence in parameter estimation.

While an developing an algorithm to minimize the influence of missing prices is a worthwhile topic for future research, there is a simple approach for achieving a reasonable result in the interim. We merely need to create *brand-absence* dummy variables, which would take a value of one when then brand is absent and a value of one when present. If we then replace the missing (log) price with a zero, the parameter of the brand-absence measure show the penalty uniquely associated with not distributing the brand. This approach will be illustrated in the next section.

5.12   The Coffee-Market Example

To illustrate the use of these estimation techniques on POS data, consider the ground, caffeinated coffee market. Data, provided by Information Resources, Inc., from BehaviorScan stores in two cities, report price, newspaper feature, in-store display and store-coupon activity for all brands. The small-volume, premium brands were aggregated into an "All Other Branded" (AOB) category, and the small "Private Label" (PL) brands were aggregated into an "All Other Private Label" (AOPL) category. Consequently, twelve brands of coffee were analyzed: Folgers, Regular Maxwell House, Maxwell House Master Blend, Hills Bros., Chock Full O'Nuts, Yuban, Chase & Sanborne, AOB, PL 1, PL 2, PL 3, and AOPL. For eighteen months, each week's data for a brand were aggregated over package weights, and over stores-within-grocery chains in the two cities. These are aggregate data from stores, not discrete-choice data from BehaviorScan consumer panels. Price for each brand was aggregated into average price per pound, net of coupons redeemed. Feature, display and coupon were represented as percent of volume sold on promotions of each type to allow for aggregation over stores with slightly differing promotional environments. The data were divided into a year for calibration of the market-share model, and six months for cross-validation. The average price and market share of each brand appear in Table 5.12.

5.12.1   The Market-Share Model

With four marketing instruments per brand the full cross-effects model would have 587 parameters ($4 \times 12 \times 12 + 11$). To avoid estimating so many parameters an asymmetric market-share model was estimated by procedures similar to those discussed in Carpenter, Cooper, Hanssens, and Midgley [1988].[38] The distinctiveness of marketing efforts were incorporated by using exp(z-scores) for each marketing instrument. A differential-effects model was estimated with a unique parameter for each brand's price, feature, display, and store coupons, and a brand-specific intercept for the qualitative features of each brand using OLS proce-

---

[38]Carpenter et al. suggest forming dynamically weighted, attraction components to deal with the lagged effects of marketing instruments. Chapter 3 discusses alternative methods for specifying the dynamic components, but neither of these approaches was used in this illustration. Store-week data are sufficiently disaggregate that they rarely have the complex time-series properties dealt with in Carpenter et al., so that no dynamically weighted, attraction components were needed.

Table 5.12: Coffee Data — Average Prices and Market Shares

Brand	Average Price/lb.	Average Share
Folgers	$2.33	28.5
Maxwell House	$2.22	24.2
Master Blend	$2.72	7.8
Hills Bros.	$2.13	4.3
Chock Full O Nuts	$2.02	15.3
Yuban	$3.11	0.2
Chase & Sanborne	$2.34	0.3
All Other Branded	$2.64	2.4
Private Label 1	$1.99	3.9
Private Label 2	$1.95	3.6
Private Label 3	$1.93	3.7
All Other Private Labels	$1.95	5.7

dures. The brand-specific intercept which was closest to zero (PL 2) was set to zero to avoid singularity. The residuals from this differential-effects model were cross-correlated brand by brand with the transformed contemporaneous explanatory variables for all other brands. The cross-competitive effects which were significant in the residual analysis were entered into the model.[39]

This specification approach leads to a generalized attraction model:

$$\mathcal{A}_{it} = \exp(\alpha_i + \epsilon_{1i}) \prod_{k=1}^{K} [\exp(z_{kit})]^{\beta_{ki}} \prod_{(k^*j^*)\epsilon C_i} [\exp(z_{k^*j^*t})]^{\beta_{k^*ij^*}}$$

where α_i is brand i's constant component of attraction, ϵ_{1i} is specification error, β_{ki} is brand i's market-response parameter on the kth marketing–mix element, $\exp(z_{kit})$ is brand i's attraction component for the kth marketing-mix element (standardized over brands within a store-week), C_i is the set of cross-competitive effects on brand i, $\exp(z_{k^*j^*t})$ is the standardized attraction component of the cross-competitive influence of brand j^*'s marketing-mix element k^* on brand i, $(k^*j^*)\epsilon C_i$, and $\beta_{k^*ij^*}$ is the cross-effect parameter for the influence of brand j^*'s attraction component k^* on brand i's market share.

---

[39]The criteria for inclusion of a cross effect were that it had to be based on more than 52 observations and the correlation had to be significant beyond the .05 level.

For the final model the residuals from the OLS estimation were used to estimate the error variances for each brand. The weights for a WLS regression were formed as

$$w_i = \frac{1}{(1 - \frac{1}{m})\hat{\sigma}_i} \ .$$

These weights compensate for heteroscedasticity of error variances over brands, but do not treat the possibility of nonzero error covariances. The results for the calibration period of 52 weeks appear in Table 5.13.

The resulting model has an R^2 of .93 with 140 parameters estimated and 2,051 residual degrees of freedom ($F_{2051}^{140} = 181$). Since the model is estimated without an intercept, R^2 is redefined as is noted on the regression output. In models estimated without an intercept R^2 is like the congruence coefficient discussed in section 5.6. If the mean of the dependent measure is equal to zero, the lack of an intercept doesn't matter, and R^2 has the normal interpretation as the proportion of linearly accountable variation in the reduced form of the dependent measure. The dependent measure in the OLS-estimation phase does have a mean of zero (and an R^2 of .92) but rescaling by the WLS weights affects the mean of the dependent measure. So while it is obvious that the cross-effects model fits extremely well, it is not strictly proper to interpret .93 as the proportion of explained variation.[40]

We cross validate these models by combining the parameter values in Table 5.13 with fresh data to form a single composite prediction variable, and then correlate the predicted dependent measure with the actual dependent measure for the new observations; 26 weeks of fresh data were used in cross validation. The squared cross-validity correlation is .85 using the parameters in Table 5.13. This is an excellent result for a relationship that uses just one composite variable to predict over 1,000 observations ($F_{1012}^1 = 5808$). The OLS differential-effects model has a squared cross-validity correlation of .79, indicating that the cross effects do enhance the model in a stable manner.

---

[40]Because reweighting changes the interpretation of R^2, to assess the incremental contribution of the cross effects, it is simpler to compare the OLS differential-effects model to the OLS cross-effects model. In this case the OLS differential-effects model has an R^2 of .82, so that the cross effects represent a substantial improvement over the good-fitting differential-effects model.

Table 5.13: WLS Regression Results for Cross-Effects Model (MCI)

Coffee Data Base For Pittsfield And Marion Markets
Ground-Caffeinated Coffee Brands Only
MCI WLS Regression

Model: Coffee
Dep Variable: LCSHARE Log-Centered Share

Analysis Of Variance

Source	DF	Sum of Squares	Mean Square	F Value	Prob>F
Model	140	11556.72	82.55	181.54	0.01
Error	2051	932.62	0.45		
U Total	2191	12489.34			

Root MSE	0.67	R-Square	0.93	
Dep Mean	0.18	Adj R-Sq	0.92	
C.V.	383.34			

Note: No intercept term is used. R-Square is redefined.

Parameter Estimates

Variable	DF	Parm Est	Std Err	T For H_0: Parm=0	Prob> $|T|$
Folg Intercept	1	2.54	0.17	15.07	0.01
Folg Price Z-Score	1	−0.96	0.07	−13.07	0.01
Folg Featv Z-Score	1	0.06	0.04	1.52	0.13
Folg Dispv Z-Score	1	0.16	0.05	3.56	0.01
Folg Coupv Z-Score	1	−0.13	0.05	−2.53	0.01
RMH Intercept	1	1.92	0.12	15.50	0.01
RMH Price Z-Score	1	−0.58	0.06	−10.02	0.01
RMH Featv Z-Score	1	0.00	0.03	0.12	0.91
RMH Dispv Z-Score	1	0.06	0.03	1.74	0.08
RMH Coupv Z-Score	1	0.11	0.04	2.92	0.01
MHMB Intercept	1	1.79	0.17	10.27	0.01
MHMB Price Z-Score	1	−0.24	0.07	−3.21	0.01
MHMB Featv Z-Score	1	0.19	0.04	5.33	0.01
MHMB Dispv Z-Score	1	0.22	0.05	4.79	0.01
MHMB Coupv Z-Score	1	−0.08	0.06	−1.43	0.15
HlBr Intercept	1	−0.50	0.11	−4.49	0.01
HlBr Price Z-Score	1	0.04	0.07	0.57	0.57
HlBr Featv Z-Score	1	0.48	0.05	8.96	0.01
HlBr Dispv Z-Score	1	0.23	0.05	4.57	0.01
HlBr Coupv Z-Score	1	1.52	0.19	7.97	0.01
CFON Intercept	1	0.61	0.11	5.37	0.01
CFON Price Z-Score	1	−1.33	0.09	−14.50	0.01
CFON Featv Z-Score	1	0.12	0.05	2.27	0.02
CFON Dispv Z-Score	1	−0.04	0.04	−0.94	0.35
CFON Coupv Z-Score	1	−0.22	0.07	−3.35	0.01
Yub Intercept	1	−0.15	0.21	−0.71	0.48
Yub Price Z-Score	1	−0.77	0.09	−8.70	0.01
Yub Featv Z-Score	1	0.21	0.21	0.98	0.33
Yub Dispv Z-Score	1	0.70	0.25	2.82	0.01
Yub Coupv Z-Score	1	0.15	0.22	0.70	0.49
C&S Intercept	1	−0.42	0.17	−2.48	0.01
C&S Price Z-Score	1	−0.27	0.14	−2.01	0.05
C&S Featv Z-Score	1	−0.07	0.31	−0.22	0.83
C&S Dispv Z-Score	1	1.19	0.33	3.65	0.01
C&S Coupv Z-Score	1	0.78	0.24	3.21	0.01

Parameter Estimates, Continued				
		Parm	Std	T For H_0:	Prob>
Variable	DF	Est	Err	Parm=0	$|T|$
AOB Intercept	1	0.50	0.12	4.00	0.01
AOB Price Z-Score	1	−0.49	0.06	−8.28	0.01
AOB Featv Z-Score	1	−0.24	0.06	−3.75	0.01
AOB Dispv Z-Score	1	0.13	0.04	2.87	0.01
AOB Coupv Z-Score	1	0.16	0.09	1.84	0.07
PL1 Intercept	1	0.28	0.16	1.75	0.08
PL1 Price Z-Score	1	−1.07	0.09	−11.64	0.01
PL1 Featv Z-Score	1	−0.06	0.04	−1.47	0.14
PL1 Dispv Z-Score	1	−0.06	0.04	−1.62	0.10
PL1 Coupv Z-Score	1	0.03	0.03	0.79	0.43
PL2 Price Z-Score	1	−1.11	0.17	−6.68	0.01
PL2 Featv Z-Score	1	0.06	0.14	0.43	0.67
PL2 Dispv Z-Score	1	0.12	0.13	0.91	0.36
PL2 Coupv Z-Score	1	0.41	0.42	0.97	0.33
PL3 Intercept	1	−0.30	0.22	−1.36	0.17
PL3 Price Z-Score	1	−1.00	0.15	−6.53	0.01
PL3 Featv Z-Score	1	0.02	0.06	0.28	0.78
PL3 Dispv Z-Score	1	0.35	0.41	0.84	0.40
PL3 Coupv Z-Score	1	0.05	0.05	0.95	0.34
AOPL Intercept	1	0.25	0.15	1.68	0.09
AOPL Price Z-Score	1	−0.21	0.06	−3.47	0.01
AOPL Featv Z-Score	1	0.07	0.03	2.62	0.01
AOPL Dispv Z-Score	1	−0.04	0.05	−0.68	0.50
AOPL Coupv Z-Score	1	0.02	0.04	0.43	0.67
Crs Of RMH Price Effect On Folg	1	−0.27	0.07	−3.96	0.01
Crs Of MHMB Price Effect On Folg	1	−0.10	0.08	−1.29	0.20
Crs Of HlBr Price Effect On Folg	1	0.06	0.06	0.98	0.33
Crs Of CFON Price Effect On Folg	1	0.05	0.06	0.92	0.36
Crs Of Yub Price Effect On Folg	1	−0.32	0.06	−5.85	0.01
Crs Of AOB Price Effect On Folg	1	−0.31	0.06	−5.20	0.01
Crs Of RMH Featv Effect On Folg	1	−0.13	0.03	−3.75	0.01
Crs Of Yub Featv Effect On Folg	1	−0.04	0.18	−0.24	0.81
Crs Of RMH Dispv Effect On Folg	1	−0.09	0.04	−2.40	0.02
Crs Of MHMB Dispv Effect On Folg	1	0.12	0.05	2.72	0.01
Crs Of Yub Dispv Effect On Folg	1	0.01	0.21	0.04	0.97
Crs Of AOB Dispv Effect On Folg	1	0.02	0.04	0.44	0.66
Crs Of RMH Coupv Effect On Folg	1	0.03	0.04	0.68	0.50
Crs Of MHMB Coupv Effect On Folg	1	0.03	0.05	0.47	0.64
Crs Of HlBR Coupv Effect On Folg	1	1.04	0.17	6.06	0.01
Crs Of Yub Coupv Effect On Folg	1	0.30	0.18	1.66	0.10
Crs Of AOPL Coupv Effect On Folg	1	−0.06	0.04	−1.70	0.09
Crs Of Folg Price Effect On RMH	1	−0.10	0.06	−1.54	0.12
Crs Of Yub Price Effect On RMH	1	−0.05	0.04	−1.31	0.19
Crs Of AOB Price Effect On RMH	1	−0.22	0.04	−4.83	0.01
Crs Of AOPL Price Effect On RMH	1	0.17	0.04	4.63	0.01
Crs Of Folg Featv Effect On RMH	1	−0.00	0.03	−0.09	0.93
Crs Of Yub Featv Effect On RMH	1	0.19	0.17	1.12	0.26
Crs Of AOB Featv Effect On RMH	1	−0.12	0.05	−2.24	0.03
Crs Of Folg Dispv Effect On RMH	1	−0.04	0.04	−0.92	0.36
Crs Of HlBr Dispv Effect On RMH	1	−0.08	0.03	−2.37	0.02
Crs Of Yub Dispv Effect On RMH	1	−0.49	0.20	−2.46	0.01
Crs Of HlBr Coupv Effect On RMH	1	0.31	0.15	2.09	0.04
Crs Of CFON Coupv Effect On RMH	1	−0.05	0.05	−0.87	0.39

Parameter Estimates, Continued				
Variable	DF	Parm Est	Std Err	T For H_0: Parm=0	Prob> |T|
Crs Of Yub Coupv Effect On RMH	1	0.54	0.18	3.01	0.01
Crs Of AOB Coupv Effect On RMH	1	0.20	0.07	2.76	0.01
Crs Of Yub Price Effect On MHMB	1	−0.10	0.05	−2.10	0.04
Crs Of AOB Price Effect On MHMB	1	−0.29	0.06	−4.92	0.01
Crs Of AOPL Price Effect On MHMB	1	0.38	0.04	9.73	0.01
Crs Of RMH Featv Effect On MHMB	1	−0.04	0.03	−1.27	0.21
Crs Of Yub Featv Effect On MHMB	1	0.52	0.17	3.02	0.01
Crs Of AOB Featv Effect On MHMB	1	−0.12	0.06	−2.19	0.03
Crs Of HlBr Dispv Effect On MHMB	1	−0.09	0.03	−2.69	0.01
Crs Of Yub Dispv Effect On MHMB	1	−0.43	0.22	−2.01	0.04
Crs Of AOPL Dispv Effect On MHMB	1	−0.06	0.05	−1.01	0.31
Crs Of RMH Coupv Effect On MHMB	1	0.08	0.04	2.19	0.03
Crs Of HlBr Coupv Effect On MHMB	1	0.50	0.16	3.04	0.01
Crs Of Yub Coupv Effect On MHMB	1	0.42	0.16	2.56	0.01
Crs Of AOB Coupv Effect On MHMB	1	0.14	0.07	1.89	0.06
Crs Of AOPL Coupv Effect On MHMB	1	−0.00	0.04	−0.14	0.89
Crs Of MHMB Price Effect On HlBr	1	0.19	0.07	2.71	0.01
Crs Of AOB Price Effect On HlBr	1	0.29	0.05	5.82	0.01
Crs Of MHMB Featv Effect On HlBr	1	−0.05	0.07	−0.78	0.44
Crs Of MHMB Dispv Effect On HlBr	1	−0.00	0.08	−0.02	0.99
Crs Of CFON Dispv Effect On HlBr	1	0.03	0.04	0.78	0.43
Crs Of AOB Dispv Effect On HlBr	1	−0.04	0.05	−0.76	0.44
Crs Of RMH Price Effect On CFON	1	0.31	0.08	3.70	0.01
Crs Of MHMB Price Effect On CFON	1	−0.69	0.06	−10.81	0.01
Crs Of HlBr Price Effect On CFON	1	−0.17	0.07	−2.48	0.01
Crs Of Folg Featv Effect On CFON	1	0.10	0.06	1.72	0.09
Crs Of AOB Featv Effect On CFON	1	0.01	0.06	0.11	0.91
Crs Of AOB Dispv Effect On CFON	B	−0.03	0.05	−0.70	0.49
Crs Of Folg Coupv Effect On CFON	0	−0.07	0.08	−0.90	0.37
Crs Of MHMB Coupv Effect On CFON	1	−0.63	0.14	−4.39	0.01
Crs Of HlBr Coupv Effect On CFON	1	0.01	0.19	0.05	0.96
Crs Of Folg Price Effect On Yub	1	0.10	0.06	1.58	0.12
Crs Of Folg Dispv Effect On Yub	1	−0.12	0.08	−1.48	0.14
Crs Of MHMB Dispv Effect On Yub	1	0.49	0.10	4.92	0.01
Crs Of Folg Coupv Effect On Yub	1	−0.07	0.06	−1.27	0.21
Crs Of Folg Price Effect On AOB	1	0.52	0.10	5.43	0.01
Crs Of RMH Price Effect On AOB	1	0.94	0.09	10.61	0.01
Crs Of HlBr Price Effect On AOB	1	0.35	0.08	4.36	0.01
Crs Of CFON Price Effect On AOB	1	−0.00	0.08	−0.03	0.98
Crs Of Yub Price Effect On AOB	1	0.33	0.05	6.06	0.01
Crs Of AOPL Price Effect On AOB	1	0.91	0.07	13.87	0.01
Crs Of Folg Featv Effect On AOB	1	0.01	0.04	0.25	0.80
Crs Of Yub Featv Effect On AOB	1	0.09	0.05	1.74	0.08
Crs Of Folg Dispv Effect On AOB	1	−0.14	0.05	−2.88	0.01
Crs Of Yub Dispv Effect On AOB	1	−0.18	0.06	−2.97	0.01
Crs Of RMH Coupv Effect On AOB	1	0.15	0.04	3.32	0.01
Crs Of CFON Coupv Effect On AOB	1	−0.19	0.07	−2.91	0.01
Crs Of Yub Coupv Effect On AOB	1	0.06	0.13	0.46	0.65
Crs Of Folg Price Effect On AOPL	1	−0.21	0.09	−2.30	0.02
Crs Of RMH Price Effect On AOPL	1	−0.48	0.07	−6.66	0.01
Crs Of MHMB Price Effect On AOPL	1	0.09	0.03	2.66	0.01
Crs Of AOB Price Effect On AOPL	1	−0.08	0.06	−1.33	0.18

These results differ in minor fashion from those previously summarized by Cooper.[41] There are two sources of difference. First, the article
is based on the OLS results. Second, the brand-specific effects estimated
in that article are based on z-scores, rather than the more traditional
brand-specific intercepts adopted in this book. Only the parameter values for the brand-specific effect are substantially affected by the differences between the two approaches. A brand-by-brand summary follows.

Folgers has the largest brand-specific intercept indicating a relatively
high baseline level of attraction. If all brands were at the market average
for prices and all other marketing instruments, so that only the differences in brand intercepts were reflected in the market share, Folgers
would be predicted to capture 36% of the market. This is what we will
call a *baseline market share*.[42] Folgers has a very strong and significant
price parameter. Being priced above the market average will sharply
reduce its baseline market share, while price reductions will sharply increase share. There is a positive but insignificant feature effect. There is
a strong positive effect for in-store displays. The effect of store coupons
is negative and statistically extreme. While we would normally expect
store-coupon promotions to have a positive effect, we should note two
things. First, the average number of pounds-per-week of Folgers sold on
store coupons is 1,175 compare to 2,018 pounds sold on in-store displays
and 1,397 pounds sold per week of newspaper features. So there is some
indication in these data that this might not be a spurious coefficient.
Second, the price measure is net of coupons redeemed. While this reflects the influence of manufacturers coupons as well as store coupons,
it does mean that some of the benefits of store coupons are folded into
the price effect. There are four significant cross-price effects impacting
Folgers. Regular Maxwell House, Maxwell House Master Blend, Yuban,
and the AOB category all have significantly less price impact on Folgers
than reflected in the differential-effects model. Folgers has significantly
more of a price effect on the AOB category and significantly less price

[41]Cooper, Lee G. [1988], "Competitive Maps: The Structure Underlying Asymmetric Cross Elasticities," *Management Science*, 34, 6 (June), 707-23.

[42]Baseline shares can differ substantially from the average shares reported in Table 5.12. Average shares are a straightforward statistical concept, but baseline shares
reflect something of a brand's fundamental franchise, all other things being equal. But
all other things are rarely equal. Market power can come from the way a brand uses
its marketing instruments (i.e., its promotion policy) as well as from its fundamental
franchise. Baseline share figures are reported for each of the brands. These can be
usefully compared to the average-share figures, but should not be thought of as a
prediction of long-run market share.

impact on the AOPL brands than would otherwise be expected. For features, only the increased competitive impact of Regular Maxwell House is significant. For displays, Regular Maxwell House has more of an effect, while Master Blend has less of an effect than otherwise expected. Folgers' displays exert more pressure on the AOB category than otherwise expected. Hills Bros. coupons put significantly less pressure on Folgers than expected from differential effects alone.

Regular Maxwell House also has a strong, positive brand-specific intercept, which translates into a baseline market share of 19%. It has significant price and coupon effects. Regular Maxwell House has significant competitive price effects on Chock Full O'Nuts and the AOB category, but it exerts significantly less competitive pressure on Folgers and AOPL with its price. AOPL has a significant competitive price effect, while the AOB category exerts significantly less price pressure. RMH features attack Folgers, and features for the AOB category exert significant pressure on RMH. RMH displays exert significant competitive pressure on Folgers, while Hills Bros. and Yuban attack RMH with their displays. RMH coupons have less competitive effect on Master Blend and the AOB category than would otherwise be expected, and coupons for Hill Bros., Yuban and the AOB category have significantly less impact on RMH in return.

Maxwell House Master Blend has a significant intercept which translates into a baseline share of 17%. Price, feature, and display effects are significant in the expected directions. The coupon effect is insignificant and wrong signed. Master Blend receives more price pressure from AOPL, but less from Yuban and the AOB category than would otherwise be expected. In return Master Blend exerts more price pressure on Hills Bros. and AOPL, and less pressure on CFON and Folgers than the differential-effects models could reflect. AOB features are more competitive and Yuban features are less competitive due to their significant cross effects on Master Blend. Master Blend displays are less competitive with both Folgers and Yuban than otherwise expected, while displays for Hills Bros. and Yuban exert extra pressure on Master Blend. Store coupons for Regular Maxwell House, Hills Bros. and Yuban all have less effect than otherwise expected. Store coupons for Master Blend do exert pressure on Chock Full O'Nuts.

Hills Bros.' intercept translates into a baseline share of 2%. It shows strong effects for features, displays, and coupons. The self-price effect is not significant, but it does have a significant competitive price effect on the AOB category. It has less price effect on CFON than otherwise expected. Master Blend and the AOB category exert stable competitive price effects on Hills Bros. There are no feature cross effects, but Hill Bros. has significant competitive display effects on Regular Maxwell House and Maxwell House Master Blend (as already noted).

Chock Full O'Nuts has a small baseline share (5%), but strong price and feature effects. Its use of these instruments helps it maintain the third largest average market share (15%). The Regular Maxwell House has a strong, competitive price effect on Chock Full O'Nuts. But both Master Blend and Hills Bros. exert significantly less price pressure on CFON. There are no significant feature or display cross effects, but CFON's store coupons exert extra pressure on the AOB category and Master Blend's store coupons exert extra pressure on CFON.

Yuban has a baseline share of 2%, but its high price results in a much smaller average share. It has significant price and display effects. Yuban exerts less price pressure on Folgers and Master Blend, but more pressure on the AOB category than otherwise expected. Features for Yuban have less impact on Master Blend than reflected in simpler models. Yuban displays have significant competitive effect on both Maxwell House brands and the AOB category, while Master Blends displays are less competitive in return. The display effect of both Maxwell House brands is reversed in the only two coupon effects concerning Yuban. This is such a small brand in these markets that it probably should have been folded into the AOB category. Its stronger position on the West Coast may have led the authors astray.

Chase & Sanborne also has a baseline share of 2%. Its average share is even less, due to its high price and the infrequency of promotions. Its price, display, and coupon effects are statistically significant. There are no cross effects involving Chase & Sanborne.

The premium brands in the AOB category collectively have a baseline share of 5%. There are strong price and display effects, but the feature effect is statistically extreme in the expected direction. With aggregates of brands such as AOB, it may be hard to get a clear signals from all the parameters. AOB exerts additional competitive price pressure on Hills Bros., but seems to complement Folgers and both Maxwell House brands. The AOB category receives extra price pressure from Folgers, Regular Maxwell House, Hills Bros., Yuban, and AOPL. Features for the AOB category have an extra competitive effect on both Maxwell House brands. Store coupons for AOB and Regular Maxwell House have less effect on each other than otherwise expected, but store coupons for CFON do hurt the AOB category.

The private-label brands (PL 1, PL 2, PL 3 and AOPL) collectively have a baseline share of 13%. All four have significant price effects, and AOPL has a significant feature effect. AOPL exerts price pressure on both Maxwell House brands and the AOB category. While Master Blend returns the press, both Folgers and Regular Maxwell House are less price competitive than otherwise expected. There are no cross effects for features, displays, or store coupons for the private label brands.[43]

That price is a major instrument in this market is reflected in having 11 of 12 self-price effects significant. Four self-feature effects, six self-display effects, three self-coupon effects, and seven brand-specific intercepts were significant.

Residual analysis seems to be a practical means for identifying cross effects. The criterion identified 29 cross-price effects, of which 22 were statistically significant in the final model. There were 12 cross-feature effects, 4 of which were significant in the final model; 18 display effects were identified and half of these were significant in the final model. Of the 20 cross-coupon effects identified in the residuals from the differential-effects model, 10 were significant in the final model.

Reading through a regression output like this is a tedious but useful step in developing an initial understanding of market and competitive structure. But two more elements are needed before responsible brand planning can take place. First, parameters have to be converted to elasticities before an overall picture of the structure can be achieved (see Chapter 6). And second, a category-volume model must be calibrated before a market simulator can be developed. This is the topic of the next section.

5.12.2 The Category-Volume Model

A category-volume model of the style in equation (5.33) is reported in Table 5.14.[44] The private-label brands were aggregated into a single

---

[43]This was in part dictated by the criterion for a minimum of 53 observations before a significant residual correlation could qualify as a cross effect. This excluded all but the AOPL brand. In the category-volume model presented later in this chapter and in the brand planning exercise in Chapter 7 all the private label brands are aggregated together. If this had been done in the market-share model, more cross effects involving these brands might have been identified. If market-share analysis is done as an iterative process (as was discussed early in this book), this refinement could be undertaken.

[44]Only data from grocery chains 1 – 3 are used in this model so that the results would correspond to the competitive maps developed in Chapter 6 and the market simulator developed in Chapter 7.

Table 5.14: Regression Results for Category-Volume Model

Dep Variable: LTWVOL

		Analysis of Variance			
		Sum of	Mean		
Source	DF	Squares	Square	F Value	Prob>F
Model	31	42.88	1.38	38.29	0.01
Error	124	4.48	0.04		
C Total	155	47.36			
Root MSE		0.19	R-Square	0.91	
Dep Mean		7.55	Adj R-Sq	0.88	
C.V.		2.52			

		Parameter Estimates			
		Parm	Std	T for H$_0$	
Variable	DF	Est	Err	Parm=0	Prob> $|T|$
INTERCEP	1	6.73	0.84	7.98	0.01
BA4-HLBR	1	−0.13	0.35	−0.36	0.72
LPR1-Folg	1	−0.74	0.38	−1.96	0.05
LPR2-RMH	1	−0.73	0.40	−1.83	0.07
LPR3-MHMB	1	0.56	0.51	1.09	0.28
LPR4-HLBR	1	−0.13	0.40	−0.33	0.74
LPR5-CFON	1	−2.09	0.42	−4.97	0.01
LPR6-Yub	1	−0.32	0.73	−0.43	0.67
LPR7-CAS	1	0.77	1.02	0.75	0.45
LPR8-AOB	1	3.25	0.25	13.08	0.01
LPRPL-APL	1	−0.67	0.45	−1.50	0.14
D1-Folg	1	0.62	0.14	4.47	0.01
D2-RMH	1	0.50	0.10	4.79	0.01
D3-MHMB	1	0.29	0.12	2.53	0.01
D4-HLBR	1	0.13	0.06	1.98	0.05
D5-CFON	1	−0.05	0.09	−0.50	0.62
D8-AOB	1	0.38	0.12	3.13	0.01
DPL-APL	1	0.05	0.10	0.48	0.63
C1-Folg	1	−0.13	0.18	−0.70	0.49
C2-RMH	1	0.08	0.10	0.81	0.42
C3-MHMB	1	0.04	0.40	0.10	0.92
C4-HLBR	1	−2.06	0.95	−2.16	0.03
C5-CFON	1	0.30	0.23	1.28	0.20
C8-AOB	1	−0.68	0.59	−1.14	0.26
CPL-APL	1	0.17	0.12	1.44	0.15
F1-Folg	1	−0.08	0.12	−0.67	0.50
F2-RMH	1	0.01	0.09	0.07	0.95
F3-MHMB	1	0.03	0.08	0.39	0.70
F4-HLBR	1	−0.01	0.10	−0.14	0.89
F5-CFON	1	0.06	0.09	0.63	0.53
F8-AOB	1	0.56	0.12	4.68	0.01
FPL-APL	1	0.01	0.10	0.06	0.95

PL brand. A preliminary model showed that lagged volume had no significant effect ($t = -.96$), that there were no features, displays, or coupons in Chains 1 – 3 for either Yuban or Chase & Sanborne (so that these effects were deleted). Only Hills Bros. had a distribution pattern that required a brand-absence coefficient (BA4).

The overall fit of the model is quite good ($R^2 = .91$).[45] The strongest price influences on total volume come from discounts for Folgers, Maxwell House, and Chock Full O'Nuts. Discounts for these brands clearly expand the weekly volume. As prices for the aggregate AOB category increase, total volume increases — perhaps reflecting supply conditions or prestige effects for these premium brands. Displays for Folgers, both Maxwell House brands, Hills Bros., and AOB drive up category volume. Hills Bros. store coupons seem to contract total volume, reflecting the infrequent (and apparently counter-cyclical) store-couponing policy for this brand. The only significant feature effect is associated with the AOB category.

5.12.3   Combining Share and Category Volume

The choice of measures incorporated into both the market-share and category-volume models was dictated in large part by the need for a diagnostically useful market simulator. To the extent that the variables inside these markets can explain market behavior, we obtain a way of translating market history into elasticities. Chapter 6 develops methods for mapping the market and competitive structure implied by the elasticities — as well as methods for visualizing the sources driving changes in competitive structure. In Chapter 7 the market-share and category volume models are combined into a market simulator for evaluating the consequences of marketing actions for all brands.

5.13   Large-Scale Competitive Analysis

This section addresses two questions. The first concerns whether or not market-share analysis can be done on a large enough scale to be practical. Simply stated, the issue is *how large is too large?* The second issue centers on the fixation managers seem to have concerning the signs

---

[45]This would be boosted to .99 by the inclusion of chain-specific intercepts. But this category-volume model is destined for use in the market simulator to be used in Chapter 7. We feel that the generality of the planning frame used in that chapter is enhanced by predicting volume for a generic chain rather than chain by chain.

of parameters developed using best linear-unbiased estimation. Simply stated, the issue is *is BLUE always best?* Both of these topics will be discussed using experience arising from the implementation of market-share models on optical-scanner (POS) records of weekly store sales from Nielsen Micro-Scantrack databases and IRI store-level databases.

There are 15 steps which have been integrated into a SAS$^{(R)}$ macro program to perform the analytical tasks in estimating asymmetric market-share models.

1. Form the flat file containing variables [Sales plus Marketing Instruments] and observations [Brands × Stores × Weeks].

2. Choose the model form (MCI or MNL) and the transformations of variables (zeta-scores, exp(z-scores), or raw scores).

3. Form the differential-effects file containing the expanded set of variables [Sales + (Instruments + 1) × Brands] for the same observations.

4. Form the differential-effects covariance matrix and store.

5. Estimate the differential-effects model.

6. Find the brand intercept nearest zero and delete.

7. Re-estimate the differential-effects model.

8. Compute the residuals and sort by brand.

9. Cross correlate each brand's residuals with the marketing instruments of every competitor.

10. Tally the significant cross correlations.

11. Form the differential cross-effect variables.

12. Compute and store complete covariances (differential effects and cross-competitive effects).

13. Simultaneously re-estimate the parameters for all the effects in the calibration data.

14. Estimate WLS or GLS weights and re-estimate parameters.

15. Cross validate on fresh data.

5.13.1 How Large Is Too Large?

The size implications of two applications are summarized in Table 5.15. The two applications reported there involve data from IRI and A.C. Nielsen. The IRI data are those just summarized for the ground, caffeinated coffee market. The Micro-Scantrack data involve a mature category of a frequently purchased, branded good. There were around 30 brands which were represented at the brand-size level — leading to 66 competitors in the model. The IRI data tracked four marketing instruments: prices, newspaper features, store coupons, and in-store displays. These data predate the size grading of newspaper features now standard with IRI data. The Nielsen data tracked five marketing instruments: prices, major ads, line ads, coupon

ads, and in-store displays. Including the brand-specific intercepts, the Step 3 differential-effects file for the IRI example has 60 variables, while the Nielsen application contains 396 differential-effect variables. With seven grocery chains reporting 52 weeks of sales, the IRI example has about 2200 observations in the calibration data set. The Nielsen example has up to 155 stores reporting each week, which translates to about 113,000 observations in 26 weeks.

Step 10 involves a user-controlled, statistical criterion for which residual correlations are translated into cross-competitive effects. In the IRI application any correlation with more than 52 observations and a significance level more extreme than .05 was selected. This produced 81 cross effects involving all marketing instruments and leading to a Step 12 covariance matrix around 140×140. Using the same criterion on the Nielsen example led to the identification of around 4,000 potential cross-competitive effects. This would require the computation of a $4,400 \times 4,400$ covariance matrix, which is too large to compute in SAS$^{(R)}$ on an IBM 3083. Making the required number of observations much larger and the required significance level wildly extreme still lead to around 700 potential cross-competitive effects. Finally only the 200 statistically most extreme, cross-competitive effects were selected. These most-extreme effects all involved prices.

The comparison of timing results are somewhat exaggerated by the differences in the mainframes involved. The IBM 3090 model 200 on which the smaller example was run is a enormously capable computer.

While neither the vector or parallel capabilities of this machine were really involved in this illustration, the size of the problem did not tax the resources of the 3090. All 15 steps in the analysis took around

Table 5.15: Computer Resources for Two Applications

IRI Chain-Level Data		Nielsen Micro Scantrack Data	
12	Brands	66	Brand-Sizes
4	Instruments	5	Instruments
	Price		Price
	Features		Major Ads
			Line Ads
	Store Coupons		Coupon Ads
	Displays		Displays
60	Differential Effects	396	Differential Effects
7	Chains/Week	Up to 155	Stores/Week
52 Weeks	~ 2200 Obs.	26 Weeks	~ 113000 Obs.
Cross Effects			
Obs > 50	$p < .05$	Obs > 50	$p < .05$
79	Cross Effects	~ 4000	Cross Effects
			Pick 200 Most Extreme
Timing			
On IBM 3090		On IBM 3083	
~ 32 CPU Seconds		~ 120 CPU Minutes	
Steps 1 – 15		Steps 1 – 10	
		~ 120 CPU Minutes	
		Steps 11 – 12	
		~ 10 CPU Minutes	
		Step 13	

32 CPU seconds. The IBM 3083 used in the large application is an
extended architecture (XA) machine, but the time and space required
still reflected a substantial strain on the machine resources. The first
ten steps required two hours of CPU time, most of which was spent
forming the large ($\sim 400 \times 400$) covariance matrix. Forming the extended
covariance matrix, including 200 cross effects, required another two hours
of CPU time. Once the covariance matrix was stored, however, trying
out different specifications in search of a final model only took about 10
CPU minutes per run. The WLS estimation step was not run on the
large example.

The huge number of initial cross effects in the 66-competitor example makes it clear that we can get too large unless careful judgment is exercised. The size of the analysis is quite sensitive to the number of competitors for which a full differential-effects specification is attempted. This application would have been more manageable if the 30 brands were considered the basis of the differential-effects specification, and size had been treated as a simple variable in most cases.

The 66-competitor illustration is near the limit of practicality using the system of models employed here. For comparison, however, it is useful to assess the resources needed to estimate this size illustration using the analytical methods developed by Shugan[46] for data such as these. Shugan's method requires the computation of many simple regressions. If a very fast machine required only 40 nanoseconds to compute a regression, it would take 2×10^{83} CPU seconds to complete the 66-competitor illustration. This means that if a super computer had begun at the moment of the creation of the universe, it would still not be done. In fact, the age of the universe could be taken to the seventh power and computation would still be incomplete.

5.13.2   Is BLUE Always Best?

Best linear-unbiased estimation provides the robust foundation on which the competitive-analysis system relies for its parameter estimates. But, as every analyst knows, some parameters can turn up with the "wrong signs." Price parameters which are positive are difficult to explain except perhaps in prestige product classes. Negative parameters for promotions or advertising are difficult to explain — particularly to the managers running the promotions.

It seems to be left to the analyst to explain such events, as managers seem to presume that they are the consequences or quirks of the models. Analysts assume that the explanation is in the data, and the managers typically know the market conditions reflected in the data far better than the analysts.

There are several basic problems with this scenario. First is a problem of salience — are wrong-signed parameters more salient than they should be? The second problem concerns orientation. In simple constant-elasticity models the parameters are the elasticities. But complex market-response models recognize that elasticities vary as market conditions

---

[46]Shugan, Steven M. [1987], "Estimating Brand Positioning Maps from Supermarket Scanning Data," *Journal of Marketing Research*, XXIV (February), 1-18.

change. Management needs to know how markets respond to a firm's marketing efforts, but that knowledge is reflected far better in elasticities than in parameters. Third, there is an organizational problem. In the tension between management science and management, analysts should be more responsible for the models and managers more responsible for the data and how results are interpreted. But what one side does not understand should be the responsibility of both sides to figure out. Management scientists must develop and apply techniques across a number of managerial domains. They should not be expected to know the data of a domain with the kind of intimacy needed to manage. The second and third problems are addressed in more depth in Chapter 7, so that only the first is considered further here.

The problem of salience asks if wrong-signed parameter estimates get more attention than their frequency should command. Tables 5.16 and 5.17 summarize the parameter estimates for the two illustrations.

Table 5.16: Summary of BLUE Parameters — IRI Data

	Differential-Effects Model $R^2 = .83$ $F_{2184}^{59} = 180$			Cross-Effects Model $R^2 = .93$ $F_{2051}^{140} = 181$		
Marketing Instruments	Right Sign	No. Signif.	Wrong Sign $p < .05$	Right Sign	No. Signif.	Wrong Sign $p < .05$
Prices	11/12	9/12	0/12	11/12	11/12	0/12
Features	7/12	3/12	1/12	9/12	4/12	1*/12
Displays	9/12	8/12	0/12	9/12	6/12	0/12
Coupons	8/12	1/12	1/12	9/12	3/12	2/12
Totals	35/48	21/48	2/48	38/48	24/48	3*/48

* One aggregate brand.

In Table 5.16 we see that in the differential-effects model 21 of 48 parameters are statistically significant in the expected direction, while only 2 of 48 parameters are statistically extreme with the wrong sign. Moving to the cross-effects model, 24 of 48 differential effects are statistically significant in the expected direction, in spite of the inclusion of 81 cross effects. In the cross-effects model there are 3 of 48 differential-effect parameters which are statistically extreme in the unexpected direction, and one of these relates to a brand aggregate. Since brand aggregates are not expected to behave as regularly as brands, these parameters probably present no problems for the management scientist or the manager. This is certainly not different than one might expect by random chance. Yet it is very likely that these parameters will be the ones questioned

Table 5.17: Summary of BLUE Parameters — Nielsen Data

Marketing Instruments	Cross-Effects Model $R^2 = .67 \quad F_{113000}^{446} = 503$		
	Right Sign	Significant	Wrong Sign $p < .05$
Prices	62/66	55/66	4/66
Major Ads	50/66	35/66	1/66
Line Ads	57/66	29/66	1/66
Coupon Ads	43/66	21/66	7/66
Displays	55/66	47/66	2/66
Totals	267/330	187/330	15/330

by managers. The analyst is forced to track the stability of the pattern of coefficients between the differential-effects model and the cross-effects model, as well as check the possible sources of collinearity of the variables or lack of variability in the instruments in question. But because of the strong prior hypotheses of managers about the directions of marketing effects, the focus is often on the two unusual parameters, rather than the 24 significant differential effects or the 45 significant cross effects which seem to be driving the market. The burden of explanation is on the analysts who may know little about the market data from which these parameters arise.

The problem is tractable perhaps, when only a few parameters require special explanation. But with large-scale applications the number of parameters to follow can reasonably grow large. Table 5.17 summarizes the cross-effects model for the 66-competitor example. While 187 of 330 differential effects are significant in the expected direction, 15 of 330 have the wrong sign and p < .05. 15 of 330 beyond the .05 level is well within expectation, but explaining the source of these potentially anomalous effects is at least time consuming and diverting from the main task of understanding market response.

Given the strong prior hypotheses of managers, there is another approach to parameter estimation which merits study. Quadratic programming would allow us to specify a set of inequality constraints on the parameters which would correspond to the prior hypotheses of managers. Consider an estimation scheme in which the differential-effect parameters estimated in Steps 5 and 7 would be bounded by a quadratic program to conform to the prior hypotheses. The residual analysis in Steps 8 – 11 would proceed as before. But at Step 13 the cross-competitive effect parameters would be estimated against the full set of residuals, rather than recombined with the differential effects in a BLUE scheme for overall recalibration against market shares. This approach gives primacy to the explanatory power of the differential effects. Whatever they can explain which is consistent with prior hypotheses is given to them. The cross-competitive effects are used to explain the systematic part of whatever is left over.

Whenever one considers moving away from BLUE schemes, caution and study are advised. But given the strong priors regarding the effects of marketing instruments, this avenue of research should be pursued.

5.14 Appendix for Chapter 5

5.14.1 Generalized Least Squares Estimation

Nakanishi and Cooper [1974] showed that the total covariance matrix of errors Σ_ϵ is approximately the sum of the variance–covariance matrix among sampling errors, Σ_{ϵ_2}, and the variance-covariance matrix among specification errors, Σ_{ϵ_1}. For the simplified estimation procedures the estimate of $\Sigma_{\epsilon_{2t}}$ comes from

$$\widehat{\Sigma}_{\epsilon_{2t}} = \frac{1}{n_t}(\widehat{\Pi}_t^{-1} - J) \qquad (5.34)$$

where n_t is the number of individuals (purchases) in time period t, $\widehat{\Pi}_t^{-1}$ is an $(m_t \times m_t)$ diagonal matrix with entries equal to the inverse of the market shares estimated by the OLS procedure for the m_t brands in this period, and J is a conformal matrix of ones.

The variance-covariance matrix of specification errors, Σ_{ϵ_1}, is assumed to be constant in each time period and is estimated by $\widehat{\sigma}_{\epsilon_1}^2 I$ where

$$\widehat{\sigma}_{\epsilon_1}^2 = \frac{Q - \sum_{t=1}^T \text{tr}\widehat{\Sigma}_{\epsilon_{2t}} + \text{tr}[(\sum_{t=1}^T Z_t' Z_t)^{-1}(\sum_{t=1}^T Z_t' \widehat{\Sigma}_{\epsilon_{2t}} Z_t)]}{\sum_{t=1}^T m_t - gK - T} \qquad (5.35)$$

where Q is the sum of squares of the OLS errors, and Z_t is an $(m_t \times [K + T])$ matrix containing the logs of the K explanatory variables with the T time-period dummy variables concatenated to it. This formula for $\widehat{\sigma}_{\epsilon_1}^2$ is considerably simpler than the one in Nakanishi and Cooper [1974, p. 308)] and also corrects a typographical error in that equation.

The total variance-covariance matrix $\widehat{\Sigma}_\epsilon$ is a block-diagonal matrix in which each block is the sum of $\widehat{\Sigma}_{\epsilon_{2t}} + \widehat{\Sigma}_{\epsilon_1}$.

Chapter 6

Competitive Maps

We are concerned in this chapter with the conversion of analytical results into decision-related factors. Any such discussion must center on the use of elasticities. A marketing plan should contain an instrument-by-instrument account of the actions to be taken — what prices to charge and what discounts to offer, what print ads to commission, how much to allocate to radio and television, what coupons to offer as a manufacturer and what coupons to cosponsor with retailers. To make these decisions on a sensible basis one needs to estimate the expected market response to changes in each of these elements of the marketing mix. Elasticities provide that instrument-by-instrument account of expected market response. The marketing literature provides many examples. Research on optimal advertising expenditures[1] provides many insightful special cases of the general, elasticity-based rule that you allocate resources to advertising in proportion to the marginal effectiveness of advertising in generating contributions to profits. Similarly, the literature on optimal price,[2] and general issues of optimal marketing mix and marketing

---

[1]Dorfman, Robert A. & Peter D. Steiner [1954], "Optimal Advertising and Optimal Quality," *American Economic Review*, 44 (December), 826-36. Clarke, Darral G. [1973], "Sales-Advertising Cross-Elasticities and Advertising Competition," *Journal of Marketing Research*, 10 (August), 250-61. Bultez, Alain V. & Philippe A. Naert [1979], "Does Lag Structure Really Matter in Optimal Advertising Expenditures?" *Management Science*, 25, 5 (May), 454-65. Magat, Wesley A., John M. McCann & Richard C. Morey [1986], "When Does Lag Structure Really Matter in Optimal Advertising Expenditures?" *Management Science*, 32, 2 (February), 182-93.

[2]Bass, Frank M. & Alain V. Bultez [1982], "A Note On Optimal Strategic Pricing of Technological Innovations," *Marketing Science*, 1, 4 (Fall), 371-78. Kalish, Shlomo [1983], "Monopolistic Pricing With Dynamic Demand and Production Cost," *Marketing Science*, 2, 2 (Spring), 135-59. Rao, Ram C. & Frank M. Bass [1985], "Com-

effectiveness[3] use elasticities in describing optimal decisions.

The problem is that much of this literature deals with an elasticity as if it were a fixed quantity or at best a random variable whose expected value completely summarizes it. Even if some of these studies oversimplify the case for expository purposes, managers seem most often interested in the single number that represent their brand's price elasticity or advertising elasticity.

Studies of the relation between price and product life cycle[4] deal with expected changes in elasticities as a function of the developmental stage of a product. Such efforts are steps in the right direction, for they recognize that elasticities are not fixed and invariant. This is a view we support. First, we have seen in Figures 2.1 and 3.3 four functional forms describing the changes in elasticities with changing market conditions. Second, we believe that managers should be interested in the whole changing pattern of elasticities and cross elasticities in a market. So instead of a single estimate of own-price elasticity, we advocate dealing with a matrix of price elasticities in each time and place.

In this chapter we present ways to visualize and understand the complex pattern of elasticities. A special case of multimode factor analysis portrays the systematic structure driving changes in these asymmetric cross elasticities. Continuing the coffee-market example introduced in the last chapter, we will see that the analysis of the variation in elasticities over retail outlets and weeks reveals competitive patterns showing that this market shifts during sales for the major brands. Analysis of the brand domain results in a map with each brand appearing twice. One set of brand positions portrays how brands exert influence over the competition. The other set of points portrays how brands are influenced by others. The interset distances (angles) provide direct measures of

petition, Strategy, and Price Dynamics: A Theoretical and Empirical Investigation," *Journal of Marketing Research*, XXII (August), 283-96.

[3]Lambin, Jean-Jacques, Philippe A. Naert, & Alain V. Bultez [1975], "Optimal Market Behavior in Oligopoly," *European Economic Review*, 6, 105-28. Karnani, Aneel [1983], "Minimum Market Share," *Marketing Science*, 2, 1 (Winter), 75-93. Morey, Richard C. & John M. McCann [1983], "Estimating the Confidence Interval for the Optimal Marketing Mix: An Application to Lead Generation," *Marketing Science*, 2, 2 (Spring), 193-202.

[4]Parsons, Leonard J. [1975], "The Product Life Cycle and Time-Varying Advertising Elasticities," *Journal of Marketing Research*, XVI (November), 439-52. Simon, Hermann [1979], "Dynamics of Price Elasticities and Brand Life Cycles: An Empirical Study," *Journal of Marketing Research*, XVI (November), 439-452. Shoemaker, Robert W. [1986], "Comments on *Dynamics of Price Elasticities and Brand Life Cycles: An Empirical Study*," *Journal of Marketing Research*, XXIII (February), 78-82.

competitive pressures.

Our approach is founded on an understanding of how elasticities reflect the competitive structure in a market. Elasticities serve as measures of competition — indicators of market structure. We combine the visual emphasis coming out of psychometrics with the mathematical emphasis of economics.

The traditional psychometric approach to market-structure analysis has developed mainly without reference to or use of elasticities. This approach uses multidimensional scaling (MDS) to map perceived similarities or preferences among the brands, or to model consumer choice as some function of how far each brand is from the most preferred position in a brand map.[5] People are asked one of the most neutral questions in all of social science (e.g., "How similar are the brands in each pair?"), and MDS provides from the answers powerful visual methods for portraying the dimensions underlying consumer perceptions. In new-product research, MDS provides a basis for understanding how consumers might react to new offerings. But, for the management of mature brands, particularly frequently purchased branded goods (FPBGs), this approach's *power of discovery* contributes to an important representational problem. Depending on the context, substitutable and complementary products could both appear close together in the perceptual space. For example, hot dogs and Coke (complements) could be near each other in one perceptual space, while Coke and Pepsi (substitutes) could be close together in another perceptual space.[6] Since substitutes are competitors and complements are not, we would want these very different products to take very distinct positions in any visual representation. While careful consideration of market boundaries is helpful, the ambiguity between the treatment of substitutes versus complements can diminish the utility of traditional MDS for brand management.

Approaches to market structure using panel data may be able to overcome this ambiguity. The record of interpurchase intervals available in panel data can reveal information about substitutes versus complements. In the extreme case, co-purchase of two brands on a single buy-

---

[5] For a summary of this research see Cooper, Lee G. [1983], "A Review of Multidimensional Scaling in Marketing Research," *Applied Psychological Measurement*, 7 (Fall), 427-50.

[6] Factor analysis of consumer rating scales has less difficulty here than does MDS, since the attributes of substitutes should be much more highly correlated than the attributes of complements — leading to similar locations for substitutes, but quite dissimilar positions for complements.

ing occasion indicates complementarity, while switching between brands with equal interpurchase times indicates substitutability.[7] Fraser and Bradford[8] used this kind of information in a panel-based index of revealed substitutability which they decomposed using principal components. But their method is more of a market partitioning than a competitive mapping. There is also a whole stream of research based on panel or discrete-choice data beginning with Lehmann's[9] use of brand-switching data as similarity measures in MDS. The Hendry Model,[10] the wandering vector model,[11], Genfold2[12], Moore & Winer's[13] use of panel data in Levine's[14] *pick-any analysis*, and the powerful maximum-likelihood procedures in Elrod's Choice Map[15] can be thought of as part of the general effort to develop market-structure maps from disaggregate choice data. Moore & Winer [1987] distinguish their effort by using a multiple-equation system to integrate panel data with market-level data, but only Fraser & Bradford [1983] specifically address the potential of panel data to resolve the representational ambiguity involving substitutes and complements.

[7] This can be muddled, however, since panel records are mostly of household purchases. Co-purchase may simply indicate that different members of the household like different brands. So-called *super-position processes* are discussed by Kahn, Barbara E., Donald G. Morrison & Gordon P. Wright [1986], "Aggregating Individual Purchases to the Household Level," *Marketing Science*, 5, 3 (Summer), 260-68.

[8] Fraser, Cynthia & John W. Bradford [1983], "Competitive Market Structure Analysis: Principal Partitioning of Revealed Substitutabilities," *Journal of Consumer Research*, 10 (June), 15-30.

[9] Lehmann, Don R. [1972], "Judged Similarity and Brand-Switching Data as Similarity Measures," *Journal of Marketing Research*, 9, 331-4.

[10] Kalwani, Manohar U., & Donald G. Morrison [1977], "Parsimonious Description of the Hendry System," *Management Science*, 23 (January), 467-77.

[11] Carroll, J. Douglas [1980], "Models and Methods for Multidimensional Analysis of Preferential Choice (or Other Dominance) Data," in Ernst D. Lantermann & Hubert Feger (editors), *Similarity and Choice*, Bern: Hans Huber Publishers, 234-89. DeSoete, Geert & J. Douglas Carroll [1983], "A Maximum Likelihood Method of Fitting the Wandering Vector Model," *Psychometrika*, 48, 4 (December), 553-66.

[12] DeSarbo, Wayne S. & Vitalla R. Rao [1984], "GENFOLD2: A Set of Models and Algorithms for GENeral UnFOLDing Analysis of Preference/Dominance Data," *Journal of Classification*, 1, 2, 147-86.

[13] Moore, William L.& Russell S. Winer [1987], "A Panel-Data Based Method for Merging Joint Space and Market Response Function Estimation," *Marketing Science*, 6, 1 (Winter), 25-42.

[14] Levine, Joel H. [1979], "Joint-Space Analysis of 'Pick-Any' Data: Analysis of Choices from an Unconstrained Set of Alternatives," *Psychometrika*, 44, 85-92.

[15] Elrod, Terry [1987], "Choice Map: Inferring Brand Attributes and Heterogeneous Consumer Preferences From Panel Data," *Marketing Science*, forthcoming.

The modeling efforts using aggregate (store-level) data have had difficulty dealing with both complements and substitutes. Shugan[16] has developed methods to represent the market structure specifically implied by the demand function in the Defender model.[17] This market-structure map contains price-scaled dimensions. The elasticities implied by the Defender model can be computed as simple relations among the angles brands make with these per-dollar dimensions. While brand positions have the advantage of relating directly to the rich strategic implications of the Defender model, choice sets have to be very carefully defined to screen out complements. Otherwise brands may be forced to have negative coordinates on some dimension. There is still uncertainty about the meaning of a negative coordinate on a per-dollar dimension. Vanhonacker[18] is one of the few to use elasticities to map market structure. He has worked on methods which result in two separate structural maps — one for negative cross elasticities and one for positive cross elasticities. But how we integrate information across these two maps is, as yet, unresolved.

Yet the full set of elasticities provides a very natural and conceptually appealing basis for portraying market and competitive structure. The brands could be represented as vectors from the origin. The stronger the cross elasticity between two brands, the more correlated those brand vectors should be. The more complementary two brands are in the market, the more opposite they should be in the map. If two brands do not compete at all (zero cross elasticity), their vectors should be at right angles (orthogonal). Thus the patterns of substitutability, complementarity, and independence could be represented in a single map. These are the properties of a map we would get by viewing cross elasticities as cosines (or scalar products) between brand positions in a multidimensional space. What we gain is a way of visualizing a whole matrix of elasticities — a competitive map.

---

[16]Shugan, Steven M. [1986], "Brand Positioning Maps From Price/Share Data," University of Chicago, Graduate School of Business, Revised, July. Shugan, Steven M. [1987], "Estimating Brand Positioning Maps From Supermarket Scanning Data," *Journal of Marketing Research*, XXIV (February), 1-18.
[17]Hauser, John R. & Steven M. Shugan [1983], "Defensive Marketing Strategies," *Marketing Science*, 2, 4 (Fall), 319-360.
[18]Vanhonacker, Wilfried [1984], "Structuring and Analyzing Brand Competition Using Scanner Data," Columbia University, Graduate School of Business, April.

6.1   *Asymmetric Three-Mode Factor Analysis

Consider a three-way array of the cross-elasticities as depicted in Figure 6.1. If we think of it as a loaf of sandwich bread, each slice summarizes the elasticities in a time period. The entries in each row of a slice of this loaf summarize how all the brands' prices (promotions) affect that row brand's sales. The entries in a column from any slice summarize how one brand's prices (promotions) affect all brands' sales. Then the elements in an elasticities matrix are represented by the inner (scalar) product of (1) a row from a matrix R reflecting how receptive or vulnerable each brand is to being influenced by some small number of underlying market-place forces, and (2) the elements in a row from a matrix C reflecting how much clout each brand has in the market. We can think of a series of basic factors that reflect the clout or power of brands in a market. How influential each basic source of power is in the overall clout of a particular brand would be reflected in the scores of that brand in the C matrix. Similarly, we can think of a series of basic factors that reflect vulnerability in a market. How influential each basic source of vulnerability is in the overall vulnerability of a particular brand would be reflected in the scores of that brand in the R matrix. A cross elasticity is the inner (scalar) product of the clout of one brand times the receptivity/vulnerability of the other brand.

After developing this representation for a single time period, it is generalized by assuming that the competitive patterns underlying time periods are related by simple nonsingular transformations (i.e., that the dimensions of a common space can be differentially reweighted and differentially correlated to approximate the pattern of influences in any single time period). Establishing a common origin and units of measure for the R and C matrices allow plotting in a joint space.

Equation (6.1) represents the cross elasticities E in a particular time period t as the scalar product of a row space R (reflecting scores for brands on receptivity/vulnerability factors) for time period t and a column space C (reflecting scores for brands on clout factors) for time period t plus a matrix Δ of discrepancies (lack of fit).

$$_iE_j^{(t)} = {}_iR_q^{(t)}C_j^{(t)} + {}_i\Delta_j^{(t)} \tag{6.1}$$

Similar entries in the row space for t indicate similarities between brands in the way they are influenced by competitive pressures — receptivity or vulnerability. Similar entries in the column space for t indicate similarities between brands in how they exert influence on others —

Figure 6.1: Three-Mode Array of Elasticities

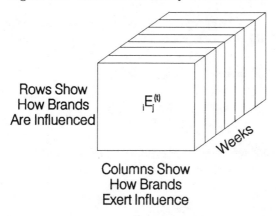

Rows Show
How Brands
Are Influenced

$_iE_j^{(t)}$

Weeks

Columns Show
How Brands
Exert Influence

clout. So while the inner (scalar) product across R and C reflects cross elasticities, the inner product within R reflects similarity in the pattern of how brands are influenced (i.e., receptivity or vulnerability), and the inner product within C indicates similarity in the pattern of how brands exert influence on other brands (i.e., clout).

We can think of the row space for a particular period t as being related to a common row space $\mathbf{R}$. The dimensions of the space for a particular period could be a simple reweighting (shrinking or stretching) of the dimensions of the common space and/or the dimensions of the common space might have to be differentially correlated to reflect what is going on in a particular period. The combinations of shrinking or stretching of each dimension and differential correlation between the dimensions of the common space to reflect a particular period can be summarized in a nonsingular transformation Q for relating the particular period t to the common row space $\mathbf{R}$.

$$_iR_q^{(t)} = {}_i\mathbf{R}_q Q_q^{(t)} \tag{6.2}$$

Similarly, we can think of the column space for t as a nonsingular transformation U of common column space $\mathbf{C}$:

$$_qC_j^{(t)} = {}_qU_q^{(t)}\mathbf{C}_j \ . \tag{6.3}$$

Tucker[19] developed this basic formulation as an extension of his pio-

---

[19]Tucker, Ledyard R [1969], "Some Relations Between Multi-Mode Factor Analysis

neering work on three-mode factor analysis.[20] Elasticities in each period
are represented, in terms of the common row and column spaces, as the
sum (over time-factors $l = 1, \ldots, L$) of the triple matrix-product — the
row space times the appropriate layer of the core matrix $G^{(l)}$ times the
common column space. Each term in the triple product is weighted by
a coefficient w_{tl} showing the association of each time period with each
time-factor (like factor scores for time periods).

$$_iE_j^{(t)} = \sum_{l=1}^{L} {}_i\mathbf{R}_q G_q^{(l)} \mathbf{C}_j w_{tl} + {}_i\Delta_j^{(t)} \tag{6.4}$$

A joint space represents brand competition on each time-factor.[21]
Each layer of the core matrix is diagonalized using singular-value decomposition:

$$_qG_q^{(l)} = {}_qV_q^{(l)}\Gamma_q^{(l)2}Y_q^{(l)} \tag{6.5}$$

where $V^{(l)}$ contains the left principal vectors of a particular layer of
the core matrix, $Y^{(l)}$ contains the right principal vectors, and $\Gamma^{(l)2}$ is a
diagonal matrix of singular values.

$$_iR_q^{(l)} = {}_i\mathbf{R}_q(V_q^{(l)}\Gamma_q^{(l)}) \tag{6.6}$$

$$_qC_j^{(l)} = ({}_q\Gamma_q^{(l)}Y_q^{(l)})\mathbf{C}_j \tag{6.7}$$

In this joint space, $R^{(l)}$ reflects the similarities in how brands are
influenced, $C^{(l)}$ reflects the similarities in how brands exert influence,

and Linear Models for Individual Differences in Choice, Judgmental and Performance
Data," Paper presented to the Psychometric Society Symposium: Multi-Mode Factor
Analysis and Models for Individual Differences in Psychological Phenomena, April 18.

[20]Tucker, Ledyard R [1963], "Implications of Factor Analysis of Three-Way Matrices
for Measurement of Change," in Chester W. Harris (editor), *Problems in Measuring
Change*, Madison: University of Wisconsin Press, 122-37. Tucker, Ledyard R [1966],
"Some Mathematical Notes On Three-Mode Factor Analysis," *Psychometrika*, 31, 4
(December), 279-311. Closely related developments are reported in Tucker, Ledyard
R [1972], "Relations Between Multidimensional Scaling and Three-Mode Factor Anal-
ysis," *Psychometrika*, 37, 1 (March), 3-27, and illustrated in Cooper, Lee G. [1973],
"A Multivariate Investigation of Preferences," *Multivariate Behavioral Research*, 8
(April), 253-72. In these latter two articles symmetric, brand-by-brand arrays make
up each layer of the three-mode matrix, making the analysis a very general model for
individual differences in multidimensional scaling. In the current context, individual
differences are replaced by differences in the competitive mix from one time to another, and the symmetric measures of brand similarity are replaced by asymmetric
measures of brand competition.

[21]See Kroonenberg, Pieter M. [1983], *Three-Mode Principal Components Analysis:
Theory and Applications*, Leiden, The Netherlands: DSWO Press, 164-67.

and the proximity (cosine between the vectors) of row and column points reflects how much the brands compete. From the joint-space coordinates, we approximate the elasticities corresponding to any particular week or any simulated pattern of marketing activity, using:

$$_i\widetilde{E}_j^{(t)} = \sum_{l=1}^{L} {}_iR_q^{(l)}C_j^{(l)}w_{tl} \ . \tag{6.8}$$

Thus if the analysis of differences in competitive contexts reveals particularly interesting patterns, we could approximate the elasticities which reflect those competitive conditions. Repeating the analysis on just the approximated elasticities for some special condition, we create a competitive map specific to this context. With only one layer this is a two-mode analysis which amounts to a singular-value decomposition of the E matrix, in which the variance is split between the left principal vectors and the right principal vectors. The result is the asymmetric three-mode equivalent of idealized-individual analysis developed by Tucker and Messick[22] for the individual-differences model for multidimensional scaling. For any idealized competitive pattern t^* in which the elasticities have been approximated by equation (6.8), we get the simplest representation:

$$_i\widetilde{E}_j^{(t^*)} = {}_iR_q^{(t^*)}C_j^{(t^*)} \ . \tag{6.9}$$

This provides a very direct visualization of the idealized elasticities because the inner product of the coordinates in $C^{(t^*)}$ for brand j and the coordinates in $R^{(t^*)}$ for brand i will reproduce the (ij) entry in $\widetilde{E}^{(t^*)}$. These idealized competitive patterns are isolated and interpreted in the illustration that follows.

6.2 Portraying the Coffee Market

The price parameters from the market-share model for the Coffee-Market Example were used to generate market-share-price cross elasticities for each grocery chain in each week. The average elasticities are shown in Table 6.1. The greatest price elasticity is for Chock Full O'Nuts (-4.71). The clear policy of this brand is to maintain a high shelf price and generate sales through frequent promotions. Over 80% of Chock Full O'Nuts

---

[22]Tucker, Ledyard R & Samuel Messick [1963], "An Individual Differences Model for Multidimensional Scaling," *Psychometrika*, 28, 4 (December), 333-67.

sales in these two cities are on price promotions. Chock Full O'Nuts maintains the third largest market share with this policy. The substantial price elasticities for Folgers, Maxwell House, and All Other Branded result from a similar policy, but with less frequent and less predictable price-promotions. Master Blend, Hills Bros., and Yuban have elasticities more like the private label brands (i.e., PL 1, PL 2, PL 3, and AOPL). Since the private-label brands have so little to offer other than price, we might expect them to have greater price elasticities. But with an every-day-low-price strategy these brands do not generate enough variation in price to achieve the elasticities of the more frequently promoted brands. As we see in the subsequent analyses, the average elasticities in Table 6.1 reflect an aggregation of widely differing competitive conditions. There are shelf-price elasticities which are quite different from the promotion-price elasticities one obtains during sales for the three major brands in these markets.

6.2.1   Signalling Competitive Change

Three-mode factor analysis is a technique for structured exploration. Although elasticities help researchers understand the raw data, the average elasticities are too aggregate to reflect the diversity of the competitive environment. The first task of the analysis is to signal when particular competitive events are part of a systematic pattern. Knowing that say five particular weeks in particular grocery chains constitute a pattern, we can go back to the original data to seek the meaning of that pattern in the antecedent conditions (e.g., these are weeks of deep price cuts for Folgers). This reduces the noise, so that signals are more easily detected. Next, the three-mode analysis determines the competitive building blocks for the elasticities. There is a pair of matrices R and C for each time factor $(l = 1, 2, \ldots, L)$ in the matrix $W = \{w_{tl}\}_{T \times L}$. Equation (6.8) approximates the elasticities for any particular competitive pattern as a linear combination of the building blocks, where the entries in a row of W serve as the linear combining weights. While each pair of matrices R and C can be interpreted, we find it best to form the linear combinations implied by particularly interesting competitive patterns and interpret the competitive maps resulting from the approximated elasticities. The building blocks may include more dimensions than are operative in any particular competitive pattern, and thus may be more difficult to interpret.

The three-mode factor analysis in this illustration was implemented

Table 6.1: Average Market-Share Elasticities of Price

	Fol-gers	Max Hse	Mstr Bln	Hills Bros.	CF ON	Yu-ban
Fol	−4.37	0.59	2.53	0.32	1.41	−0.34
RMH	1.95	−3.89	0.56	0.01	0.71	0.19
MB	1.48	−0.05	−0.88	0.02	0.68	0.10
HB	−0.53	−0.45	−0.17	−0.54	0.30	0.11
CFN	1.50	1.55	−1.90	−0.32	−4.71	0.35
Yub	0.73	−0.16	−0.25	−0.19	−0.03	0.12
C&S	0.19	0.24	0.09	0.20	0.47	0.05
AOB	1.43	3.47	−0.15	−0.87	−0.28	0.59
PL1	−0.06	0.03	0.02	0.08	0.42	0.00
PL2	0.07	0.08	0.22	0.12	0.42	0.00
PL3	0.16	0.07	−0.14	0.00	0.00	0.05
AO	1.29	0.15	−1.00	0.00	0.00	0.18

	C&S	AOB	PL1	PL2	PL3	AO PL
Fol	−0.44	0.35	−0.06	−0.12	0.06	0.06
RMH	0.26	−0.05	0.15	−0.06	0.10	0.06
MB	−0.73	0.48	−0.07	−0.09	−0.11	0.15
HB	0.09	1.23	0.03	−0.08	0.00	0.00
CFN	0.78	1.55	0.86	0.35	0.00	0.00
Yub	0.07	−0.16	0.00	0.00	−0.02	−0.10
C&S	−1.47	0.19	0.00	0.04	0.00	0.00
AOB	−0.07	−3.46	−0.25	−0.35	−0.47	0.40
PL1	0.00	−0.01	−0.47	0.00	0.00	0.00
PL2	0.06	−0.09	0.00	−0.89	0.00	0.00
PL3	0.00	−0.03	0.00	0.00	−0.14	0.03
AO	0.00	0.04	0.00	0.00	0.03	−0.69

using the matrix-algebra routines in SAS$^{(R)}$. The limit of 32,767 elements in the maximum array size in SAS$^{(R)}$'s PROC MATRIX meant that only three of the seven grocery chains reporting each week could be analyzed.[23] This limitation resulted in exclusion of Private Label 3 and All Other Private Labels from the subsequent analyses, because these brands were not distributed in Chains 1 – 3.

We choose the number of dimensions to investigate by inspecting a plot showing how the proportion of variance explained by each factor trails off as the number of factors increases. Variance is information and we look for the last relatively large drop in variance — indicating all

---

[23]The PROC MATRIX routine is available from the authors. Real applications of much larger size are currently feasible. First, SAS IML apparently removes the size restriction. Second, a general three-mode program, developed by Pieter Kroonenberg, is available for a small fee from the Department of Data Theory, University of Lieden, P.O. Box 9507, 2300 RA Leiden, The Netherlands.

subsequent factors have relatively little information. Figure 6.2 shows
this plot for the structure over chains and weeks. The factor structure
over the 52 weeks for the three chains shows that the last large drop
is between factors 4 and 5. Consequently we retain four dimensions,
accounting for almost 93% of the variation over chains and weeks. The
dominant first factor accounts for over 74% of the variance, but we must
look for the last large drop, not the first. The next three factors account
for 9%, 6.5%, and 3% respectively, while none of the remaining factors
accounts for even 1%.[24]

Figure 6.2: The Number of Factors Over Chains and Weeks

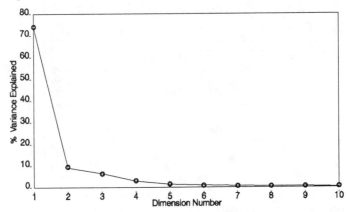

Figures 6.3 and 6.4 plot the weights w_{tl} showing the influence of the
time-factors ($l =1 - 4$) on the weeks t — with Figure 6.3 depicting the
first two factors over time, and Figure 6.4 portraying factors 3 and 4 over
time. The symbols $\bigcirc$ (circles) and $\diamond$ (diamonds) correspond to grocery
chains 2 and 3, respectively. The $\square$ (boxes) some of which have letters
inside, represent Chain 1. To help reflect the third dimension

---

[24]Choosing factors in this way is of course judgmental, but has a long tradition
in psychometrics. The idea is that there are three classes of factors in any data set
— major-domain factors, minor, but systematic factors and error or random factors.
While statistical criteria attempt to exclude the random factors, psychometricians
traditionally have used factor analysis to isolate only the major domain. While the
minor factors are present and systematic, exploratory factor analysis gives clearest
focus on the major domain. Confirmatory factor analysis and latent-variable causal
modeling, use statistical criteria for choosing the dimensionality, and are consequently
more useful in better developed domains, where the minor-systematic influences are
well known.

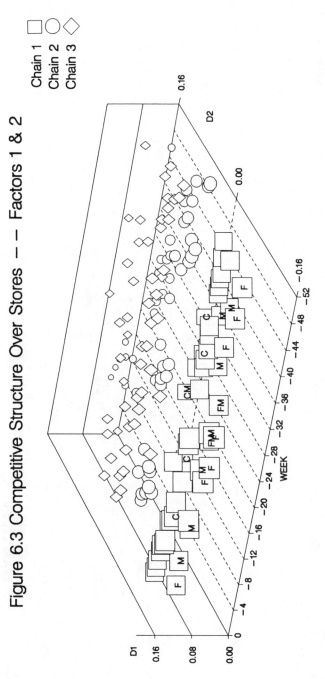

Figure 6.3 Competitive Structure Over Stores — — Factors 1 & 2

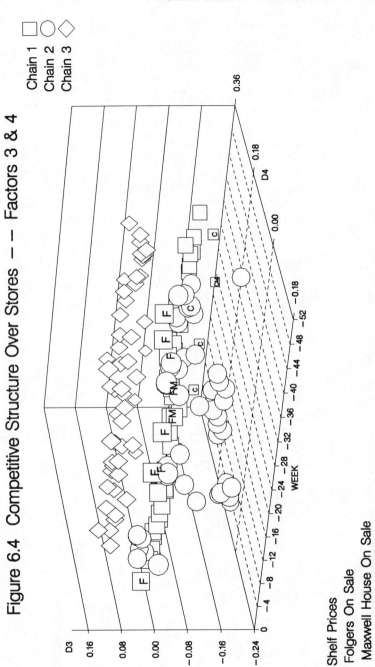

Figure 6.4 Competitive Structure Over Stores — — Factors 3 & 4

in these figures the size of the symbol decreases the farther away the observation is from the "Week" axis. The coefficients for the grocery chains are indicators of systematic structure of events in these weeks. Each of these four factors corresponds to a fundamental building block which collectively can represent any pattern of competition in the data.

The goal is to interpret the patterns of competition. First we note that it is easy to see that the grocery chains are quite distinct, reflecting substantial differences in promotion policies among chains. It is easier to summarize the differences over chains after we understand the pattern within a chain. Let us look at Chain 1. We are directed in this inquiry by the fact the original measures are price elasticities. Do the weeks that stand out correspond to recognizable *price events*? The weeks marked by blank boxes ($\Box$) indicate *Shelf Prices* — weeks in which there are no price promotions in Chain 1. "F," "M," and "C" indicate big price cuts for Folgers, Maxwell House, and Chock Full O'Nuts, respectively. Note that the weeks in Chain 1 which have high weights on the first factor reflect shelf-price competition — weeks in which no major brand is being promoted. These weeks had an average loading of about .11 on Factor 1 and $-.08$ on Factor 2, but very little weight on Factor 3 ($-.02$) or Factor 4 ($-.04$). These linear-combining weights were used to develop approximate or idealized shelf-price elasticities from the basic building blocks. These *shelf-price* elasticities were mapped and are discussed below.

The weeks with Folgers on sale have somewhat less weight on Factor 1 than the Shelf-Price weeks. Sale weeks for Chock Full O'Nuts have the weights closest to zero on Factor 2 (see Figure 6.3). Folgers sale weeks have slightly positive weights on Factor 3, while Chock Full O'Nuts sale weeks have the greatest negative weight (see Figure 6.4). This pattern is reversed in Factor 4, with Folgers sale weeks have the most negative weights and Chock Full O'Nuts sale weeks having strong positive weights. The positive weights on dimension 3 for Folgers are neutralized when Folgers and Maxwell House promote simultaneously. These weeks, marked "FM" in Figure 6.4, look much more like shelf-price weeks, indicating head-to-head promotions partially cancel each other. In general, Maxwell House sale weeks have less weight on the first factor than the shelf-price weeks, but are otherwise relatively indistinguishable from the pattern for shelf-price weeks.

Now that we see that the patterns within a chain differentiate brand promotions from shelf-price conditions, we can look at the patterns across chains. The factor structure clearly differentiates Chain 2 as having less weight on the first, dominant factor (see Figure 6.3). Since the highest weights on this first factor reflect shelf-price conditions in Chain 1, we shouldn't be surprised to find out that Chain 2, which has the lowest weight on this factor, has the fewest weeks of shelf-price competition. Chain 2 tends to run features for majors for up to eight weeks in a row, and run features for more than one major brand head-to-head — leaving the fewest weeks without promotions.[25] Chain 3 has the highest positive weights on the third factor (see Figure 6.4). This seems to correspond to the policy of having very high feature prices for the major brands.[26] So it seems that these differences in promotion policies are summarized in the relatively distinct locales for each grocery chain in this factor space. We can further note that within each general chain location, the brand promotions seem to have similar impacts. For instance, in Figures 6.3 and 6.4, the shelf-price weeks have the highest position on Factor 1 relative to the position of each chain, Folgers or Maxwell House promotions have the lowest positions on Factor 1 and the highest positions on Factor 3, while Chock Full O'Nuts promotions have the most positive weights on Factors 2 and 4 and the most negative weights on Factor 3. Similar to the interpretation of any factor structure, we must note the events which stand out and use the associated market conditions and other information to guide us in finding meaningful patterns. In this sense any factor structure is an information space into which the available data are reflected in the search for meaning. First we reflected chain number, and then promotions for different brands, and so on until we understand the pattern. For all the power of the analysis, it still takes the ability of the analyst to recognize substantive patterns.

When we isolate a pattern of interest — a particular week or average of similar weeks, we simply note its coordinates. From these we can use equation (6.9) to create idealized elasticities corresponding to the competitive pattern. So far we have focused on Chain 1 and noted the patterns associated with shelf-price weeks, Folgers-on-sale weeks, Maxwell House-on-sale week, and Chock Full O'Nuts-on-sale weeks. Ross[27] advises that idealized individuals be placed very near the positions of real individuals to minimize the possibility that averaging several locations

---

[25]Chain 2 had over 36 deal-weeks for the three largest brands combined, compared to 19 deal-weeks for Chain 1 and 24 deal-weeks for Chain 3 for these brands.

[26]Chain 3 tends to feature Folgers or Maxwell House at about $2.32, while the corresponding price-on-feature is about $1.91 and $2.10 for Chains 1 and 2, respectively.

[27]Ross, John [1966], "A Remark on Tucker and Messick's *Points of View* Analysis," *Psychometrika*, 31, 1 (March), 27-31.

could create unreal dimensional structures. Following this advice, the idealized shelf-price elasticities correspond to the coordinates in the W matrix for Chain 1 Week 2, the idealized Folgers-on-sale elasticities come from the coordinates for Chain 1 Week 1, the Maxwell House-on-sale elasticities come from Chain 1 Week 11, and the Chock Full O'Nuts-on-sale elasticities come from Chain 1 Week 25. The linear-combining weights for these patterns are shown in Table 6.2. The idealized elasticities for these four competitive patterns appear in the appendix (see Table 6.7). The competitive maps are developed and interpreted in the next section.

Table 6.2: Coordinates of the Idealized Competitive Conditions

Competitive Condition	Weights on Factors			
	1	2	3	4
Shelf-Price Competition	0.11	−0.08	−0.02	−0.04
Folgers On Sale	0.07	−0.09	0.01	−0.08
Maxwell House On Sale	0.07	−0.10	−0.04	−0.00
CFON On Sale	0.06	−0.03	−0.23	0.32

6.2.2 Competitive Maps: The Structure Over Brands

The common scaling space developed by a three-mode factor analysis of asymmetric cross elasticities, as well as the two-mode representations of idealized competitive patterns, both provide maps of competitive interactions, *rather than necessarily portraying attribute relations among the brands.* These are competitive maps, rather than product perceptual spaces. In this illustration all the maps relate to price as an attribute, since price elasticities are used to develop the maps. In applied contexts the maps derived from all other promotional instruments would be investigated.

A competitive map involves two sets of points plotted in the same space, corresponding to the two processes reflected in the elasticities. Elasticities show how a percent change in the price of a brand, j, translates into change in the market share of brand i. The first process involved deals with how much clout brand j has. We can think of brands which just seem more able to influence others, or brands which pressure no others. Correspondingly, the first set of points — symbolized by circles ○ — represents the way brands exert influence on one another.

Similar positions for two brands indicate they exert a similar pattern of influence on the market place. The second process deals with how able some brands are to resist the advances of competitors, while others seem quite vulnerable. And so the second set of points — symbolized by squares □ — represents the way brands are influenced by competitive pressures. Similar positions for two brands indicate they are similarly vulnerable to pressures from other brands.

Most joint-space, multidimensional-scaling methods deal with different rows than columns (e.g., with brands for columns and consumer preferences for row the joint space would locate ideal points in a brand map). But this multidimensional-scaling method has some very special properties. Because we are using ratio-scale quantities (i.e., elasticities have a meaningful zero-point and unit of measure), the origin of the space has great importance. Most MDS methods are based on interpoint distances and the origin is arbitrarily placed at the centroid of all the brands — merely for convenience since the interpoint distances are unaffected by a translation of origin. But this model doesn't work with estimates of interpoint distances. Brands are vectors from a fixed origin. For the ○ brands, the distance of a brand from the origin of the space is a measure of how much *clout* the brand has.[28] For the □ brands, the distance from the origin is a measure of how *vulnerable* or *receptive* a brand's sales are to price competition.[29] Hence, two ○ brands on the same vector from the origin exert the same pattern of pressure on the other brands, but differ in the amount of clout each possesses. Two □ brands on the same vector from the origin are pressured by the same competitors, but could be differentially vulnerable or receptive. A ○ brand on the same vector as a □ brand would exert its greatest cross-elastic pressure on that □ brand. The cross elasticity falls off as the cosine between the angles of the brands drops toward zero (brands at right angles). Brands on opposite sides of the origin (angles greater than 90°) reflect complementary cross elasticities, rather than competitive pressures.

In the ground, caffeinated coffee market under study there are four major dimensions describing the relations among brands on each time-factor. The dimensionality is chosen, as before, by inspecting the vari-

---

[28] Formally it is a function of the sum of squares of the cross elasticities of other brands' shares with respect to this brand's price.

[29] Formally it is a function of the sum of squares of the cross elasticities of this brand's share with respect to the other brands' prices. Elasticities reflect percentage changes. So if a brand with small share can lose a large percent of its share to other brands, it can appear far from the origin and be very vulnerable in percentage terms.

ance accounted for by each dimension. In the appendix to this chapter Table 6.3 shows the coordinates of the brands in the common row scaling space and the common column scaling space, Table 6.4 lists the variance on each of the common dimensions for the row space and the column space, Table 6.5 displays the four planes in the core matrix G, and Table 6.6 lists the coordinates of the joint-space, building blocks corresponding to each core plane. Even though these building blocks are four-dimensional, the linear combinations representing each of these four special cases are three-dimensional. Any particular competitive pattern need not involve all the basic factors.

Figure 6.5 portrays the competitive map accounting for 98.7% of the idealized shelf-price elasticities in Table 6.7. The size of the symbol for each brand represents the distance from the fixed origin of this space. This reflects the clout or receptivity/vulnerability of the brand. We see that Folgers and Maxwell House exert a similar pattern of pressure, with Maxwell House having more clout at shelf prices. They are both aligned to exert the greatest pressure on the premium brands in the All-Other-Branded category, which are quite vulnerable to their attack. Even though □ Chock Full O'Nuts is separated from ○ Folgers and Maxwell House by a sizeable angle, its extreme receptivity translates into its being strongly pressured by both Folgers and Maxwell House. The almost 180° angle between Folgers ○ and Folgers □ indicates that Folgers helps itself quite directly with price cuts. The most extreme example of this involves Chock Full O'Nuts which has a great deal of clout and is very vulnerable. The pattern in Figure 6.5 shows Chock Full O'Nuts competing much more with Folgers than with Maxwell House, while being very receptive to its own price moves. ○ Master Blend is positioned to exert its greatest pressure on Folgers at shelf prices. But Folgers is not in the best position to return the pressure on either Regular Maxwell House or Master Blend.

Yuban (unlabelled in the figure) resides at the fixed origin of this space, and the private-label brands PL 1 and PL 2 sit very near the origin, exhibiting no role in the competitive interplay. This is expected since the shelf-price map reflects an idealization of condition in Chain 1 which does not distribute Yuban or its own private label. If we were to create idealized elasticities closer to the position of a shelf-price week in Chain 2, which distributes this brand, it might behave more like the other premium brands in the AOB category. If we were to create idealized elasticities closer to the position of a shelf-price week in Chain 3, we

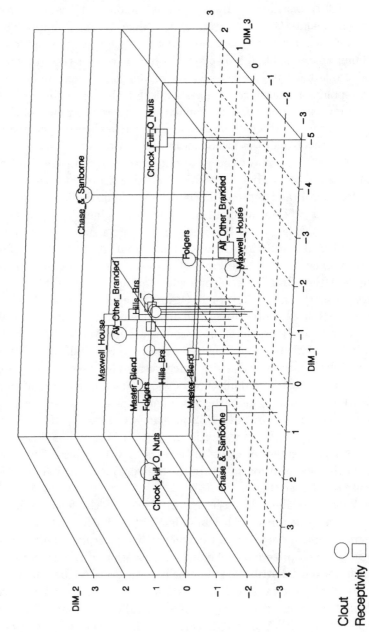

Figure 6.5 The Competitive Map – – Shelf Prices

would see a greater role for the private labels.[30]

When Folgers goes on sale the pattern in Figure 6.6 is operative (accounting for 99.8% of the corresponding idealized elasticities in Table 6.4). First, note that Folgers has less clout on sale. Shelf-price elasticities are like potential energy. When the brand actually goes on sale some of this energy is dissipated, in this case by being translated into sales. The reduction in the angle between ○ and □ for Folgers on sale indicates at least a small dissipation of Folgers' influence over its own market share. An approximately 90° between ○ and □ for Folgers would indicate that Folgers cannot help itself by further price reductions. On sale, Folgers is substantially less vulnerable to both Chock Full O'Nuts and AOB. Folgers can still attack the All-Other-Branded category and Chock Full O'Nuts, but the reduced shares for these brands during a Folgers promotion provide less incentive to Folgers.

When Maxwell House goes on sale Figure 6.7 depicts the action. As clearly indicated Maxwell House puts the greatest pressure on All Other Branded. While the premium brands which make up the AOB category possess considerable clout of their own, and are aligned to be able to help themselves, they are not particularly well aligned to return the pressure on Maxwell House. Only Chase & Sanborne is aligned for counter attack and potent enough to be a threat. Chock Full O'Nuts is a potent force under these market conditions, but is aligned to impact Folgers much more than it can impact Maxwell House. Note that in the one week of coincident promotions for Maxwell House and Chock Full O'Nuts (Week 24), the coefficients look like those for Chock Full O'Nuts sale weeks, rather than other Maxwell House sale weeks (see Figures 6.3 and 6.4). Brand managers for Maxwell House might do well to incorporate this information into planning the timing of their promotional events.

When Chock Full O'Nuts goes on sale (see Figure 6.8) it exerts a great deal of pressure directly on Folgers, which is vulnerable to the attack. Chock Full O'Nuts also pressures Hills Bros. and Master Blend. Maxwell House seems not very vulnerable to Chock Full O'Nuts on sale. Chock Full O'Nuts is not vulnerable to counter attack, although Chase & Sanborne's alignment makes it the most potent threat. Almost all the brands have near-zero loadings on the second dimension — making this

---

[30]It has already been noted that Chain 3 has a much higher feature price for the major brands than the other chains. Combined with the very frequent in-store displays and lower shelf prices for its private-label brand, the policy seems to be to draw shoppers in with a major-brand feature and encourage them to switch through the displays at the coffee aisle.

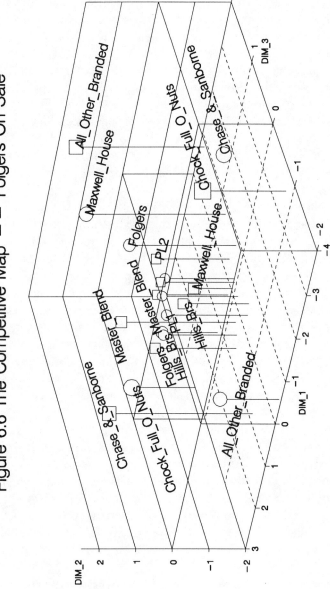

Figure 6.6 The Competitive Map − − Folgers On Sale

Figure 6.7 The Competitive Map – Maxwell House On Sale

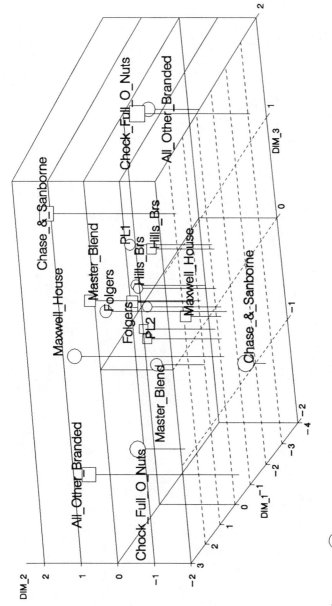

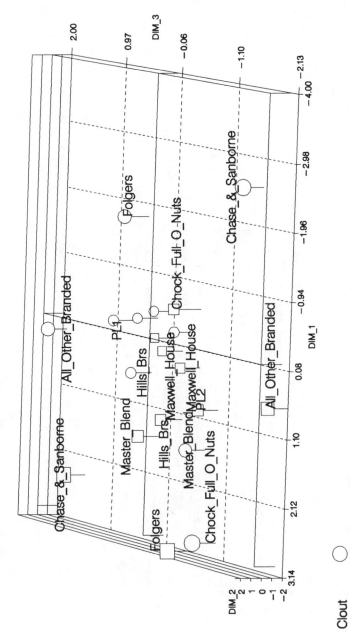

Figure 6.8   The Competitive Map – – Chock Full O Nuts On Sale

map almost two-dimensional.

Overall, these patterns show substantial asymmetries which would not have been revealed by any other market-structure map.

There are very simple relations between the maps and the idealized elasticities in Tables 6.7. As implied by equation (6.9), one need only multiply the clout coordinate of brand j times the receptivity coordinate of brand i, and sum over dimensions to produce the elasticity of brand i's market share with respect to brand j's price. For those who are more comfortable with maps than with matrices, these maps provide a visual representation of the richly asymmetric competitive patterns resulting from price changes in the coffee market. As in other categories of frequently purchase branded goods, price is used as a major weapon of promotional strategy. What one can read from these maps is what brands constitute the major threats to others with their price policy and where the major opportunities for competitive advantage may reside. These maps offer many signals which are new and very different from the market-structure maps of the past. Only a very few of these signals have been mentioned in this illustration. The full meaning of these signals is better interpreted by managers and management scientists involved in these markets than by academic researchers involved in methods development.

6.3 *Elasticities and Market Structure

The value of much of the developments so far rests on the propriety of using cross elasticities to reflect market structure. There are at least three deficiencies to elasticities as measures of competition:[31] 1) they are static measures as they assume no competitive reaction to change in a marketing-mix variable, 2) because they are static measures, they do not account well for structural change in markets, and 3) they can be difficult to measure when price changes are infrequent or are of low magnitude.

First, both historic lags and competitive reactions can be included in elasticity calculations. This was indicated by Hanssens,[32] although misspecification of his equation (2) precluded computation. Lagged in-

---

[31] Thanks are due to an anonymous reviewer for *Management Science* who pointed out these potential problems.

[32] Hanssens, Dominique M. [1980], "Market Response, Competitive Behavior, and Time Series Analysis," *Journal of Marketing Research*, XXVII (November), 470-85.

fluences on brand i's market share can be represented as $e^{(k)}_{ijt*t}$. This is the influence that brand j's price (k^{th} marketing instrument) in historic time-period t^* has on brand i's market share in period t. But for a competitive reaction to influence a current elasticity, a combination of events must occur. There must be an action involving marketing instrument k' by some brand i' in historic period t' which produces a significant price reaction by brand j in some historic period t^*, *and* there must be a nonzero elasticity for the effect of brand j's price in period t^* on brand i's market share in period t. We can represent the reaction elasticity as $e_{k'i't'\overline{R}kjt^*}$, where the subscripts before $\overline{R}$ indicate the antecedents producing the reaction, while the subscripts after $\overline{R}$ indicate where the reaction occurs. Then the market-share cross elasticity is represented as:

$$e^{(k)}_{ijt} = \sum_{t^*=(t-h)}^{t} e^{(k)}_{ijt^*t} + \sum_{t^*=(t-h)}^{t} \sum_{t'=(t^*-h)}^{t} \sum_{k'=1}^{K} \sum_{i'=1}^{N} e_{k'i't'\overline{R}kjt^*} \cdot e^{(k)}_{ijt^*t} \quad (6.10)$$

where h is the maximum relevant historic lag. Note that if either $e_{k'i't'\overline{R}kjt^*}$ or $e^{(k)}_{ijt^*t}$ is zero, the entire term makes no contribution to $e^{(k)}_{ijt}$. In the current illustration there were no significant lagged effects (or cross effects) on market share, nor were there any significant competitive reactions. Given the highly disaggregate nature of the modeling effort (i.e., modeling marketing shares for brands in each grocery chain each week) and the irregular timing of major promotions, the absence of such effects is not surprising.

Second, exploration of the time mode (chain-weeks in the current illustration) can help minimize the limitations of elasticities in reflecting structural changes. While a regular lag structure may not be evident, one of the attractive features of the three-mode factor analysis is in its ability to highlight structural events which occur at irregular intervals over the study period. In the coffee market, promotions for major brands signalled the big structural changes. These will most likely occur at irregular intervals to minimize competitive reaction as well as consumers delaying purchase in the certain anticipation of a sale for their favorite brand.

Third, if there is too little variation in a marketing instrument, elasticities can be hard to estimate accurately. In the retail coffee market there are very frequent price promotions, features, displays, and considerable couponing activity. About 50% of all sales are made on a promotion of some kind. But in warehouse-withdrawal data, more temporally or regionally aggregated data, or in categories with less frequent retail promotions (e.g., bar soap), lack of variation would be more of a concern.

The benefits of this style of analysis become clearer when we consider the task of intelligently using scanner data for brand planning. We could plot sales, prices, features, displays, and coupons for each brand, each chain and each week. But the points of information become so numerous that without further guidance, the ability to assimilate soon suffers. In the current illustration this would entail a scatter plot for each brand in each chain over 52 weeks or a pie chart summarizing each week in each chain over all the brands. Market-response models provide an enormous concentration of information. But how do we assimilate the implications of a market-response model? Simulations and forecasts are very valuable, but they reverse the concentration of information achieved by the market-response model. For each simulation run we must track the competitive strategies of all brands as well as all the outcomes — estimates of sales and profits for all manufacturer and all retailers.

The parameters of the market-response model can be a source of insight. We could even factor the matrix B using the model in equation (6.9). While we might obtain some sense of the structure of competitive forces, we would have no idea of how that structure changes with changes in competitive patterns. The notion of reflecting changes is one of the most basic and appealing features of elasticities.

Elasticities can provide quantitative understanding of a market. Like simulations, however, elasticities reverse the information concentration achieved by market-response models. Using asymmetric three-mode factor analysis summarizes the 22,464 elasticities (3 Chains × 52 Weeks × [12 × 12] Brands) into only two plots for the factors differentiating grocery chains over weeks, and a plot for each of the idealized competitive situations. The plots representing the structure over time can be helpful in planning the timing of promotions, tracking promotional effectiveness, and detecting promotional wear-out. Looking at over-time patterns helps counteract some of the limitations imposed by the static nature of each week's elasticity estimates. In the analysis of these data aggregated to the weekly level over grocery chains, these plots have revealed the market-wide expansion of elasticities in key pay-weeks. It is during the key-pay week that all Federal checks (Social Security, Aid to Families with Dependent Children, welfare, government pensions, etc.) arrive. These Federal checks are often cashed at supermarkets and then banked in the form of food purchases for the month. These first-week customers, typically being of limited means, are some of the most price-sensitive shoppers and are purchasing a disproportionate share of their monthly needs in this week.[33] Other applications could reveal temporal or seasonal patterns of interest. This format signals what are the systematic structural events in a dataset which otherwise might be too large to explore. The structure over brands is contained in figures describing the idealized competitive contexts which characterize this market. Shelf-price competition, and the structure of competition during sales for each of the three largest-selling brands, are differentiated in a manner which could never be detected from the average elasticities. The planning exercise in Chapter 7 shows how the competitive maps can be used to help focus the path of inquiry and limit the number of simulations.

6.4   *Interpretive Aids for Competitive Maps

The limitations of this approach stem mainly from its being descriptive, rather than prescriptive. The dimensions of a competitive map describe the terrain. While there is no guarantee that the map can easily be labelled in terms of brand attributes, the structure over brands could perhaps be made more useful if ideal points or property vectors were located in the space. Ideal points describe the most preferred position in a perceptual map. Property vector describe directions such as the direction of increasing economy or sportiness often seen in maps of the car market. Two special logit models[34] were designed to do this for competitive maps. These models provide an external analysis of preference, perceptions, or brand attributes. Internal analysis of preferences attempts to develop both the brand map and ideal points from ratings or ranking of consumer preferences. In external analysis of preferences we must have a pre-existing brand map, and we simply wish to estimate the most popular region(s) of the map. The competitive map contains the scale values for the brand — fulfilling the need for a pre-existing brand map, while sales data provide the relative choice frequencies required for locating the ideal points for each week.[35]

---

[33]Special thanks is due to J. Dennis Bender and John Totten for helping me understand the meaning and significance of this finding.

[34]Lee G. Cooper & Masao Nakanishi [1983b], "Two Logit Models for External Analysis of Preferences," *Psychometrika*, 48, 4, 607-20.

[35]The relative choice frequencies were originally supposed to come from paired-comparison judgments gathered in an experimental setting, but we can substitute the number of choices (sales) for on brand compared to the number of choices (sales) for the other brand for the required paired comparisons as long as most of the buyers

The basic idea of this style of analysis is that preference increases as brands get closer to an ideal point in a map. We can consider a distance function d_i^* which reflects how far brand i is from the ideal location.

$$d_i^* = \sum_{h=1}^{H} \beta_{hi}(X_{hi} - X_h^*)^2$$

where:

X_{hi} = the known coordinates of brand i on the given dimensions $h = 1, 2, \ldots, H$ of a map

X_h^* = the unknown coordinates of the ideal point on dimension h, and

β_h = the unknown weights reflecting the importance of dimension h in capturing the preferences.

The statistical problem is to be able to estimate the ideal coordinates X_h^* and the dimensional importance weights β_h from the relative choice frequencies. Let $\bar{f}_{ij}$ be the expected relative frequency of choice of brand i over brand j.

$$\bar{f}_{ij} + \bar{f}_{ji} = 1$$

The model for $\bar{f}_{ij}$ is given by:

$$\bar{f}_{ij} = \frac{\exp(d_i^*)\varepsilon_i}{\exp(d_i^*)\varepsilon_i + \exp(d_j^*)\varepsilon_j} \tag{6.11}$$

where d_i^* is as previously defined and ε_i is a log-normally distributed specification-error term, unique to the alternative.[36] This model actually allows for three different views of the relations between ideal points and choices. If all the weights β_h are negative, we have the standard ideal-point model in which preference declines smoothly in any direction away from the ideal point. This is portrayed in Figure 6.9 with the ideal point at (0,0). But sometimes preferences are more readily characterized by what we don't like than what we do. In such cases all the weights β_h are positive and we can locate an anti-ideal point, the least desirable point.

---

purchase a single unit (pound of coffee, for example) at a time.

[36] The function in equation (6.11) is formally derivable from the generalized extreme value distribution for a random utility model. See appendix 2.9.3 and Yellott, J. I. [1977], "The Relationship Between Luce's Choice Axiom, Thurstone's Theory of Comparative Judgments, and the Double Exponential Distribution," *Journal of Mathematical Psychology*, 15, 109-44, for further details.

As is pictured in Figure 6.10 preferences increase as we diverge in any direction away from the anti-ideal point at (0,0). If some of the weights β_h are positive and others are negative, preferences are represented by a saddle point, as is shown in Figure 6.11. The classic example of saddle points involves tea drinks. Some people like iced tea and some like hot tea. But on the temperature dimension there is an anti-ideal point at tepid tea. On the sweetness dimension some people like two lumps of sugar and their preference declines if either more or less sugar is used. The combination of an anti-ideal dimension of temperature and the ideal dimension of sweetness creates a saddle point.

Figure 6.9: Preference and the Ideal Point

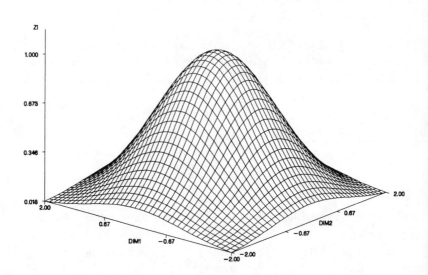

In addition to ideal dimensions and anti-ideal dimensions there are many dimensions on which only the most preferred direction is known. *Price* is an obvious example. The ideal price is almost always lower than any offered price. We know the direction of increasing preference but cannot isolate an ideal point. Such special cases are known as vector models.[37] Corresponding to the logit ideal point model in (6.11) we have

---

[37]The ideals in a vector model do not have to be infinite. Any time the ideal is outside the configuration of points in a map a vector model may be more apt than an

Figure 6.10: Preference and the Anti-Ideal Point

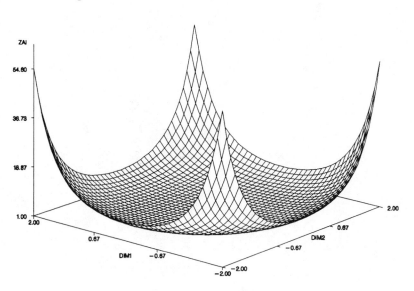

the following logit vector model.

$$\bar{f}_{ij} = \frac{\exp(\sum_{h=1}^{H} \alpha_h X_{hi})\varepsilon_i}{\exp(\sum_{h=1}^{H} \alpha_h X_{hi})\varepsilon_i + \exp(\sum_{h=1}^{H} \alpha_h X_{hj})\varepsilon_j} \qquad (6.12)$$

where α_h is the coordinate of the preference vector on dimensions h (the greater the coordinate the more influence that dimension has on preference).

Both the logit ideal-point model and the vector model can be estimated by regression techniques. Taking the logit of the expected, relative choice frequencies, reveals a linear form

$$\log\left(\frac{f_{ij}}{f_{ji}}\right) = d_i^* - d_j^* + (\log \varepsilon_i - \log \varepsilon_j) \ .$$

We can see how to estimate both the importance weight and the ideal

---

ideal point model.

Figure 6.11: Preference and the Saddle Point

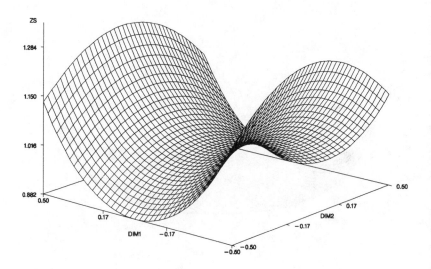

coordinate on each dimension by noting

$$d_i^* - d_j^* = \sum_{h=1}^{H} \beta_h [(X_{hi}^2 - 2X_{hi}X_h^* + X_h^{*2}) - (X_{hj}^2 - 2X_{hj}X_h^* + X_h^{*2})]$$

$$= \sum_{h=1}^{H} \beta_h [X_{hi}^2 - X_{hj}^2 - 2X_h^*(X_{hi} - X_{hj})]$$

$$= \sum_{h=1}^{H} [\beta_{h1}(X_{hi}^2 - X_{hj}^2) - \beta_{h2}(X_{hi} - X_{hj})]$$

where the importance of each dimension is reflected in the parameter associated with the difference in squared scale values ($\beta_{h2} = \beta_h$), and the ideal coordinate on each dimension can be found by solving a simple function involving the parameter associated with the difference in scale values ($\beta_{h1} = -2\beta_h X_h^*$).

Taking the logit of the observed, relative choice frequencies reveals the estimation form of the ideal-point model as:

$$\log\left(\frac{f_{ij}}{f_{ji}}\right) = \sum_{h=1}^{H} \beta_{h1}(X_{hi} - X_{hj}) + \beta_{h2}(X_{hi}^2 - X_{hj}^2) + u_{ij} \qquad (6.13)$$

where u_{ij} is a stochastic-disturbance term which represents the combined influences of specification errors ε_i and ε_j and sampling error for the departure of the observed, relative choice frequency, f_{ij}, from its expectation, $\bar{f}_{ij}$.[38]

The logit vector model is estimated as:

$$\log \left(\frac{f_{ij}}{f_{ji}} \right) = \sum_{h=1}^{H} \alpha_{h1}(X_{hi} - X_{hj}) + u_{ij} \ . \tag{6.14}$$

The difference between these two models is simply that the ideal-point model has one additional parameter associated with the differences in the squares of the scale values. Thus it is very straightforward to test if the logit ideal-point model or the logit vector model is most appropriate. Estimation and reduced-model tests are discussed in the original article.

There are several uses for this style of analysis. First, sales data from each time period or region can be transformed into relative choice frequencies and used to locate ideal points. If panel data are available, we could locate ideal points for each segment. In surveys consumers could be asked to pick any of a variety of attributes which are descriptive of each brand. The relative choice frequencies could come from such *pick-any data* as well as from more traditional, paired comparisons. The added benefit is that we can readily assess if an attribute vector or an ideal point is most appropriate for each property fit into the competitive map.[39]

Although we may always attempt to imbed property vectors in the space to help interpret the dimensions, the fit may not be good even in a good map. A map does not tell us *how* to reposition a brand to avoid competitive pressures. It merely reflects *what* those pressures are.

Kamakura and Srivastava[40] develop an alternative to the market-share model and the logit ideal-point model. They first create a probit version of the Cooper and Nakanishi logit ideal-point model (which they call the CN model), and then further generalize that model to estimate the distribution of ideal points in any choice situation. In so doing they end up with a model which can predict choice probabilities (market

---

[38]The nonspherical error-covariance matrix requires generalized least-square estimation procedures which are fully presented in Cooper & Nakanishi [1983b].

[39]The ideal points or vector could be positioned with respect to either the scale values representing the clout of each brand or its vulnerability. For most applications it is probably appropriate to use the scale values representing clout. For sales data we would then see how *clout* translates into sales.

[40]Kamakura, Wagner A. & Rajendra K. Srivastava [1986], "An Ideal-Point Probabilistic Choice Model for Heterogeneous Preferences," *Marketing Science*, 5, 3 (Summer), 199-218.

shares) in a way not bound by Luce's IIA assumption. Their models can be thought of as asymmetric, probit-based alternatives to asymmetric market-share models.

In comparing these efforts there are two technical issues and one general issue. Kamakura and Srivastava [1986] claim the CN model is a Luce-type model, subject to the problems inherent in the IIA assumption. When the CN model is used as they use it, this is true. But used as part of the system of models for competitive analysis, it is not true. In any system of models the problem of differential substitutability need only be solved once. In our case, the asymmetric market-share model solves this problem by estimating specific cross-competitive effects and by modeling the distinctiveness of marketing activities with zeta-scores or exp(z-scores). Both the competitive maps and the ideal points imbedded into them are not limited by Luce-type assumptions. The second technical point concerns the Kamakura and Srivastava claim that the CN model estimates only a single ideal point. The CN model was developed to estimate an ideal point in each time period, each consumer segment, each region, or each other delineation of choice situations. The example included in the original article (Cooper & Nakanishi [1983b]) specifically estimated ideal points for differing orders-of-presentation, just to illustrate this potential. In our current example there could be 156 ideal points — one for each store in each week. The idea is that, in coordination with market-share models and competitive maps, we could see how the competitive structure changes over time or competitive conditions and how those changes were translated into sales (or shares). Kamakura and Srivastava estimate the distribution of ideal points in any one context, but their efforts would have to be extended to estimate the distribution of ideal points in possibly many different competitive contexts.

The general issue involves the prediction of choice probabilities or market shares. Kamakura and Srivastava indicate that their methods were developed especially for predicting shares of choices. It is an empirical matter, but hard to imagine that a mapping procedure could predict market shares better than a market-share model. In our multimodel system there is specialization of purpose. The forecasting is done by the market-share model. Visualizations of competitive structures are accomplished with maps, while interpretation and opportunity analysis may be aided by ideal points. Thus no single model in the system is required to do more than what it does best. The Kamakura and Srivastava model seems to provide representations useful in product positioning or repositioning, which competitive maps are not designed to do. But forecasting market shares does not seem to be their model's strength.

The market-share models, the procedures for estimating elasticities from those models, three-mode factor analysis for representing the structure underlying those elasticities both over time and over brands, and the ideal-point model are a major part of the system of models for competitive analysis. Rather than proposing specific behavioral models of consumer response, these models provide the structural relations between the entities in a market information system. Although this system of models can be used for many purposes, the scientific goal is to provide a more systematic basis for using market information, while the practical goal is to provide a graphic understanding of the competitive structure and dynamics of a marketplace. Chapter 7 discusses how these methods can be used to provide a firmer empirical base for brand planning.

6.5 *Appendix for Chapter 6

This appendix presents the tables which resulted from the asymmetric three-mode factor analysis of the coffee-market example. While the technical development in the body of the chapter focused on the basic matrix concepts involved in the analysis, this appendix will deal more with the estimation methods. In particular the focus will be on the eigenvalue-eigenvector approach, in the belief it is easier to understand the mechanics of three-mode analysis from this perspective. Once the problem to be solved is understood it is easier to accept that alternating least-squares procedures (see Kroonenberg [1983]) can provide an overall least-squares solution to the problem, while the eigenvalue-eigenvector approach provides just an approximate least-squares solution (albeit a good approximation).

To understand the three views of the data we obtain from three-mode analysis it helps to review briefly some properties of two-mode tables. Consider a matrix $_nX_p$ with n rows for *individuals* and p columns for *variables*. Let us assume X is of rank $r \leq min(n,p)$. We can always represent X as a triple product.

$$_nX_p = {_nW_r}\Lambda_r U'_p$$

where $_nW_r$ is an orthonormal matrix containing coefficients relating the *individuals* to the *factors*, $_r\Lambda_r$ is a diagonal matrix containing the square roots of the variance of each factor on the diagonal, and $_pU_r$ is an orthonormal matrix containing coefficients which relate the *variables* to the *factors*. We speak of *factors* loosely, since this basic-structure model relates more to a principal-axes model than the formal factor-analytic model. Since W is orthonormal we know

$$_rW'_nW_r = I_r .$$

If we form the scalar products showing the associations between variables we get

$$_pX'_nX_p = {}_pU_r\Lambda^2{}_rU'_p .$$

Since U is orthonormal we know

$$_rU'_pU_r = I_r .$$

If we form the scalar products showing the associations between individuals we get

$$_nX_pX'_n = {}_nW_r\Lambda^2{}_rW'_n .$$

In this form we should be able to recognize W as the *left-principal vectors* (also known as eigenvectors or characteristic vectors), and U as the *right principal vectors* and the diagonal entries in Λ^2 as the eigenvalues (also known as latent roots or characteristic roots). We have long had the numerical algorithms to solve for the eigenvalues and eigenvectors of the symmetric matrices $X'X$ and XX'. Algorithms which solve directly for W, Λ and U are called *singular-value-decomposition* algorithms, where Λ contains the singular values (square roots of the eigenvalues).

This system sets up a series of orthogonal (independent) axes. The axes are linear combinations of the original variables. The first axis contains the greatest variance (information) which any single axis can hold; the next contains the greatest variance in any direction independent of the first axis. The third axis contains the greatest amount of variance in any direction that is independent of the first two, etc. The value of this kind of a representation becomes more apparent when we realize that if we discard the smallest dimension, we retain the most information we can pack into an $(r - 1)$-dimensional representation. The best two-dimensional approximation to the information in the original matrix comes from retaining the first two principal axes. The concept of approximating the information in a matrix, by a lower-dimensional system has been around for over 50 years.[41] It underlies much of the thinking which led Tucker to develop three-mode factor analysis.

---

[41] Eckart, Carl & Gale Young [1936], "The Approximation of One Matrix by Another of Lower Rank," *Psychometrika*, 1, 211-18.

The common scaling space for the columns can be found from a singular value decomposition of a matrix **E** formed by vertically concatenating the elasticity matrices for each chain-week:

$$\mathbf{E_j} = \begin{pmatrix} E^{(1)} \\ E^{(2)} \\ \vdots \\ E^{(T)} \end{pmatrix} .$$

We need only the right principal vectors of this matrix which are the same as the eigenvectors of $_j\mathbf{E'E_j}$. As previously stated, these vectors will reflect the similarity among the columns of an elasticities matrix — the structure underlying how brands exert influence on the marketplace. These vectors appear in Table 6.3 as the Column Space.

Table 6.3: Common Scaling Space

Brand	Row Space				Column Space			
	1	2	3	4	1	2	3	4
1	0.39	−0.10	0.59	−0.33	0.38	−0.25	0.03	−0.72
2	0.14	−0.24	0.05	−0.39	0.34	−0.59	0.21	0.56
3	0.06	0.22	0.31	0.16	−0.38	−0.02	−0.06	0.29
4	0.00	−0.23	0.33	−0.21	−0.09	0.08	0.13	−0.01
5	−0.87	−0.26	0.34	−0.06	−0.73	−0.26	−0.00	−0.23
6	−0.04	0.01	0.05	−0.08	0.06	0.01	−0.07	−0.04
7	0.10	0.14	0.53	0.66	0.17	0.21	−0.85	0.14
8	−0.21	0.86	0.10	−0.34	0.08	0.67	0.41	0.10
9	0.06	0.04	−0.04	−0.03	0.11	0.12	0.17	0.00
10	0.04	0.06	0.19	−0.34	0.07	0.03	0.04	−0.08

The corresponding eigenvalues (shown in Table 6.4 as the Clout Factors) are used to select the dimensionality of the common scaling space for columns. Note that the last large drop is from the 7.4% of the variance in the fourth factor to the 4.1% of the variance contained in the fifth factor, so that four factors are retained for the common scaling space matrix **C** introduced in equation (6.4).

The common scaling space for the rows can be found from a singular value decomposition of a matrix **E** formed by horizontally concatenating the elasticity matrices for each chain-week:

$$_i\mathbf{E} = (E^{(1)}|E^{(2)}|\cdots|E^{(T)}) .$$

We need only the left principal vectors of this matrix which are the same as the eigenvectors of $_i\mathbf{EE_i'}$. These vectors will reflect the similarity

Table 6.4: Dimensionality of Common Scaling Space

	Clout Factors		Vulnerability Factors	
	Eigen- values	Percent Variance	Eigen- value	Percent Variance
1	46895.1	49.4%	45716.4	48.1%
2	19917.4	21.0%	20617.8	21.7%
3	9297.1	9.8%	9661.6	10.2%
4	7070.7	7.4%	7287.2	7.7%
5	3866.6	4.1%	5822.9	6.1%
6	3079.8	3.2%	2600.2	2.7%
7	2237.8	2.4%	1702.9	1.8%
8	1542.3	1.6%	660.0	0.7%
9	1050.8	1.1%	575.6	0.6%
10	0.0	0.0%	312.8	0.3%

among the rows of an elasticities matrix — the structure underlying how brands are influenced by marketplace forces. These vectors appear in Table 6.3 as the Row Space.

The corresponding eigenvalues (shown in Table 6.4 as the Vulnerability Factors) are used to select the dimensionality of the common scaling space for rows. It is possible, though inconvenient, that the dimensionality of the row space and that of the column space could differ. In fact, in this case there is some evidence that there might be a fifth factor among the rows. For, though there is a striking alignment of the variance controlled by the first four factors in the two spaces, the fifth factor among the rows is somewhat larger than that for the columns. It is a minor point, indeed, but choosing a common dimensionality for both the row space and column space is advisable. In this case we decided to select four factors for each space.

So far we have seen that there are two ways to organize the data, each corresponding to a different view of the brands. There is yet another way to view the data. Each matrix $E^{(t)}$ could be strung out into a column vector, $\mathbf{e_t}$, containing m^2 elements. These column vectors could be horizontally concatenated into a matrix $\mathbf{E_t}$

$$\mathbf{E_t} = (\mathbf{e_1}|\mathbf{e_2}|\cdots|\mathbf{e_T}) \ .$$

We may represent $\mathbf{E_t}$ by

$$\mathbf{E_t} = SW$$

where W contains the right principal vectors of $\mathbf{E_t}$ — the elements w_{tl} introduced in equation (6.8). The right principal vectors of this matrix are the same as the eigenvectors of $_t\mathbf{E'E_t}$. These vectors will reflect the similarities among stores and weeks — the structural forces leading to the representations in Figures 6.3 and 6.4.

These three different views of the data are tied together by the core matrix, G, introduced in equation (6.4). The core planes can be found one at a time, by taking each column of S and reorganizing it into an $m \times m$ matrix $S^{(l)}$, essentially reversing the process by which $E^{(t)}$ was strung out into $\mathbf{e_t}$. The lth layer or the core matrix can be found from

$$_qG_q^{(l)} = {}_qR'S^{(l)}C_q \ .$$

The core matrix is presented in Table 6.5

In the general three-mode factor-analysis model, the core matrix is very important in understanding how factors on one mode relate to factors on the other modes. We simplify the issue in this special case by diagonalizing each core plane as shown in equation (6.5), and forming the matrices $_iR_q^{(l)}$ and $_qC_j^{(l)}$ developed in equations (6.6) and (6.7) and displayed for the coffee-market example in Table 6.6.

These joint-space coefficients are the building blocks from which the idealized elasticities are created from equation (6.8) corresponding to particular competitive patterns of interest. The idealized elasticities for the four conditions highlighted in the coffee-market example are presented in Table 6.7.

As a result of this presentation we hope it will be clearer from where the spatial representations come. While the eigenvalue-eigenvector development can help provide such insight, numerically it creates only an approximate least-squares solution to the systems of equations. Kroonenberg [1983] shows how all the components can be estimated using an alternating least-squares (ALS) algorithm. Whether this numerical refinement makes a practical difference will have to be determined in future research.

Table 6.5: The Core Matrix for the Coffee-Market Example

Core Plane 1			
1	2	3	4
1 202.01	5.13	3.00	1.80
2 −10.62	132.57	6.56	−5.60
3 −2.79	−10.50	−39.02	−32.94
4 −6.84	−0.05	−42.68	21.53

Core Plane 2			
1	2	3	4
1 −1.43	18.90	−34.48	9.81
2 7.04	−3.51	−19.57	7.57
3 −17.16	15.74	−29.30	13.86
4 32.10	7.42	−35.47	0.49

Core Plane 3			
1	2	3	4
1 −8.33	−9.61	−22.26	−4.59
2 2.44	−0.73	−13.13	−1.30
3 45.48	4.60	−14.71	−1.37
4 −18.91	7.39	−18.53	6.36

Core Plane 4			
1	2	3	4
1 7.69	3.08	−2.25	3.85
2 −3.25	−9.97	−2.74	−4.10
3 −21.48	−4.62	5.76	2.34
4 1.98	1.25	−0.09	−0.20

Table 6.6: Joint-Space Coefficients for Chain-Week Factors

Chain-Week Factor 1

Brand	Vulnerability Factors				Clout Factors			
	1	2	3	4	1	2	3	4
1	5.65	1.47	1.87	3.87	−5.33	−2.65	−0.78	−4.50
2	2.42	2.56	−1.75	1.96	−5.06	−6.67	2.71	2.98
3	0.43	−2.11	2.78	0.52	5.36	−0.40	0.05	1.82
4	0.28	2.93	0.67	2.27	1.32	0.99	0.89	−0.22
5	−12.24	3.90	1.18	1.63	10.39	−3.02	−0.06	−1.43
6	−0.48	−0.08	−0.08	0.57	−0.86	0.05	−0.57	−0.14
7	0.81	−0.80	6.39	−0.96	−2.13	1.52	−6.29	1.93
8	−3.56	−9.76	−0.57	2.23	−1.15	8.17	2.77	0.27
9	0.78	−0.54	−0.33	−0.01	−1.62	1.60	1.18	−0.18
10	0.63	−0.66	−0.51	2.36	−0.93	0.41	0.11	−0.53

Chain-Week Factor 2

Brand	Vulnerability Factors				Clout Factors			
	1	2	3	4	1	2	3	4
1	2.27	4.50	−0.00	−0.32	−1.61	−3.78	0.42	−0.54
2	−1.62	2.29	−0.10	−0.62	−1.61	−2.02	−0.36	2.23
3	2.79	0.46	0.11	0.61	0.36	2.60	−0.06	0.68
4	−0.34	2.42	0.14	−0.43	−0.91	0.62	−0.02	−0.29
5	−3.77	0.36	0.66	0.43	−2.19	3.32	0.39	0.67
6	−0.32	0.46	0.02	0.14	0.55	−0.39	0.02	−0.06
7	6.07	−0.64	0.33	0.11	7.38	−0.26	0.07	0.17
8	−0.27	0.82	−0.12	3.08	−0.96	0.81	−0.36	−2.09
9	0.06	0.03	−0.06	0.05	−0.79	−0.45	−0.11	−0.51
10	−0.61	2.21	−0.04	0.43	−0.23	−0.46	0.02	−0.26

Chain-Week Factor 3

Brand	Vulnerability Factors				Clout Factors			
	1	2	3	4	1	2	3	4
1	4.31	1.09	−0.21	−1.47	2.81	−0.38	0.37	−2.28
2	0.96	−1.22	−0.17	−1.35	1.71	−1.36	−0.64	−0.91
3	1.78	1.73	0.08	0.47	−2.73	0.64	−0.18	0.54
4	2.53	−0.73	−0.19	−0.33	−0.74	−0.69	0.05	0.22
5	2.93	−3.73	−0.02	2.35	−5.15	0.61	0.10	−1.23
6	0.55	−0.30	0.02	−0.09	0.52	0.34	0.02	−0.04
7	2.01	3.77	−0.08	1.89	1.99	4.82	−0.02	1.04
8	2.08	−0.01	0.72	−0.57	0.43	−2.61	0.20	2.36
9	−0.22	0.14	0.02	−0.26	0.68	−1.12	0.04	0.37
10	2.02	−0.59	0.05	−0.92	0.47	−0.26	0.06	−0.07

Chain-Week Factor 4

Brand	Vulnerability Factors				Clout Factors			
	1	2	3	4	1	2	3	4
1	2.04	−1.11	−0.05	1.01	−1.31	1.98	0.03	−0.99
2	−0.12	−0.82	−0.08	0.26	−0.44	0.59	0.13	1.20
3	1.48	0.29	0.05	0.32	1.70	−0.55	−0.03	0.49
4	1.32	−1.01	−0.04	0.11	0.46	−0.38	0.01	−0.16
5	2.77	−0.56	−0.03	−1.45	3.78	0.61	−0.04	−0.24
6	0.34	0.02	−0.01	−0.01	−0.37	0.15	−0.01	−0.02
7	2.09	−0.27	0.15	0.33	−2.04	0.34	−0.15	0.65
8	1.89	2.74	−0.05	0.22	−0.94	−2.34	0.02	−0.57
9	−0.22	0.13	−0.01	0.10	−0.51	−0.45	0.03	−0.19
10	1.00	0.03	−0.06	0.29	−0.31	0.05	0.01	−0.17

Table 6.7: Elasticities for Idealized Competitive Conditions

Idealized Shelf-Price Elasticities

	Fol-gers	Max Hse	Mstr Bln	Hills Bros.	CF ON	Yu-ban	C&S	AOB	PL1	PL2
Fo	−3.92	−1.32	2.90	0.98	4.39	−0.64	−2.81	1.14	−0.25	−0.48
MH	−2.43	−2.78	1.29	0.14	0.80	0.01	2.56	0.98	−0.33	−0.23
MB	0.42	2.56	0.18	0.30	1.29	−0.34	−3.96	−0.61	0.18	−0.04
HB	−1.41	−0.93	0.00	0.18	−1.65	0.02	0.80	2.43	0.51	0.05
CF	4.63	4.17	−6.82	−1.60	−15.91	1.27	5.68	4.77	2.59	1.24
Yu	0.12	0.46	−0.25	−0.14	−0.79	0.07	0.51	−0.05	0.05	0.02
CS	0.45	2.43	0.16	1.16	2.35	−0.74	−8.69	1.75	1.00	0.14
OB	3.84	8.78	−1.50	−1.58	−1.78	0.32	0.28	−7.31	−0.94	−0.11
P1	−0.25	−0.14	0.46	0.03	1.05	−0.06	−0.11	−0.63	−0.26	−0.10
P2	−0.70	0.85	0.39	−0.23	−0.18	0.04	1.06	−0.81	−0.28	−0.15

Idealized Folgers Sale-Price Elasticities

	Fol-gers	Max Hse	Mstr Bln	Hills Bros.	CF ON	Yu-ban	C&S	AOB	PL 1	PL 2
Fo	−0.90	−0.06	0.76	0.41	1.50	−0.26	−1.91	0.51	0.06	−0.10
MH	−1.03	−1.46	0.47	−0.06	0.01	0.09	1.99	0.31	−0.22	−0.10
MB	0.70	1.75	−0.21	0.21	0.47	−0.20	−2.89	−0.16	0.27	0.06
HB	−0.13	−0.16	−0.56	−0.05	−1.89	0.11	0.81	1.35	0.40	0.13
CF	2.91	2.66	−4.61	−1.21	−11.20	0.93	4.83	3.19	1.68	0.82
Yu	0.19	0.33	−0.27	−0.12	−0.72	0.07	0.44	−0.01	0.05	0.04
CS	0.78	1.82	−0.18	0.83	1.45	−0.52	−6.50	1.34	0.82	0.17
OB	2.55	5.17	−1.32	−0.99	−2.01	0.27	0.47	−3.81	−0.36	0.03
P1	−0.17	−0.11	0.31	0.03	0.72	−0.04	−0.12	−0.40	−0.16	−0.07
P2	0.15	0.74	−0.24	−0.27	−0.89	0.11	0.97	−0.49	−0.07	−0.01

Idealized Maxwell House Sale-Price Elasticities

	Folg gers	Max Hse	Mstr Bln	Hills Bros.	CF ON	Yu-ban	C&S	AOB	PL1	PL2
Fo	−2.11	−0.40	1.73	0.74	3.09	−0.49	−3.03	0.76	−0.04	−0.26
MH	−1.53	−1.80	0.72	−0.05	0.07	0.09	2.45	0.46	−0.27	−0.15
MB	0.47	1.89	0.15	0.39	1.42	−0.34	−4.00	−0.22	0.24	0.00
HB	−0.82	−0.52	−0.03	0.09	−1.08	0.02	0.58	1.43	0.30	0.03
CF	2.64	2.19	−4.18	−1.21	−10.27	0.92	5.18	2.61	1.40	0.72
Yu	0.09	0.27	−0.17	−0.11	−0.54	0.06	0.45	−0.08	0.01	0.01
CS	0.56	2.09	0.23	1.18	2.76	−0.75	−8.66	1.56	0.91	0.13
OB	2.66	5.48	−1.00	−1.01	−0.97	0.21	0.11	−4.79	−0.63	−0.06
P1	−0.14	−0.08	0.28	0.02	0.64	−0.04	−0.08	−0.39	−0.16	−0.06
P2	−0.32	0.56	0.18	−0.20	−0.22	0.05	0.89	−0.65	−0.20	−0.09

Idealized Chock Full O'Nuts Sale-Price Elasticities

	Folg gers	Max Hse	Mstr Bln	Hills Bros.	CF ON	Yu-ban	C&S	AOB	PL1	PL2
Fo	−7.85	−2.70	5.99	1.90	9.26	−1.27	−5.31	1.70	−0.70	−1.01
MH	−3.41	−2.69	1.84	0.24	1.18	−0.08	2.44	1.19	−0.37	−0.34
MB	−1.16	1.31	1.77	0.83	4.48	−0.67	−5.49	−0.62	−0.15	−0.29
HB	−4.01	−2.22	2.71	0.78	3.53	−0.46	−0.87	1.32	−0.32	−0.45
CF	0.66	−0.37	−0.44	−0.46	−0.91	0.28	2.50	−0.98	−0.31	0.02
Yu	−0.49	−0.10	0.44	0.03	0.66	−0.05	0.11	−0.32	−0.18	−0.10
CS	−1.08	1.73	1.86	1.69	5.92	−1.13	−10.78	1.34	0.61	−0.15
OB	1.44	4.66	1.17	−0.62	4.23	−0.17	−1.58	−7.03	−1.60	−0.48
P1	0.02	0.10	0.01	−0.04	0.00	0.01	0.14	−0.18	−0.05	−0.01
P2	−2.80	−0.69	2.34	0.32	3.41	−0.32	−0.16	−0.89	−0.73	−0.48

Chapter 7

Decision-Support Systems

The main thrust of this book has been the analysis of market-share figures with an explicit objective of improving the marketing manager's understanding of the market and competition. We have presented in Chapters 1 through 3 a framework and models which we consider the best to achieve this end. The data collection and estimation techniques for calibrating these models were discussed in Chapters 4 and 5. A competitive-mapping technique which is useful in interpreting the calibration results was presented in Chapter 6. Yet those chapters have not entirely achieved our objective because the manager is obviously not content with merely analyzing and describing the competitive interactions in the marketplace. Whatever understanding the manager gains through market-share analysis will have to be converted eventually into concrete marketing programs. We turn next to this last stage of market-share analysis.

It has been our position in this book that the competitive conditions in a market may be chiefly described by a set of model parameters, especially the elasticities of market shares with respect to marketing variables. However, we recognize that designing a marketing program based on the knowledge of elasticities is not an automatic process. With only a limited number of brands and marketing variables one may have to deal with a surprisingly complex pattern of competitive interrelationships, indicated by the large number of elasticities and cross elasticities. The manager needs to interpret such a pattern and to select one set of levels for the marketing variables which presumably maximizes the firm's (long-term) profits. But there are no easy rules for converting a given pattern of competition into an implementable marketing program.

Some might think of designing marketing programs as large-scale mathematical-programming problems, but such a conception is unrealistic for several reasons. For one thing, the future environment for a firm's marketing program is full of uncertainties which affect its performance. Economic conditions change unexpectedly; variations in consumer tastes are sometimes illogical; weather and climate substantially impact demand, etc. Statistical decision theory may be employed to cope with future uncertainties, but its application to market-share analysis is complicated by the fact that those factors that cause uncertainties must be explicitly brought into the model and the strength of their influence must be calibrated beforehand. Many important factors cannot be treated in this manner. How, for example, does one calibrate the impact of one-time events, such as new governmental regulations, on one's market share?

For another thing, even if other uncertain factors can be correctly guessed, the best (optimal) marketing program for a firm is still dependent on the willful and often unpredictable actions of the competitors. One may guess competitors' marketing actions and plan one's own program accordingly. But will they guess that our actions are about to be modified and adjust their actions again? As we discuss later, game theory, which is one possible solution technique to decision making under this type of circular reasoning, is not advanced enough to give the marketing manager practical solutions in competitive situations involving many brands and a large number of marketing variables.

Lastly, designing an optimal *marketing mix* (i.e., the best combination of marketing variable) presumes the existence of a definite objective. In formal theories the objective is assumed to be maximizing either long-run or short-run profits, but in many practical decision situations profit maximization is not always pursued. The real-world managers may have difficulties in conceptualizing long-run profits, yet they are too astute to try to maximize short-run profits. In the context of market-share analysis, it is often a planned level of market share that becomes the main objective and is pursued vigorously. To complicate the matter further, the brand manager at a manufacturing firm may have an entirely different objective than that of a store manager for a supermarket chain. Both the brand manager and the store manager may feel that the objective of the other is wrong. There is no sophisticated theory of mathematical programming which enables one to find an optimal marketing mix when one is not sure of the objective to achieve.

We believe that the present state of the art in decision theory and game theory is such that the marketing manager will find little use for these theories in their planning work. Lacking an easily applicable theory, the manager may resort to the simplest approach, in which he/she forecasts the most likely pattern (or *scenario*) of the future environment and the competitors' actions, and designs a single marketing program to meet this pattern. This approach, however, is not a very logical one, especially when the likelihood that the chosen scenario occurs is small.[1] It is far more practical for the manager to create several likely scenarios of the future environment and competitors' actions, initially choose one program that corresponds to the most likely scenario, and keep the others as *contingency* plans. If the initially-chosen plan turns out to be the wrong one in view of the subsequent developments, one may easily move to another plan which fits the new situation best.

This contingency-planning approach appears to us to be the most practical solution to marketing planning under environmental and competitive uncertainties. But if the marketing manager wishes to take this planning approach he/she will need a planning tool which permits him/her to design many marketing programs, each of which corresponds to a likely scenario. Even with only a few brands and several marketing variables, the computation of the optimal marketing mix could be a formidable task. The manager must first collect the data on past market shares and marketing variables, calibrate the model, and forecast the effects of environmental and competitive factors. He/she must then compute, for each likely scenario, the value of profits (or some other objective function) for each combination of marketing variables, and select that combination which maximizes the objective. Unless we supply him/her with an efficient computational tool to perform this task, the manager is likely to revert back to a more naive approach.

In the following sections we present an example market information system, the main purpose of which it to facilitate market-share analysis. Although our example system, which is called CASPER (Competitive Analysis System for Promotional Effectiveness Research), may seem small compared to real-world market information systems (which tend to be immense), it attempts to integrate the data collection, model estimation, interpretation, and the marketing-planning process. Real-world systems can be designed as natural extensions of our proposed system.

---

[1]This may sound contradictory, but when the events which constitute the chosen scenario are independent and numerous, the joint probability that all of the events occur simultaneously may indeed be very small — even for the most likely scenario — because it is the product of probabilities for the individual events.

7.1   CASPER

The most practical component of a market information system is the decision-support system. The functions of a decision-support system must be broad enough to enable managers to:

1. learn from history (and graphic summaries of history are often far better for learning than are tables of numbers);

2. simulate the consequences of their plans in terms of both sales and profits, for both the manufacturers and the retailers; and

3. test selected strategies in a dynamic, competitive environment.

CASPER has been developed to illustrate the kinds of functions encompassed by this mandate. CASPER contains a HISTORY file with a year's worth of weekly data, from three grocery chains, summarizing sales in the ground, caffeinated coffee market. These historical data were used to calibrate the market-share and category-volume model.[2] As indicated in the development of the category-volume model (see section 5.12.2), the private-label brands (PL 1–3 and AOPL) were combined into a single APL brand aggregate.

CASPER's Standard Graphic Library summarizes each of the nine brands in this category. Each brand is traced over time, and each week is traced over brands for a comprehensive, visual record of the marketplace. Looking at the data is an indispensable step in building the kind of expertise needed for good decisions. CASPER also contains a menu-driven market simulator. One inquires into the market by specifying the competitive conditions for a particular occasion or series of occasions, with the results being accumulated in an OCCASIONS file. CASPER contains graphing and tabling functions to help summarize simulation results. All basic results are in the form of spreadsheets so that one can use the capabilities of FRAMEWORK to create a wide variety of summary reports.[3]

The dynamic simulator in CASPER is structured as a game. The GAME provides a way of putting marketing plans to the test. In the

---

[2]The market-share model used data from all seven grocery chains to estimate parameters.

[3]FRAMEWORK is a product of Ashton-Tate, 20101 Hamilton Avenue, Torrance, CA 90502-1319. While FRAMEWORK is necessary to run CASPER, any of the resulting spreadsheets can be imported to other spreadsheet programs for further analysis.

GAME module three Brand Teams (for Folgers, Regular Maxwell House, and Chock Full O'Nuts) develop promotion plans and support material to try to convince three Retailer Teams to promote their brands during an eight- or nine-week promotion period. All six teams can compete for profits or the roles of the Retailer Teams can be played by a Game Master. In either case the teams receive results back in the form of three spreadsheets. First is a summary of sales and estimated profits achieved by the real brands and retailers during this period under the profit assumptions of the GAME. Second, each Brand Team receives a summary of how they would have fared against the real brands' actions. And finally all teams receive a summary of the sales and profits in head-to-head competition. By triangulation, each team gets a comprehensive summary of its performance. The complete GAME involves three promotion periods of nine, nine, and eight weeks, respectively. These 26 weeks of data were the ones following the 52 weeks used to calibrate the market-share and category-volume models.

The simulator in CASPER is driven by a high-parameter asymmetric market-share model,[4] which incorporates the basic premise that marketing actions must be distinctive to be effective, and by a 31 parameter, category-volume model.[5] This version of CASPER is a brand-management tool for the coffee market, as well as a prototype for the kind of functionality managers should expect in any market covered by optical-scanner data.

7.2 Using HISTORY

CASPER's Standard Graphic Library contains plots which provide an initial summary of the history of all brands. The summary of a brands market share or sales over time is found in Plot Settings.View.Standard Libraries.XY-Plots. If one uses this menu to bring Folgers Sales – Chain 1 to the screen, the result should look like Figure 7.1. The top line reflects the price each week with values recorded on the right-hand vertical axis (from $2.64). The bottom line reflects market shares, with values demarcated on the left-hand vertical axis. Weeks with a feature (F), display (D), and/or store coupon (C) are noted just above the "Week" axis at the bottom. Note the large spikes in share or sales (up to 5,238 lbs. in week 49) which occur in weeks with price cuts combined with feature

---

[4]The parameter values are listed in Table 5.13.
[5]The parameters for the category-volume model are given in Table 5.14.

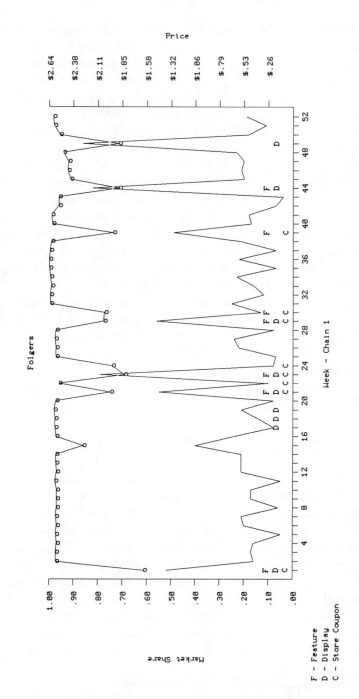

Figure 7.1: Folgers Market Share – Chain 1

(F), displays (D), and/or store coupons (C). The dramatic pulsing of sales during promotions is something which would be lost in yearly aggregated sales graphs. By looking at a chain-week record one obtains a much clearer sense of market response and the promotion policy of a grocery chain.[6]

To see the array of competition a brand faces in any given week use CASPER's Standard Pie Charts. Use Plot Settings.View.Standard Libraries.Pie Charts to look at Chain 2 weeks 10, 13, and 30. These should look like Figures 7.2 – 7.4. Note that at $1.87 per pound (with a newspaper feature and an in-store display) Chock Full O'Nuts acquires 72% of the market in week 10. In week 13 (Figure 7.3) the same offering for Chock Full O'Nuts results in a 44% share. Is there anything in the competitive environment which explains the difference in market response to Chock Full O'Nuts? Obviously the promotion for Maxwell House (low price combined with a newspaper feature, in-store display, and store coupon) has an impact. As was emphasized in prior discussions of the distinctiveness of marketing activities, whatever the value of a particular feature, it is shared by all the brands possessing the feature. In week 30 the shared feature is only the distinctively low prices for Maxwell House and Chock Full O'Nuts, since there is no overlap in the other promotional instruments.

Before beginning to exercise the market simulator, it is natural to want to know how good the simulator is at reproducing history.[7] For example, we can view Maxwell House Market Share – Chain 2 from the Standard Graphic Library. It should look like Figure 7.5. Then select file Ch2Maxms from directory \CASPER\CASOCCS\CH2SIM for comparison. It should look like Figure 7.6. The ability of these models to reflect the consequences of competitive actions on a brand's market share make these forecasts valuable as planning aids. Even if univariate time-series were more accurate (which does not appear to be the case),

---

[6]View the market share or sales figures for Chains 2 and 3. Do grocery chains seem to differ in how frequently they promote Folgers or how they use the marketing instruments? Chain 2 seems more willing to sustain a promotion over several weeks. Chain 3 seems to promote less frequently, using few, if any, store coupons or displays.

[7]Up to 52 weeks worth of historical data can be run through the market simulator a time using the Run.Run Off History menu in CASPER. This was done a grocery chain at a time. The spreadsheets summarizing these simulations are called CH1SIM, CH2SIM, and CH3SIM, respectively. How to build CASPER's Standard Graphs from these spreadsheets is described below. For now we need only note that any CASPER graphics made by the user can be viewed in CASPER by selecting Plot Settings.View.User Libraries and specifying the complete file name.

Figure 7.2: Market Shares – Week 10 Chain 2

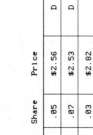

Market Shares

Week Number 10   Chain Number 2
      File   "history"

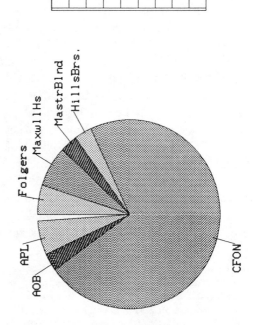

Brand	Share	Price	
Folgers	.05	$2.56	D
Maxwll Hs	.07	$2.53	D
MastrBlnd	.03	$2.82	
HillsBrs.	.03	$2.45	D
CFON	.72	$1.87	F
Yuban	.00	$.00	D
C&S	.00	$.00	
AOB	.03	$2.93	D
APL	.06	$2.19	

Figure 7.3: Market Shares – Week 13 Chain 2

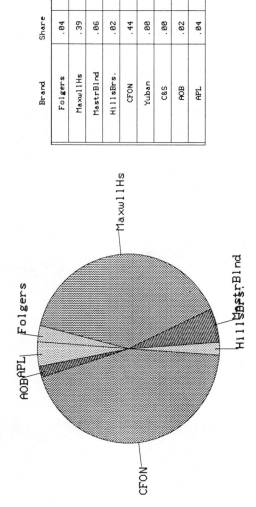

Market Shares

Week Number 13   Chain Number 2
File   "history"

Brand	Share	Price			
Folgers	.04	$2.57			C
Maxwl1Hs	.39	$2.01	F	D	
MastrBlnd	.06	$2.82			
HillsBrs.	.02	$2.46			
CFON	.44	$1.87	F	D	
Yuban	.00	$.00			
C&S	.00	$.00			
AOB	.02	$2.99		D	
APL	.04	$2.19			

Figure 7.4: Market Shares – Week 30 Chain 2

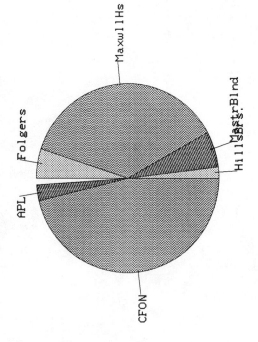

Market Shares

Week Number 30 Chain Number 2
     File   "history"

Brand	Share	Price			
Folgers	.05	$2.77			C
Maxwl1Hs	.37	$2.00	F		
MastrBlnd	.06	$2.59			
HillsBrs.	.02	$2.42		D	
CFON	.46	$1.89			
Yuban	.00	$.00			
C&S	.00	$.00			
AOB	.00	$3.46			
APL	.03	$2.19			

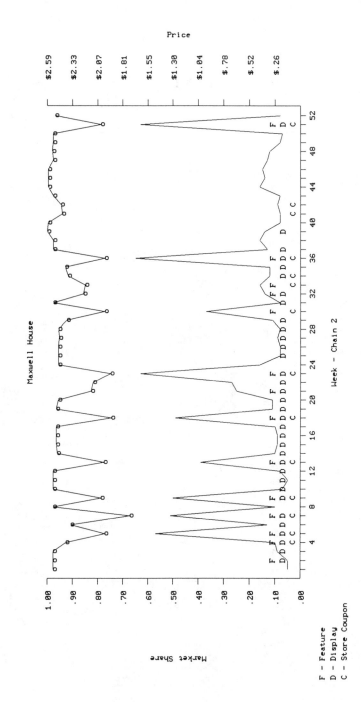

Figure 7.5: Maxwell House Actual Market Shares – Chain 2

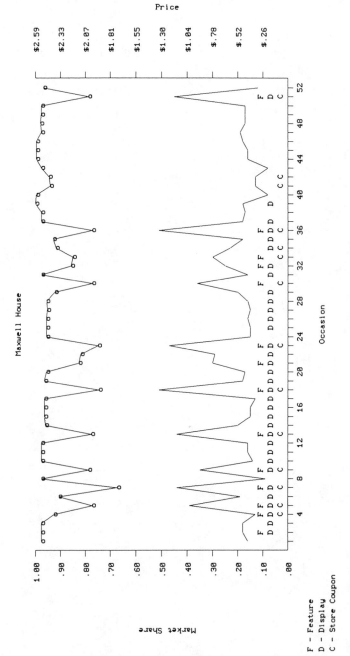

Figure 7.6: Maxwell House Estimated Market Shares – Chain 2

such models do not answer the *what-if* questions which form the core of any planning exercise.

7.3 Simulating Static Occasions

This section presents a planning exercise assessing market response to a sale for Chock Full O'Nuts. This will be a static simulation in the sense that we first want to reflect market response as if nothing preceded each occasion and nothing followed it. The occasions will be demarcated by price varying from a little lower than is reasonable ($1.60) to a little higher than is reasonable ($2.80). The sale will be supported by a newspaper feature.[8] The market response will be assessed first against the standard shelf prices for all other brands, then against a sale for Folgers, then Maxwell House, and finally against a simultaneous sale for Folgers and Maxwell House. We will set the background conditions, set the ranges of price for the simulations, and plot the results.

The defaults are the background conditions which don't change in the course of a simulation (a block of occasions). If we are going to vary Chock Full O'Nuts' price it will be set in the next section. Here we are concerned only with setting Feature, Display, and Coupon – the things which will be fixed while prices vary.

First let's look at the existing defaults. We view them in the same pop-up spreadsheet which can alter the defaults. Select the menu options Set Defaults.Set Values.Marketing Instruments.Set.Set Manually/View. A display like Table 7.1 should appear.

When CASPER is started, these default background assumptions are made. They simply reflect the average shelf prices for all brands in the HISTORY file. For easy modification, input to this sheet is *keystroke filtered* so that only sensible values can be entered. Prices must be positive numbers. Promotions are reflected as the proportion (between 0 and 1) of all category volume sold on that kind of a promotion. By using the extremes of 0 and 1, we can simulate what occurs in a single store. By using proportions we can reflect the results for less than a full week of promotion or results aggregated over stores with somewhat differing promotional environments.[9] Entering "1" for CFON Feature,

---

[8]The own-display and own-coupon parameters for Chock Full O'Nuts are not significant, and are therefore not used in this simulation.

[9]All changes to the defaults are highlighted in bold-faced type. Any unacceptable characters produce a beep and are not entered. Once any modifications are made, you exit this spreadsheet by pressing the <ESCAPE> key.

Table 7.1: Default Price and Promotion Table

Brand	Price	Feature	Display	Coupon
Folgers	$2.59	.00	.00	.00
MaxHouse	$2.31	.00	.00	.00
MasterBlend	$2.88	.00	.00	.00
Hills Brs.	$2.39	.00	.00	.00
Chock Full	$2.29	.00	.00	.00
Yuban	$3.29	.00	.00	.00
C&S	$2.39	.00	.00	.00
AOB	$2.45	.00	.00	.00
APL	$2.18	.00	.00	.00

<RETURN>, and then <ESCAPE> will set the background conditions for the first block of simulations.[10]

The background cost and profit-margin assumptions can be reviewed and modified in another pop-up spreadsheet obtained by choosing Set Defaults.Set Values.Profit.Set Costs Manually/View. The default values in this spreadsheet are summarized in Table 7.2.

Table 7.2: Default Costs

	Brand Cost per lb.		Cost per Store		
Brand	Retailers'	Manufctr's	Feature	Display	Coupon
Folgers	$1.98	$1.39	$75.00	$35.00	$20.00
MaxHouse	$1.89	$1.32	$75.00	$35.00	$20.00
MasterBlend	$2.07	$1.45	$75.00	$35.00	$20.00
Hills Brs.	$1.68	$1.18	$75.00	$35.00	$20.00
Chock Full	$1.70	$1.19	$75.00	$35.00	$20.00
Yuban	$2.69	$1.88	$75.00	$35.00	$20.00
C&S	$1.81	$1.27	$75.00	$35.00	$20.00
AOB	$1.98	$1.39	$75.00	$35.00	$20.00
APL	$1.53	$1.07	$50.00	$25.00	$15.00

These are only our crude estimates and we are not particularly well

---

[10]The original default values can be restored under Set Defaults.Set Values.Marketing Instruments.Reset CASPER Default Values.All.

informed on the specifics of costs in this market. Firms actually involved in this industry would have access to or interest in developing more accurate estimates of costs for all competitors. There are two points to be emphasized. First, in any simulation these cost assumptions should be made explicitly, not implicitly. Second, a decision-support system should allow one to change these assumptions as better information becomes available. Even in the absence of better data on costs, being able to vary cost assumptions allows one to see how sensitive the final profit results are to the initial cost assumptions.

Note that the cost structure is divided to reflect different roles of agents in the channels of distribution. The grocery stores are characterized as paying a cost per week for newspaper features, in-store displays, or store coupons. The *Store Profits* associated with each brand's simulated results are therefore a brand's estimated gross revenues (lbs. sold × retail price per pound) minus the wholesale costs (lbs. sold × retailers cost per pound) minus the fixed cost associated with features, displays and store coupons. The *Brand Profits* associated with each simulation come from the difference between the retailers' and manufacturers' cost per pound × the number of pounds sold. These are obviously elementary computations. The point is that a decision-support system should be able to reflect the profit implications of a brand's plans for the firms and for the channels of distribution. Planning which does not investigate channel profits is unreasonably myopic.

The means a manufacturer has of encouraging stores to promote a brand are in the form of per-pound discounts for features, displays, or coupons. The default assumptions in the CASPER simulator is that a $.05 discount per pound is offered for each promotional element, for each brand. Many different forms of incentives could be employed. But they can be represented on a per-pound basis without loss of generality. While stores are free to promote a brand without these incentives, the assumption here is that a brand offers a per-pound price without support (this is the price reflected in Table 7.2 as Retailers' Cost per lb.), and that the offered discounts per pound shown in Table 7.3 are only received by the retailer if they perform on that particular kind of promotion. A firm which didn't wish to use in-store displays, for example, would simply offer a zero discount per lb. for displays.[11]

The Run menu controls simulations. Since we are going to vary

---

[11] After reviewing or altering the default settings enter <ESCAPE> and the menu at the bottom of the desktop will return. Use the <END> and <RETURN> keys repeatedly to navigate out of the Set Defaults submenus.

Table 7.3: Default Discounts Offered to Retailer by Manufacturer

	Per-Pound Discount for		
Brand	Feature	Display	Coupon
Folgers	$.05	$.05	$.05
MaxHouse	$.05	$.05	$.05
MasterBlend	$.05	$.05	$.05
Hills Brs.	$.05	$.05	$.05
Chock Full	$.05	$.05	$.05
Yuban	$.05	$.05	$.05
C&S	$.05	$.05	$.05
AOB	$.05	$.05	$.05
APL	$.05	$.05	$.05

CFON's price, we can Choose Brands.CFON to toggle select Chock Full O'Nuts as the brand on which this simulation focuses.[12] The Variables menu is used for specifying the marketing instruments to vary during the simulation. Selecting Price.Set Minimum and typing 1.6 <RETURN> will set the minimum price to $1.60 per pound. Selecting Set Maximum and typing 2.8 <RETURN> will set the maximum price to $2.80 per pound. The number of steps between $1.60 and $2.80 can be set at any interval, but this simulation uses the default increment of $.10.[13] Selecting Run.Go will begin the first block of occasions.[14] We return to the Set Defaults.Set Values.Marketing Instruments.Set.Set Manually/View three times. First we set as background for the CFON simulation, a sale for Folgers using newspaper features and in-store displays to announce a

---

[12] An "X" will appear next to CFON on the desktop. Since we will be going back and forth between the Set Defaults and the Run menus we can lock this toggle switch "on" by using the Brand Lock option. Use the <END> and <RETURN> keys to move to the next higher level of the menu.

[13] Select the Default increment [.10]. Use the <END> and <RETURN> keys to move to the next higher level of the menu.

[14] The occasions will be appended to the current Occasions file on the desktop. If there are no Occasion files on the desktop CASPER will bring up a template which will simply be labeled Occasions. After the first block is completed use the File Management.Rename.Occasions menus to change the name of this file to something more mnemonically meaningful. The first three characters of this file name will be used as part of the identification of all plots generated by CASPER off the file, so that a name like C7Sim might be helpful in remembering that these are the simulations developed in Chapter 7 (up to eight characters may be used).

$2.05 (average sale price for Folgers in the HISTORY file), then return to the Run.Run Settings to reset the price ranges for CFON. Second, we reset Folgers to its default values, set a sale for Regular Maxwell House using newspaper features, in-store displays and store coupons to announce a sale price of $2.10 (average sale price for Regular Maxwell House in the HISTORY file), and return to the Run menu to reset the price ranges for CFON. For the last block of occasions we leave the Maxwell House sale in place and add back the Folgers sale values to the default settings. This simulates simultaneous sales for the three leading brands in this market.

We plot simulation results using the Plot Settings.Build.Using Occasions.Standard X-Y Plots menu. Selecting CFON will cause a pop-up menu to appear listing the following options:

Market Share

Sales

Brand Profit

Store Profit

Total Profit

Done .

Consider first the market-share plot (should be the same as Figure 7.7). The saw-tooth pattern at the top portrays the four blocks of simulations, each with its linear increase in price, in $.10 increments from $1.60 to $2.80. The downward-sloping market-share curves in each block seem to have very similar shapes – differing mainly in the maximum value in each block. In each block we can see how the market-share model deals sensibly with extreme values. A linear market-share model might well predict a negative market share for CFON at the higher prices in this simulation, but the MCI formulation shows that market shares have a natural asymptote. With all other brands at shelf price, CFON's market-share response is strongest in the first block. Facing a Folgers sale in the second block dramatically reduces the market-share potential of CFON. Facing a sale for Regular Maxwell House in the third block seems to be less damaging to CFON's market-share position. This may be partly due to the differences in brand-specific effects between Folgers and Regular Maxwell House, but the $.05 difference in average sale prices for these brands also contributes. Against sales for both Folgers and Regular Maxwell House, CFON's market share performs very like it does facing only a sale for Folgers.

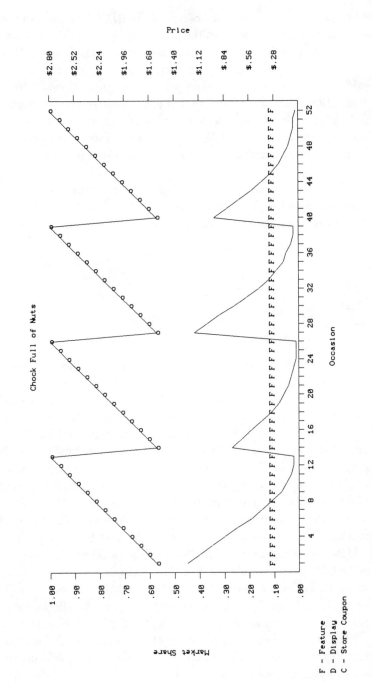

Figure 7.7: CFON's Market Shares – Simulation Results

While the market-share model helps us understand how competitive conditions affect how the total pie is shared among the brands, the category-volume model helps us forecast how large the pie is. Table 5.14 reveals that lowering prices for these three brands has the most expansive effect on total category volume. Figure 7.8 plots the total sales volume associated with this simulation.[15] Note that in the first block of occasions the variation in CFON's price leads to about 1,000 lbs.' difference in total category volume. With all three major brands on sale, the price variation leads to around three times as much variation in total category sales. What is showing here is that sales for more than one major brand bring a lot of coffee shoppers into the stores. That around 50% of all sales in the category are made on some kind of a trade deal indicates that many shoppers have been trained to look for coffee deals. That the coffee category is purchased by over 90% of household makes coffee a prime category for promotions aimed at bringing shoppers into the stores.[16] Some undoubtedly come in for a particular brand, while others may well switch brands in the store due to differences in prices, displays, and/or store coupons.

Figure 7.9 shows what these promotions imply for the sales of Chock Full O'Nuts. Even though market share declines for CFON over the four blocks in the simulation, sales increase as the total category volume expands. Some shoppers may be drawn in by the features for Folgers or Regular Maxwell House and switch based on price comparisons at the coffee display.

Whenever there is a constant promotional environment the brand profits will be a constant proportion of sales, so that the sales and brand-profit functions will have identical shapes. If plotted, profits for the brand would always be maximized at the lowest price in each block. This is quite different from the plot of profits for the store (should look like Figure 7.10). Note that $2.00 seems to be the price that maximizes CFON's contribution to store profits in each block. The sum of brand profits and the brand's contribution to store profits is plotted as *Total Profits* in Figure 7.11. The function is similar in shape to brand profits, except that the fixed cost of the features, displays, and coupons cut into profits at the lowest price levels since margins at that point are smallest.

The higher level of total profits associated with sales for all three

---

[15]This plot is formed by selecting Plot Settings.Build.Standard X-Y Plots.TCV. The prices on the right-hand vertical axis are a volume-weighted average over brands.

[16]Both statistics are from *The Marketing Fact Book*, Chicago: Information Resources Inc., 1983.

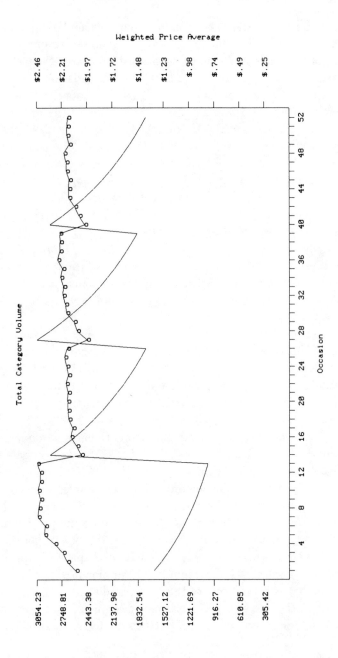

Figure 7.8: Total Category Volume – Simulation Results

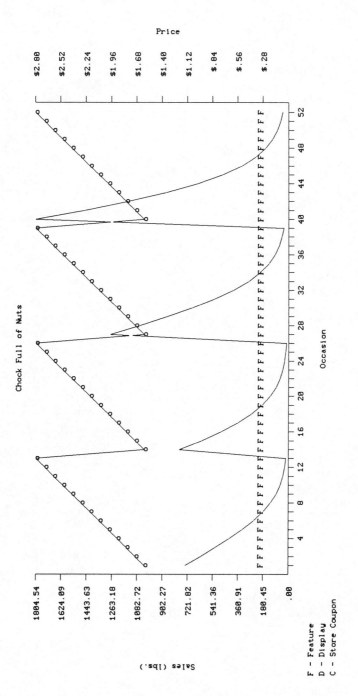

Figure 7.9: CFON's Sales – Simulation Results

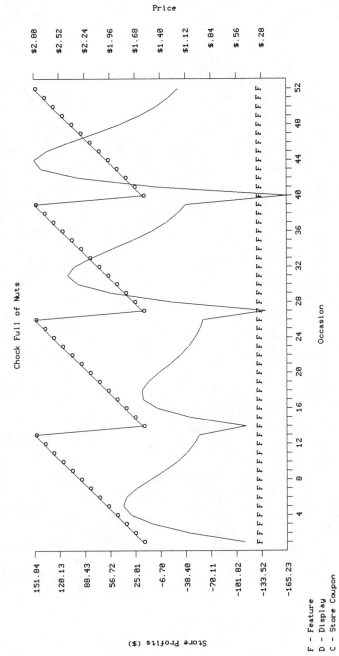

Figure 7.10: CFON's Contribution to Store Profits – Simulation Results

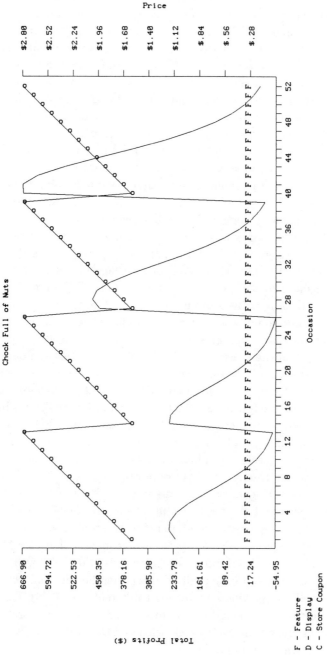

Figure 7.11: Total CFON Profits – Simulation Results

brands stems from the fact that these three brands can expand total category volume when they are on sale. Competition is normally less fierce among brands which can expand markets, but the market expansion we see here is only for a week. People will switch brands, buy earlier, or increase their inventory of coffee when dramatic sales occur, but the evidence is that in the longer term, they don't drink a lot more coffee just because of price promotions. Look at the TCV plot in CASPER's Standard Graphic Library for support of this claim. Because brand managers need to plan promotions over longer periods, it is important that they are not deluded into believing this level of sales can be sustained week after week. The competitive game incorporates the type of constraints which can only be manifest over time. Before turning to the game, however, we will first look at the simulation results from the perspective of the Folgers and Regular Maxwell House.

In this simulation Folgers' market share always increases as CFON's price increases (see Figure 7.12). Comparing the second and fourth blocks in the simulation, it appears that Folgers market share is hurt much more by the joint competition from CFON and Regular Maxwell House than it is by a promotion for CFON alone. Even facing CFON at an unreasonably low price, a promotion for Folgers at $2.05 per lb. using newspaper features and in-store displays is still expected to draw over 40% of the sales. The sales for Folgers in this simulation are shown in Figure 7.13. Note that the maximum occurs in the second block when Folgers is on promotion and CFON is at $2.30 (as close as possible to the average shelf price of $2.29). Brand profits for Folgers in this simulation would be shaped very similarly to the plot in Figure 7.13. Only the decreased margin of $.10 per lb. supporting the retailers' feature and display cost keeps the plots from being exactly proportional. Folgers' contribution to store profits are plotted in Figure 7.14. These are maximized when Folgers' sales are maximized. When Regular Maxwell House is being promoted, the store's profit contribution from Folgers declines.

From the perspective of Regular Maxwell House the results should look like Figures 7.15 – 7.17. Note that market share for Maxwell House first rises as CFON raises its price, and then Maxwell House's share either flattens out or actually drops (when Folgers undercuts it in price). Maxwell House seems to respond differently to being distinctively low priced than does Folgers. The brand and store profit for Maxwell House are maximized in each block when CFON is far below the maximum price in these simulations.

Market asymmetries are being reflected here. Only recently have

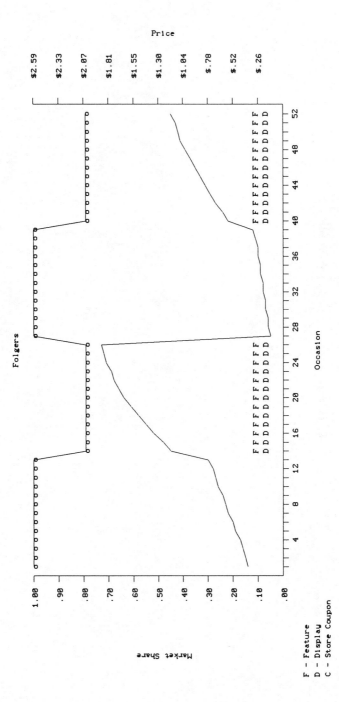

Figure 7.12: Folgers' Market Shares – Simulation Results

Figure 7.13: Folgers' Sales – Simulation Results

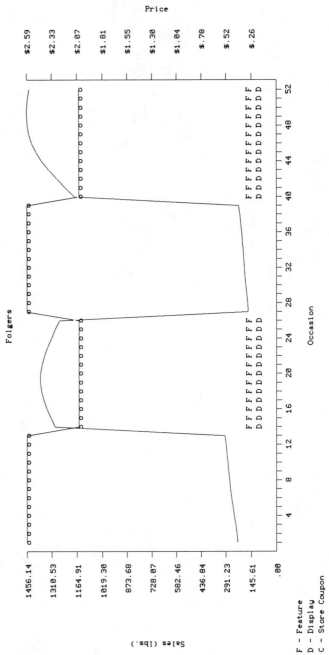

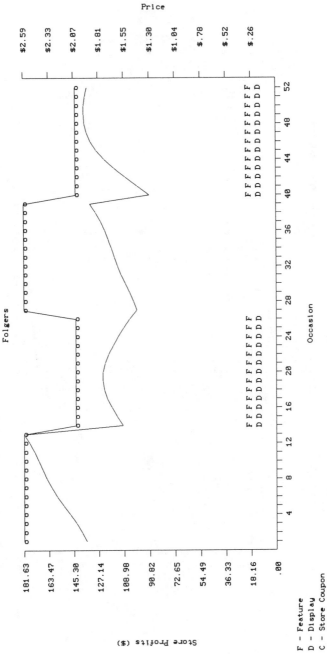

Figure 7.14: Folgers's Contribution to Store Profits – Simulation Results

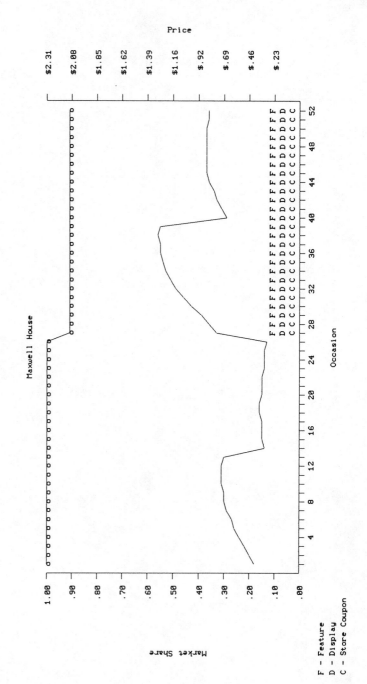

Figure 7.15: Maxwell House's Market Shares – Simulation Results

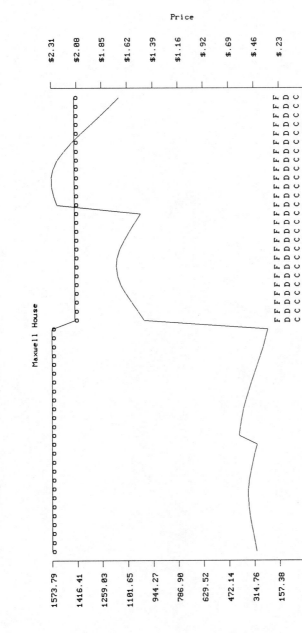

Figure 7.16: Maxwell House's Sales – Simulation Results

Figure 7.17: Maxwell House's Contribution to Store Profits – Simulation Results

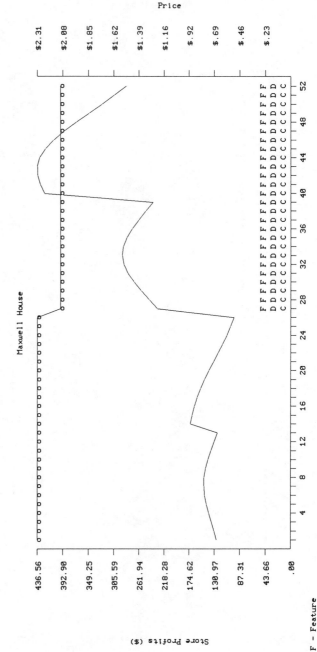

market-response models become available which can capture the diversity of asymmetric competition and yet are practical for use. Only recently have the records of retail transactions become available which allow us to see so clearly what drives consumer purchases. The coincidence of these events has created a new opportunity for brand management to develop plans based on comprehensive data and systematic inquiry. But plans are based on assumptions as well as on data. The propriety of such assumptions is the topic of the next section.

7.4 The Assumptions Underlying Planning

It was emphasized earlier that looking at the data is an indispensable part of building the expertise necessary for good decision making. One of the reasons is that *looking* makes it easier to evaluate the propriety of assumptions.

The marketing literature on optimal pricing, for example, seeks the single price that maximizes profits under certain assumptions concerning competition.[17] A look at the data and one sees that there are two price distributions: one corresponding to shelf prices and another corresponding to sale prices. The pulsing back and forth between these two distributions seems far too systematic a pulsing between sale prices and shelf prices to be a search for a single, optimal price. Some chains obviously have the policy of promoting a brand for only one week at a time. If a brand is on promotion this week in such a chain, we are very sure it will not be promoted the next.

As we aggregate store-week data, either over stores or over weeks, we know that our ability to see the underlying process diminishes. But it is just such aggregation that makes the assumptions underlying optimal marketing-mix models appear more tenable. Game-theory models are process models, which is why many of the equilibria can be sought numerically by simply *running the game*. If the process descriptions only seem apt for overaggregated results, then better models are needed.

There needs to be further development of game-theory scenarios tailored to fit what we see in these data. One interesting possibility combines a "Colonel Blotto" game with MacQueen's[18] development of N-

<hr />

[17] cf. Bass & Bultez [1982], Kalish [1983], Ram & Bass [1985].

[18] MacQueen, James [1988], "Systems of N-Person Time-Variable Games," A talk presented to the Jacob Marschak Interdisciplinary Colloquium On Mathematics in the Behavioral Sciences, Western Management Science Institute, UCLA, January 15.

person time-variable games. The Colonel Blotto game is due to Tukey,[19] but it was introduced to us by Steckel[20] in his discussion of resource allocation based on attraction models. Steckel's simulation results are based on seven assumptions:[21]

1. Only one resource is to be considered.

2. The amount of the resource a firm has to allocate is constant.

3. The firm has a fixed price and contribution margin for each unit of product it sells.

4. The maximum potential margin or profit obtainable from a given outlet is constant. No amount of resource, no matter how large, can increase primary demand.

5. The responses of each outlet are independent of each other.

6. The planning horizon is one period, with no lagged effects.

7. A firm about to make an allocation decision either knows its competitor's allocation or can anticipate it accurately.

If we think of the planning horizon as a year then these assumptions provide a well-thought-out set of assumptions. The most controversial assumptions would be items 4 and 7. But at the yearly level we would not expect to see wide swings in primary demand that we see in the weekly data. It is even reasonable to assume that firms can make good guesses of competitors' total promotional expenditures; we simply would not be able to anticipate when or where the resources would be spent.

The biggest problem is that if we calibrate an attraction model to correspond to this planning horizon, we would aggregate away all the interesting behavior. The final allocation model could tell us nothing about when or where to allocate resources. We need to decouple the planning horizon from the periodicity of the market-share model. The Colonel Blotto game helps here by proposing a scenario in which "two players contending on independent battlefields must distribute their entire forces to the battlefields before knowing the opposing deployment. The payoff to each player on the ith battlefield is a function of the opposing forces

[19]Tukey, John W. [1949], "A Problem in Strategy," *Econometrica*, 17, 73.
[20]Steckel, Joel H. [1987], "On Using Attraction Models to Allocate Resources in a Competitive Environment," Columbia University Working Paper, August 23.
[21]Steckel [1987], p.3.

committed to that battlefield."[22] If the *battlefields* are thought of as regions, the independence between them is probably not a problem. But if *battlefields* are *weeks*, then independence is less tenable. The important feature of the Colonel Blotto game is in the relaxation of item 7. Even if competitors' overall resources can be estimated, their deployment is not known. This game also makes it easier to think of a planning period as a collection of subgames, with an attraction model corresponding to the less aggregate subgames.

MacQueen's game enables a generalization to n persons (*m* brands in our case) from the two-person case, specifically acknowledges the time-varying aspect of subgames. Casting MacQueen's scenario into our context, we have *m* brands each of which follows a circuit with numerous nodes. The nodes in our case could be regions or time periods, but are probably best though of as promotional conditions (e.g., shelf prices, sale prices, features). Some of the nodes are common points on different circuits. When two brands jointly occupy the same node they play a game, which can be of different durations and payoffs.[23]

While generalizations along these lines hold promise, we are a long way from being able to calibrate a model and then just push an optimality button and receive back the best decisions to make. The lure of *push-button* management is very strong. We encounter it not only in game theory but also in the development of *expert systems*.

The essential notion of expert systems is that if we could only capture the knowledge of the experts in computer programs, then all we would have to do is to describe our particular context and the program would tell us what to do. There are three basic ingredients. We need the experts, the knowledge engineers to translate expert knowledge into conditioned-act statements, and we need the computer program to act as repository of the knowledge and as the decision-support system to prompt users through the sequence of questions needed to access the stored expertise.

The expert-systems programs (shells) exist although they will not be reviewed here. Marketing academicians with interest in behavioral

---

[22]Steckel [1987], p. 17.

[23]MacQueen's study of circuit processes and induced fields has helped him derive the stationary distributions representing the expected time a Markov process is in each particular state (node). His efforts make it mathematically easier to characterize the equilibrium solutions to these processes. Interested readers should see MacQueen, James [1979], "I. Circuit Processes. II. Notes on Markov Particle Systems with Exclusion and Induced Fields," Western Management Science Institute, Working Paper No. 294, University of California, Los Angeles, CA 90024-1481.

decision theory are developing the needed experience with knowledge engineering in areas such as advertising decision making. But analytical methods for representing market response based on scanner data are so new that we don't yet see the experts. The management expertise of tomorrow is built from the structured inquiry of today. The development of CASPER as a FRAMEWORK application is designed to provide an open environment in which expert systems can be developed by the real experts – the managers themselves. Getting from here to there requires that we ask the basic question ...

7.5   What If There Were No Experts?

What experts know is not innate. It must have been learned. So the task is to structure our inquiry into a market so that we learn. We have looked at history and done one planning exercise in earlier sections of this chapter. But much more effort is needed to understand this market. We could perform this same kind of planning exercise varying Folgers' price or Maxwell House's price. Beyond these basic exercises there are still a huge number of simulations which could be run.

We can look at the competitive maps developed in Chapter 6 for guidance in pruning possibly unfruitful branches of inquiry, and provide more focus to our efforts. From looking at the structure over stores and weeks (Figures 6.3 and 6.4) we already know that the major structural changes in price elasticities coincide with shelf-price and promotions for the three major brands: Folgers, Maxwell House, and Chock Full O'Nuts.

Going back to the map of shelf-price competition in Figure 6.5, we can consider what simulations might help determine a robust shelf price or distribution of shelf prices. For Folgers or Maxwell House simulations should include a look at the AOB category, since the AOB brands are aligned to be most vulnerable to Folgers and Maxwell House. Folgers should look at the influence CFON's and Master Blend's shelf prices on Folgers' shelf price, since Folgers is vulnerable to moves by these brands. Regular Maxwell House should look at the influence of its flanker Master Blend, since Master Blend is aligned competitively at shelf prices.

When investigating Folgers' sale price, the map in Figure 6.6 can help reduce the simulations. Folgers is vulnerable to CFON, but also Hills Bros. and Master Blend are well aligned, although they do not appear to have much clout. Simulations could tell if this alignment translates into a substantial threat. Folgers should also look at its influence on CFON and AOB, for although these brands are somewhat distant, they appear to be quite vulnerable. Simulation to help determine Maxwell House's sale price should include how the AOB category is affected, as well as how vulnerable Maxwell House is to Chase & Sanborne and Master Blend (see Figure 6.7). Chock Full O'Nuts (Figure 6.8) on sale is aligned to attack Folgers, Hills Bros., and Maxwell House (although these brands seem to differ greatly in their vulnerability) and, to a lesser extent, it is aligned to attack PL 2 and Master Blend. On the other hand it seems vulnerable to counterattack from Chase & Sanborne and Folgers.

Three things should be remembered. First, the maps from Chapter 6 relate only to prices. While prices are the major instrument in this market, maps for other marketing instruments might help complete the picture. Second, note that the idealized competitive conditions reflected mostly stores in grocery chain 1. The private-label brands might have a more active role in maps corresponding to other chains. And third, the maps are based on market-share elasticities. The brands which are able to expand the category volume in any given week have a somewhat different set of concerns than those who can only compete in a zero-sum fashion.

The simulation exercise showed that a simultaneous sale for the three biggest and most market-expansive brands are estimated to generate over 8,000 lbs. of coffee in a single week. Even if this were an accurate estimate, no one would expect the same market conditions in the following week to produce the same results. The dynamic effects have to be considered in planning promotions.

7.6 Dynamic Simulations

There is a difference between demand and consumption. All consumers adopt some inventory policy, at least implicitly. If we stimulate primary demand through promotions, we may be filling up the larder, without any influence on consumption. If this is the case, we can expect further stimulation to become less and less effective as inventories build up in the households. While many aspects of consumer behavior in such circumstances have been the basis of rational speculation in economics, we now have the data to answer some basic questions.

Since the release of IRI's Academic Database on the coffee market in 1983, the academic marketing-science community has learned a lot about the behavior of consumer panels.[24] One statistic we now have available is the average interpurchase time which is 52.5 days in this category.[25] If we wish to know how much we can expect to expand consumption we aggregate sales over some multiple of the average interpurchase time. Since we also know the variance, we could use two standard deviations above the average interpurchase interval as the range.

If we know this range, but have only the store-level data for further analysis, we could plot a centered moving average of sales for this range of weeks. If the plot is relatively flat, we have no evidence of increased consumption.[26] If there are variations we could relate them to similarly aggregated variations in the promotional conditions.

If we have the panel data for analysis we could do much more. Gupta[27] developed models for assessing when, what, and how much to buy, using the IRI coffee database. He postulates that consumers first decide *when* to buy, and then decide *what* and *how much*. This modeling framework enables Gupta to develop an overall sales elasticity which can be decomposed into the proportion of sales associated with *forward buying*, the proportion associated with brand switching, and the proportion associated with *stockpiling*. He found that "84% of the sales increase due to promotion comes from brand switching (a very small proportion of which may be switching between different sizes of the same brand). Purchase acceleration in time accounts for less than 14% of the sales increase, whereas stockpiling due to promotion is a negligible phenomenon accounting for less than 2% of the sales increase." These models are based on the characterization of the coffee category as being a mature product class, with constant *long-term* consumption rates. But since variations due to brand switching are independent of consumption rates, we can use these results to put an upper limit of 16% on the combined effects of forward buying, stockpiling, and increased consumption.[28] The

---

[24]The Academic Database reported on 78,000 transactions in the coffee market by 1,000 households in each of two small cities, Marion, Indiana, and Pittsfield, Massachusetts. The data used in Chapter 5 to develop the market-share and category-volume models are store-level data from about the same time periods, not these consumer-panel data.

[25] *The Marketing Fact Book*, Chicago: Information Resources, Inc., 1983.

[26]This plot could reveal seasonal variations in consumption, even if there are no variations resulting from efforts to stimulate demand.

[27]Gupta, Sunil [1988], "Impact of Sales Promotion on When, What, and How Much to Buy," *Journal of Marketing Research*, forthcoming.

[28]We could also reasonably assume that forward buying is far more substantial an influence than is stockpiling.

brand-switching component agrees closely with the estimates of McAlister and Totten.[29]

These percents are useful in putting constraints on a dynamic simulator. CASPER's dynamic simulator has three promotion periods of nine, nine, and eight weeks, respectively, using data from the 26 weeks reserved for cross validation of the market-share model. The total sales of all brands in any promotion period can expand by no more than 16% above the actual sales in the corresponding period. The percentage can be adjusted to reflect that 16% expansion is not expected to occur each and every period.

CASPER's dynamic simulator is structured as a game. To add a note of realism, Brand Teams develop promotional offers which are presented to the Store Teams or a Game Master. Results from the static simulator can be used to entice stores to accept a brand's promotional offer. While each brand must present the same plan to each store, the stores must act independently on the offers.

Using historic data in a dynamic simulator has some obvious advantages. Applying the cost assumptions to the historic data provides a profit baseline for the stores and the brands. This is a particularly valuable baseline if the stores are run by independent teams, rather than by a Game Master. If only the brands are managed by independent teams, the Game Master can rely on actual market decisions to fill in the unknown conditions. In addition to the pure baseline results, it is straightforward to evaluate one brand's plan against the background data, or to evaluate the brands in head-to-head competition.

One basic cycle of inquiry involves:

1. looking at the historical data,

2. evaluating how well a market-response model simulates history,

3. performing basic simulation exercises,

4. consulting the competitive maps,

5. performing simulations indicated in the maps,

6. proposing a plan,

---

[29]McAlister, Leigh & John Totten [1985], "Decomposing the Promotional Bump: Switching, Stockpiling, and Consumption Increase," Talk presented to the Atlanta ORSA/TIMS Conference, November.

7. simulating how well the plan is received by the stores as well as the ultimate market response, and

8. comparing the brand's performance against appropriate baselines.

The full cycle should precede the first promotion period. Cycles for later promotion periods could begin by trying to reconcile results with the competitive maps in item 4.

This seems to be a lot of effort, but if the information potential of scanner databases is to be tapped, this is the kind of effort which needs to be undertaken.

7.7   Management Decision Making

Those of us involved with management research and education face the dual problems of developing relevant management tools and preparing current and future managers to use them. There are obvious tensions involved. If brand managers were captivated by the complexities of choice models or market-share models, they might well have chosen to pursue academic careers. Those of us involved in methods development are rarely intrigued by the pragmatics of brand management. So where do we meet?

The design of market information systems may be as close as we can get to a common ground. This is the arena in which management science can help provide a systematic basis for utilizing data and market-response models, while management practice can use these efforts in decision making.

The emphasis on real data and real brands makes CASPER a prototype decision-support component of a market information system which could be transported to any of the hundreds of categories for which such data are available. While the development effort needed to implement CASPER-style interface in another product area is far from minor, the end result has some obvious benefits. First, brand managers spend their time learning about market response in their own product area. Second, they must make explicit the assumptions about the competition which are too often hidden or implicit in forecasts or simulations. Third, they are forced to consider the revenue and cost implications of their plans, for the firm and for the channels of distribution.

The most obvious benefit for the academicians is that their talents at research and methods development can be used to advance management theory and practice without being judged for how much they know (or don't know) about selling coffee.

Chapter 8

A Research Agenda

A number of research issues have come up in the writing of this book which will be recapitulated here. The basic topics include problems arising in estimation, decision support, integration of panel data, and trans-category research.

8.1 Estimation Problems

There are three issues here which should be high on a research agenda: methods for dealing with missing data, the issue of constrained parameter estimation, and the understanding of long-run effects.

8.1.1 Missing Data

For a category-volume model, different patterns of distribution can lead to a lot of missing data. The approach taken in Chapter 5 was simply to create *brand-absence* variables which have a zero whenever the brand is present and a one whenever it is absent. The log(price) variable corresponding to the missing brand is given a value of zero whenever the brand-absence coefficient has a value of one. This is a practical remedy for the missing explanatory variables in the category-volume model. The issue which needs to be addressed concerns how much influence these missing values have on the parameters of a category-volume model. It is possible to derive estimates of the missing values which are specifically designed to minimize the influence of missing explanatory variables.[1] It

---

[1] See Cooper [1987b].

would be very worthwhile to compare the parameters estimated by such a scheme with those in Table 5.14.

Note that for the category-volume model the missing explanatory variables are the problem, not missing dependent variables. If a brand is not distributed it simply does not increment total category volume. If $\exp(\text{z-scores})$ or zeta-scores are used in the corresponding market-share model, the missing explanatory variables can simply be given a value at the mean for that occasion. Missing dependent measures in the market-share model only affect the full cross-effects model (see section 5.7). In the other versions of the market-share model we can drop the observation corresponding to a missing dependent variable. In the full cross-effects model, the ease of parameter estimation is dependent on having a complete matrix of dependent variables. Practical methods along the lines of Malhotra's [1987] developments need to be investigated.

8.1.2   Constrained Parameter Estimation

We have the means to guarantee that the differential-effect parameters which are expected to be positive (or expected to be negative) turn out that way, or turn out to be zero. The residuals from the differential-effects model may be used to identify cross-competitive effects. The question is whether we should recombine all effects and re-estimate parameters in a best linear unbiased fashion. Alternatively we could use a two-step procedure which would estimate the parameters of the cross effects from the residuals of the constrained differential-effect parameterization.

This is a straightforward problem which simply requires thorough study before recommendations can be made.

8.1.3   Long-Run Effects

Hanssens[2] asks if marketing efforts have a permanent impact on sales; 106 tests on scanner data (instant coffees) showed the series to be stationary (*non-stationarity* is a necessary, though not sufficient condition for showing a permanent component to marketing efforts). While this means that the kinds of models developed here for the coffee market are

---

[2]Hanssens, Dominique M. [1987], "Marketing and the Long Run," Center for Marketing Studies Working Paper No. 164, Anderson Graduate School of Management, UCLA, September.

free of the time-series issues discussed in Chapter 3, we believe the issue will require more study in the future.

The *brand franchise* or *market power* is summarized, in a sense, in the brand-specific parameter α_i. These parameters are used in Chapter 5 to develop estimates of *baseline market shares*. Since the parameter estimate is a constant it will, of course, have no correlation with variations in marketing efforts. But it seems reasonable to ask if national advertising affects these brand intercepts. It may be possible to address the question if differences in these intercepts across brands have a permanent component which can be related to differences in advertising, distribution, or other longer-term influences across brands.

8.2 Issues in Decision Support

8.2.1 Game Theory

The basic message in the brief discussion on game theory in Chapter 7, is that more development is needed of games which reflect the conditions we see in the data. What we see is that manufacturers try to *push* their products through the channels by offers of trade deals as well as *pull* the products through by national advertising. While advertising budgets used to exceed greatly promotion budgets, the balance has shifted in many firms. The optimal balance between *push* and *pull* strategies is an area of study which might well help manufacturers.

Retailers in general know that the trade-promotion offers they receive from manufacturers are also received by other retailers. But they do not know what offers will be accepted or when performance on those offers will occur. While the focus of analysis here has been on a grocery chain, the *game* among the retailers is at the level of a trading area (which may be conveniently specified by the local newspapers for grocery categories). At this level it is obvious that the onset of promotions must be random, for if one retailer knows another is scheduled for a major promotion there would be substantial advantage in a preemptive sale. The amount of an advantage would, of course, be influenced by the frequency of promotions in the category, the length of time retailers have to perform on an offer, the length of the interpurchase period, and the household inventory policy for the category. Developing games which reflect all these influences will not be an easy task.

8.2.2   Expert Systems

While we recognize the desire on the part of managers and students of management to look for an expert – a guru to provide the answers would greater simplify the tasks at hand – we are not very sanguine about the possibility of finding such expertise. This is a very young field and we are reminded of a passage from Henry Adams:[3]

> What one knows is, in youth, of little moment; they know enough who know how to learn.

Thus our emphasis is on how one can learn from the vast amounts of data and the extensive development of models. Is there a way to structure the process of inquiry into these markets? Can we develop expert inquiry systems?

8.3   The Integration of Panel Data

The growing availability of consumer panels tied to store-level scanner data creates the opportunity to study many complex processes.

Disentangling the effects of forward buying, stockpiling, and increased consumption will ultimately be done using panel data. Totten and colleagues[4] have identified the consumer groups which contribute to these effects, but more research is needed to model the interrelations among these groups and how they are influenced by market forces.

This raises the fundamental issue of integrating panel data and store-level data. Connecting panel measurements and the corresponding store-level conditions to the sales results is the important step as is emphasized in Moore and Winer [1987]. When subgroups have to be incorporated as implied by Totten's research, the problem becomes more complex. We know the market conditions for each group since these conditions are homogeneous over groups within a week. If the identifying characteristics of the groups are assessable from the panel data, then a market-share model can be estimated at the group level. Oh yes, there is one thing missing. At this point we don't have a dependent measure. We don't know the market shares or sales by subgroup.

---

[3]Adams, Henry [1918], *The Education of Henry Adams*, New York: Random House, 1931.

[4]Totten, John C. & Martin P. Block [1987], *Analyzing Sales Promotion: Text and Cases*, Chicago: Commerce Communications, Inc. McAlister & Totten [1985].

If we simply aggregate the panelists' choices by group, all the advantages of the store-level data are lost. Besides, experimentation with such an approach when IRI's Academic Database was first released convinced us that even with 1,000 families per city, aggregated panel-based market shares are too sparse to allow estimation of cross effects. The real opportunity is in integrating the two data sources, not in using aggregated panel data as if they were store-level data.

Using market shares computed from the panel data for each group, deriving group-level estimates of the corresponding store-level market shares should be a solvable problem. For example, one of the most likely segmentations would be to minimize within group heterogeneity in mean purchase frequency. In Chapter 2 we emphasized that forecasting of brand sales and market shares would become more accurate if market shares are forecast for each segment and weighted by the mean purchase frequency for the segment to obtain the estimate of over-all market shares (p. 44 above). Totten and Block [1987] showed that the heavy-user group was the most likely to increase consumption due to a promotion. Chapter 4 (see Table 4.1 and section 4.2) warns that if subgroups have heterogeneous market shares, as implied by Totten's finding, then aggregation can diminish our ability to reflect the underlying process. In this example our problem can be simplified by thinking that heavy and light users form two mutually exclusive and exhaustive groups. We know that a weighted sum of the group market shares must equal the store-level market shares. Such a constraint should make the solution more useful and may make the problem easier to solve.

The constrained estimation of subgroup market shares allows us to calibrate asymmetric market-share models reflecting how the groups respond differently to market conditions. The estimation method could be used in the analysis of split-cable experiments. Market shares could be estimated based on the partitions in the experimental design. The analysis-of-covariance model from section 5.2.3 could be useful here. It may be that elaborations on the segmentation scheme could help integrate more and more of the television-viewing data now being collected in parts of panels.

Along with segment-level characteristics and records of viewing behavior, survey techniques can be used for subsamples of the panels. If the resulting interval-scale measures are transformed to zeta-scores or exp(z-scores), these measures can be used like any other variable in the market-share model. It is through this connection that we may assess if brand image or perceptual positioning can affect market shares.

With survey data connected in we can begin to ask questions about
how consumer judgments of value or importance relate to purchase behavior. Cooper and Finkbeiner[5] propose some basic models for the integration of consumers' judgments of importance into MCI models. This
should make a much more realistic platform for asking if statistically
estimated importance weights are superior to subjective estimation, or
if the combination of the two is better still.

8.4   Market-Basket Models

If we have data on the total transactions of each consumer, someone is
going to try to model them. Extrapolating the approach in this book
to that task, we would divide the market basket into categories, model
the total expenditures as we would a category-volume model, and model
the shares among categories as we would a market-share model. Within
each category we would have a nested pair of models for category volume
and brand shares.

This illustrates two levels of what might turn out to be a more ar-
ticulately leveled scheme. But the principles are the same. If the category label is beverages, the subcategories might cross hot and cold with
carbonated and noncarbonated. The hot, noncarbonated subcategory
might be divided into coffee and tea, and the coffee subsubcategory is
caffeinated, ground coffee. At some point we will get to the brand level
we have illustrated in this book, and we will know the principles involved
in modeling each level of categorization and connecting the results with
their siblings and parents.

Such an analysis would provide the elasticity needed to drive shelf-
space allocation models. While such an undertaking may be unreasonable at the present time, we believe such efforts will be more doable
as experience with these models grows and the diffusion of computing
technology continues.

---

[5]Cooper, Lee G. & Carl T. Finkbeiner [1984], "A Composite MCI Model for In-
tegrating Attribute and Importance Information," in Thomas C. Kinnear (editor),
Advances in Consumer Research, Volume XI, Provo, UT: Association for Consumer
Research, 109–13.

References

Adams, Henry [1918], *The Education of Henry Adams*, New York: Random House, 1931.

Abell, D. F. & J. S. Hammond [1979], *Strategic Market Planning: Problems and Analytical Approaches*, Englewood Cliffs, New Jersey: Prentice-Hall.

Alker, Hayward R. Jr. [1969], "A Typology of Ecological Fallacies," In Mattei Dogan & Stein Rokkan (editors), *Quantitative Ecological Analysis in the Social Sciences*, Cambridge, MA: The M.I.T. Press, 69-86.

Ashby, W. R. [1956], *Introduction to Cybernetics*, New York: Wiley.

Bass, Frank M. & Alain V. Bultez [1982], "A Note On Optimal Strategic Pricing of Technological Innovations," *Marketing Science*, 1, 4 (Fall), 371-78.

Beckwith, Neil E. [1972], "Multivariate Analysis of Sales Response of Competing Brands to Advertising," *Journal of Marketing Research*, 9 (May), 168-76.

Bell, David E., Ralph L. Keeney & John D. C. Little, John D. C. [1975], "A Market share Theorem," *Journal of Marketing Research*, XII (May), 136-41.

Belsley, David A., Edwin Kuh & Roy E. Welsch [1980], *Regression Diagnostics: Identifying Influential Data and Sources of Collinearity*, New York: John Wiley & Sons.

Berkson, Joseph [1953], "A Statistically Precise and Relatively Simple Method of Estimating the Bioassay with Quantal Response, Based on the Logistic Function," *Journal of the American Statistical Association*, 48 (September), 565-99.

Box, George E. P. & Jenkins, Gwilym [1970], *Time-series Analysis: Forecasting and Control*. San Francisco: Holden Day.

Brodie, Roderick & Cornelius A. de Kluyver [1984], "Attraction Versus Linear and Multiplicative Market share Models: An Empirical Evaluation," *Journal of Marketing Research*, 21 (May), 194-201.

Bultez, Alain V. & Philippe A. Naert [1975], "Consistent Sum-Constrained Models," *Journal of the American Statistical Association*, 70, 351 (September), 529-35.

Bultez, Alain V. & Philippe A. Naert [1979], "Does Lag structure Really Matter in Optimal Advertising Expenditures?" *Management Science*, 25, 5 (May), 454-65.

Burke, Ray & Arvin Rangaswamy [1987], "Knowledge Representation in Marketing Expert Systems," *International Workshop on Data Analysis, Decision Support and Expert Knowledge Representation in Marketing and Related Areas of Research*, University of Karlsruhe, West Germany, June 21 – 23.

Robert D. Buzzell, Bradley T. Gale and Ralph G. M. Sultan [1975], "Market-Share — A Key to Profitability," *Harvard Business Review*, January-February, 97–106.

Carpenter, Gregory S., Lee G. Cooper, Dominique M. Hanssens & David F. Midgley [1988], "Modeling Asymmetric Competition," *Marketing Science*, 7, 4 (November), forthcoming.

Carroll, J. Douglas [1980], "Models and Methods for Multidimensional Analysis of Preferential Choice (or Other Dominance) Data," in Ernst D. Lantermann & Hubert Feger (editors), *Similarity and Choice*, Bern: Hans Huber Publishers, 234–89.

Clarke, Darral G. [1973], "Sales-Advertising Cross-elasticities and Advertising Competition," *Journal of Marketing Research*, 10 (August), 250–61.

Cooper, Lee G. [1973], "A Multivariate Investigation of Preferences," *Multivariate Behavioral Research*, 8 (April), 253–72.

Cooper, Lee G. [1983], "A Review of Multidimensional Scaling in Marketing Research," *Applied Psychological Measurement*, 7 (Fall), 427–50.

Cooper, Lee G. [1985], "Sources of and Remedies for Collinearity in Differential-Effects Market-Share Models," Working Paper No. 136 Revised, Center for Marketing Studies, Graduate School of Management, University of California, Los Angeles, July.

Cooper, Lee G. [1987b], "The Minimum-Influence Approach to Missing Data in Regression." Marketing Science Conference, Centre HEC-ISA, Jouy-en-Josas, France, June 24–27.

Cooper, Lee G. [1988a], "Market-Share Analysis: Communicating Results Through Spreadsheet-Based Simulators," in Wolfgang Gaul & Martin Schader (editors), *Data, Expert Knowledge, and Decisions: An Interdisciplinary Approach with Emphasis on Marketing Applications*, Berlin: Springer–Verlag, 35–41.

Cooper, Lee G. [1988b], "Competitive Maps: The Structure Underlying Asymmetric Cross Elasticities," *Management Science*, 34, 6 (June), 707–23.

Cooper, Lee G. & Carl T. Finkbeiner [1984], "A Composite MCI Model for Integrating Attribute and Importance Information," in Thomas C. Kinnear (editor), *Advances in Consumer Research, Volume XI*,

Provo, UT: Association for Consumer Research, 109–13.

Cooper, Lee G. & Masao Nakanishi [1983a], "Standardizing Variables in Multiplicative Choice Models," *Journal of Consumer Research*, 10 (June), 96–108.

Cooper, Lee G. & Masao Nakanishi [1983b], "Two Logit Models for External Analysis of Preferences," *Psychometrika*, 48, 4 (December), 607–20.

Debreu, Gerard [1960], "Review of R. D. Luce's *Individual Choice Behavior: A Theoretical Analysis*, *American Economic Review*, 50 (1), 186–8.

DeSarbo, Wayne S., Vithala Rao, Joel H. Steckel, Yoram Wind & Richard Columbo [1987], "A Friction Model for Describing and Forecasting Price Changes," *Marketing Science*, 6, 4 (Fall), 299–319.

DeSarbo, Wayne S. & Vitala R. Rao [1984], "GENFOLD2: A Set of Models and Algorithms for GENeral UnFOLDing Analysis of Preference/Dominance Data," *Journal of Classification*, 1, 2, 147–86.

DeSoete, Geert & J. Douglas Carroll [1983], "A Maximum Likelihood Method of Fitting the Wandering Vector Model," *Psychometrika*, 48, 4 (December), 553–66.

Dorfman, Robert A. & Peter D. Steiner [1954], "Optimal Advertising and Optimal Quality," *American Economic Review*, 44 (December), 826–36.

Elrod, Terry [1987], "Choice Map: Inferring Brand Attributes and Heterogeneous Consumer Preferences From Panel Data," *Marketing Science*, forthcoming.

Finn, Jeremy D. [1974], *A General Model for Multivariate Analysis*, New York: Holt, Rinehart & Winston.

Fraser, Cynthia and John W. Bradford [1983], "Competitive Market Structure Analysis: Principal Partitioning of Revealed Substitutabilities," *Journal of Consumer Research*, 10 (June), 15–30.

Ghosh, Avijit, Scott Neslin & Robert Shoemaker [1984], "A Comparison of Market share Models and Estimation Procedures," *Journal of Marketing Research*, 21 (May), 202–10.

Guadagni, Peter M. & John D. C. Little [1983], "A Logit Model of Brand Choice Calibrated on Scanner Data," *Marketing Science*, 2, 3 (Summer), 203–38.

Gupta, Sunil [1988], "Impact of Sales Promotion on When, What, and How Much to Buy," *Journal of Marketing Research*, forthcoming.

Gurumurthy, K. & John D. C. Little [1986], "A Pricing Model Based on Perception Theories and Its Testing on Scanner panel Data," Massachusetts Institute of Technology Working Paper Draft, May.

Haines, George H., Jr. Leonard S. Simon & Marcus Alexis [1972], "Maximum Likelihood Estimation of Central-City Food Trading Areas," *Journal of Marketing Research*, 9, (May), 154–59.

Hanssens, Dominique M. [1980], "Market Response, Competitive Behavior, and Time Series Analysis," *Journal of Marketing Research*, 17 (November), 470–85.

Hanssens, Dominique M. [1987], "Marketing and the Long Run," Center for Marketing Studies Working Paper No. 164, Anderson Graduate School of Management, UCLA, September.

Hanssens, Dominique & Lon-Mu Liu [1983], "Lag Specification in Rational Distributed Lag Structural Models," *Journal of Business and Economic Statistics*, 1, 4 (October), 316–25.

Hauser, John R. & Steven M. Shugan [1983], "Defensive Marketing Strategies," *Marketing Science*, 2, 4 (Fall), 319–60.

Helmer, Richard M. & Johnny K. Johansson [1977], "An Exposition of Box–Jenkins Transfer Function Analysis with an Application to the Advertising–Sales Relationship," *Journal of Marketing Research*, 14 (May), 227–39.

Huff, David L. [1962], *Determination of Intraurban Retail Trade Areas*, Los Angeles: Real Estate Research Program. University of California, Los Angeles.

Huff, David L. [1963], "A Probabilistic Analysis of Consumer Spatial Behavior," in William S. Decker (editor), *Emerging Concepts in Marketing*, Chicago, IL: American Marketing Association, 443–61.

Hulbert, James & Norman Toy [1977], "A Strategic Framework for Marketing Control," *Journal of Marketing*, 41 (April), 12–20.

Kahn, Barbara E., Donald G. Morrison & Gordon P. Wright [1986], "Aggregating Individual Purchases to the Household Level," *Marketing Science*, 5, 3 (Summer), 260–68.

Kalish, Shlomo [1983], "Monopolistic Pricing With Dynamic Demand and Production Cost," *Marketing Science*, 2, 2 (Spring), 135–59.

Karnani, Aneel [1983], "Minimum Market Share," *Marketing Science*, 2, 1 (Winter), 75–93.

Karnani, Aneel [1984], "The Value of Market Share and the Product Life Cycle – A Game-Theoretic Approach," *Management Science*, 30, 6 (June), 646–712.

Kroonenberg, Pieter M. [1983], *Three–Mode Principal components Analysis: Theory and Applications*, Leiden, The Netherlands: DSWO Press.

Korth, Bruce & Ledyard R Tucker [1975], "The Distribution of Chance Coefficients from Simulated Data," *Psychometrika*, 40, 3 (September), 361–72.

Korth, Bruce & Ledyard R Tucker [1975], "The Distribution of Chance Coefficients from Simulated Data," *Psychometrika*, 40, 3 (September), 361–72.

Kotler, Philip [1984], *Marketing Management: Analysis, Planning, and Control*, Fifth Edition, Englewood Cliffs, NJ: Prentice-Hall, Inc.

Lambin, Jean Jacques [1972], "A Computerized On–Line Marketing mix Model," *Journal of Marketing Research*, 9 (May), 119–26.

Lambin, Jean Jacques, Philippe A. Naert & Alain V. Bultez [1975], "Optimal Marketing Behavior in Oligopoly," *European Economic Review*, 6, 105–28.

Leeflang, Peter S. H. & Jan C. Reuyl [1984a], "On the Predictive Power of Market Share Attraction Models," *Journal of Marketing Research*, 21 (May), 211–15.

Leeflang, Peter S. H. & Jan C. Reuyl [1984b], "Estimators of the Disturbances in Consistent Sum-Constrained Market Share Models," Working Paper, Faculty of Economics, University of Gronigen, P.O. Box 9700 AV Gronigen, The Netherlands.

Little, Roderick J. A. & Donald B. Rubin [1987], *Statistical Analysis with Missing Data*. New York: John Wiley & Sons, Inc.

Lukacs, E. [1965], "A Characterization of the Gamma Distribution," *Annals of Mathematical Statistics*, Vol. 26, 319-24.

Magat, Wesley A., John M. McCann & Richard C. Morey [1986], "When Does Lag Structure Really Matter in Optimal Advertising Expenditures?" *Management Science*, 32, 2 (February), 182–93.

Mahajan, Vijay, Arun K. Jain & Michel Bergier [1977], "Parameter Estimation in Marketing Models in the Presence of Multicollinearity: An Application of Ridge Regression," *Journal of Marketing Research*, 14 (November), 586–91.

Malhotra, Naresh [1987], "Analyzing Market Research Data with Incomplete Information on the Dependent Variable," *Journal of Marketing Research*, XXIV (February), 74–84.

McAlister, Leigh & John C. Totten [1985], "Decomposing the Promotional Bump: Brand Switching, Purchase Acceleration and Increased Consumption," Paper presented to the ORSA/TIMS Conference, Atlanta, November.

McCann, John M. [1986], *The Marketing Workbench: Using Computers for Better Performance*, Homewood, IL: Dow Jones–Irwin.

McFadden, Daniel [1974], "Conditional Logit Analysis of Qualitative Choice Behavior," in Paul Zarembka (editor), *Frontiers in Econometrics*. New York: Academic Press, 105–42.

McGuire, Timothy W., Doyle L. Weiss & Frank S. Houston [1977], "Consistent Multiplicative Market Share Models," in Barnett A. Greenberg & Danny N. Bellinger (editors), *Contemporary Marketing Thought*, Chicago: American Marketing Association, 129–34.

Moore, William L. & Russell S. Winer [1987]. "A Panel–Data Based Method for Merging Joint Space and Market Response Function Estimation," *Marketing Science*, 6, 1 (Winter), 25–42.

Morey, Richard C. & John M. McCann [1983], "Estimating the Confidence Interval for the Optimal Marketing Mix: An Application to Lead Generation," *Marketing Science*, 2, 2 (Spring), 193–202.

Naert, Philippe A. & Marcel Weverbergh [1981], "On the Prediction Power of Market Share Attraction Models," *Journal of Marketing Research*, 18 (May), 146–53.

Naert, Philippe A. & Marcel Weverbergh [1985], "Market share Specification, Estimation and Validation: Toward Reconciling Seemingly Divergent Views," *Journal of Marketing Research*, 22 (November), 453–61.

Nakanishi, Masao [1972], "Measurement of Sales Promotion Effect at the Retail Level – A New Approach," *Proceedings, Spring and Fall Conferences, American Marketing Association*, 338–43.

Nakanishi, Masao & Lee G. Cooper [1974], "Parameter Estimation for a Multiplicative Competitive Interaction Model — Least Squares Approach," *Journal of Marketing Research*, 11 (August), 303–11.

Nakanishi, Masao & Lee G. Cooper [1980], "Parameter Estimation of the MCI and Related Models: Revisited," University of California, Graduate School of Management, Center for Marketing Studies Paper No. 97, October.

Nakanishi, Masao & Lee G. Cooper [1982], "Simplified Estimation Procedures for MCI Models," *Marketing Science*, 1, 3 (Summer), 314–22.

Nakanishi, Masao, Lee G. Cooper & Harold H. Kassarjian [1974], "Voting for a Political Candidate Under Conditions of Minimal Information," *Journal of Consumer Research*, 1 (September), 36–43.

Parsons, Leonard J. [1975], "The Product Life Cycle and Time-Varying Advertising Elasticities," *Journal of Marketing Research*, 16 (November), 439–52.

Rao, Ram C. & Frank M. Bass [1985], "Competition, Strategy, and Price Dynamics: A Theoretical and Empirical Investigation," *Journal of*

Marketing Research, 22 (August), 283–96.

Robinson, W. S. [1950], "Ecological Correlation and the Behavior of Individuals," *American Sociological Review*, 15, 351–57.

Ross, John [1966], "A Remark on Tucker and Messick's *Points of View* Analysis," *Psychometrika*, 31, 1 (March), 27–31.

Shoemaker, Robert W. [1986], "Comments on *Dynamics of Price Elasticities and Brand Life Cycles: An Empirical Study*," *Journal of Marketing Research*, 23 (February), 78–82.

Shugan, Steven M. [1986], "Brand Positioning Maps From Price/Share Data," University of Chicago, Graduate School of Business, Revised, July.

Shugan, Steven M. [1987], "Estimating Brand Positioning Maps From Supermarket Scanning Data," *Journal of Marketing Research*, 24 (February), 1–18.

Simon, Hermann [1979], "Dynamics of Price Elasticities and Brand Life Cycles: An Empirical Study," *Journal of Marketing Research*, XVI (November), 439–52.

Sims, Christopher A. [1972], "Money, Income, and Causality," *American Economic Review*, 62, 540–52.

Theil, Henri [1969], "A Multinomial Extension of the Linear Logit Model," *International Economics Review*, 10 (October), 251–59.

Totten, John C. & Martin P. Block [1987], *Analyzing Sales Promotion: Text and Cases*, Chicago: Commerce Communications, Inc.

Tucker, Ledyard R [1951], "A Method of Synthesis of Factor Analysis Studies," *Personnel Research Section Report*, No. 984, Washington, D.C., Department of the Army.

Tucker, Ledyard R [1963], "Implications of Factor Analysis of Three-Way Matrices for Measurement of Change," in Chester W. Harris (editor), *Problems in Measuring Change*, Madison: University of Wisconsin Press, 122–37.

Tucker, Ledyard R [1966], "Some Mathematical Notes On Three-Mode Factor Analysis," *Psychometrika*, 31, 4 (December), 279–311.

Tucker, Ledyard R [1969], "Some Relations Between Multi-Mode Factor Analysis and Linear Models for Individual Differences in Choice, Judgmental and Performance Data," Paper presented to the Psychometric Society Symposium: Multi-Mode Factor Analysis and Models for Individual Differences in Psychological Phenomena, April 18.

Tucker, Ledyard R [1972], "Relations Between Multidimensional Scaling and Three-Mode Factor Analysis," *Psychometrika*, 37, 1 (March), 3–27.

Tucker, Ledyard R & Samuel Messick [1963], "An Individual Differences Model for Multidimensional Scaling," *Psychometrika*, 28, 4 (December), 333–367.

Vanhonacker, Wilfried [1984], "Structuring and Analyzing Brand Competition Using Scanner Data," Columbia University, Graduate School of Business, April.

Weiss, Doyle L. [1968], "The Determinants of Market Share," *Journal of Marketing Research*, 5 (August), 290–95.

Wildt, Albert R. [1974], "Multifirm Analysis of Competitive Decision Variables," *Journal of Marketing Research*, 11 (February), 50–62.

Yellott, J. I. [1977], "The Relationship Between Luce's Choice Axiom, Thurstone's Theory of Comparative Judgments, and the Double Exponential Distribution, *Journal of Mathematical Psychology*, 15, 109–44.

Young, Kan H., and Linds Y. Young [1975], "Estimation of Regressions Involving Logarithmic Transformations of Zero Values in the Dependent Variables," *The American Statistician*, 29 (August), 118–20.

Index

Detach Here

Place
Stamp
Here

Casper Software Products
P.O. Box 1108
Santa Monica, CA 90406-1108

CASPER Information

The CASPER software is designed to run on an IBM AT, PC/2, or compatible computer. It requires either extra RAM (2Mb for the Single-User Module or 4Mb for the Game-Master Module) or equivalent hard-disk space. FRAMEWORK III is required.

Educational discounts are available on both CASPER and FRAMEWORK III.
For more information and current prices please fill out and mail the attached postcard.

Please send me information on CASPER
☐Single-User Version
☐Site-License Version (Includes Game Module)

Name: _____
Company: _____
Street: _____
City: _____
State: _____
Zip Code: _____